*f*P

The
TRUSTED
LEADER

Bringing Out the Best in
Your People and Your Company

ROBERT GALFORD

ANNE SEIBOLD DRAPEAU

THE FREE PRESS

New York • London • Toronto • Sydney • Singapore

THE FREE PRESS

A Division of Simon & Schuster, Inc.
1230 Avenue of the Americas
New York, NY 10020

Manufactured in the United States of America

10   9   8   7   6   5   4   3   2   1

Library of Congress Cataloging-in-Publication Data Is Available

Galford, Robert M.
The trusted leader : bringing out the best in your people and your
company / Robert Galford, Anne Siebold Drapeau.
p.   cm.
Includes bibliographical references and index.
1. Leadership—Moral and ethical aspects. 2. Business ethics. 3. Organizational
behavior—Moral and ethical aspects. 4. Industrial management—Moral and ethical
aspects. 5. Employee motivation. 6. Trust. I. Drapeau, Anne Seibold. II. Title.

HD57.7 .G33 2003
174'.4—dc21
                                                                    2002034672
ISBN 0-7432-3539-8

For information regarding special discounts for bulk purchases,
please contact Simon & Schuster Special Sales at 1-800-456-6798
or business@simonandschuster.com

To Susan, Katy, and Luke

To Bob and Caroline

ACKNOWLEDGMENTS

When you write a book, you realize how dependent you are on the time, insights, generosity, and kindness of others. With the completion of *The Trusted Leader*, we feel that most deeply. We give heartfelt thanks to the people who so generously shared their stories and thoughts with us, who steered and guided us, who listened patiently through our struggles, and who supported us in so many ways throughout the entire process.

While we hope they already know how grateful we are, we thank Kathy Biro, Barnes Boffey, Mark Braverman, Ephraim Brecher, Henk Broeders, Michael Bronner, Paul Clark, Alan Colsey, Bob Garland, Mary Gegler, Diane Hessan, George Hornig, Jim Lawrence, Craig Meeker, John Peterman, Regina Pisa, Michael Rice, Jon Skinner, Tom Valerio, Michael Welles, Michael Wiklund; also, Tim Riley, George Colony, Tina Sterpe, Jon Younger, Nick Noyes for morning coffees, Kathy Lubar and the wonderful people of the Ariel Group, and *Trusted Advisor* co-author Charlie Green for his seminal work on trust. Both of us had day jobs while we were working on this project, and we are grateful to our colleagues at Digitas and the Center for Executive Development for their encouragement and flexibility, particularly, Michael Ward and David Kenny at Digitas and Rob's partners at CED.

We are grateful for early support from Bob Wallace, along with Leslie Meredith, who became our editor at The Free Press. She helped turn this into reality, along with her assistant, Dorothy Robinson. We thank Lynn Goldberg and her colleagues at Goldberg-McDuffie Associates, particularly Mark Fortier, for their early encouragement and their vision.

Finally, we consider it beyond comprehension that anyone

might ever write a book without Regina Fazio Maruca. Writer, thinker, finder of our collective voice, translator of wild and disparate thoughts into rational form, all combined with a gentle demeanor and a wicked sense of humor. What a gift Regina has been to us. We thank her (and her family) so much.

And finally, finally, we thank our families, accommodating spouses and children, who, in ways even unbeknownst to them, have made this so worthwhile.

CONTENTS

PART FIVE: BUILDING TRUST IN PERSPECTIVE

INTRODUCTION

THIS BOOK ABOUT trusted leadership is a surprising, accidental byproduct of the work Rob was doing around the skills of trusted advisors (the topic of his first book, with David Maister and Charles Green). Rob was teaching in a series of executive programs jointly delivered by the graduate business schools at Columbia and Kellogg/Northwestern, for the executives of a single firm. In each of those thirty sessions, he asked the participants to rank themselves—and then rank their colleagues—on how trusted they were as advisors to clients and customers. The striking results of that particular survey question, repeated every single time, session after session, was that a sizable percentage of the respondents had little or no confidence in their own partners' abilities to build trust! If such a gap in the level of trust existed inside the upper levels of an organization, Rob wondered, how could the organization ever develop the trust of its customers?

That question led us to explore just how to create and sustain trust among the members of a single organization. This challenge affects companies large and small, centralized and decentralized, global and local, and in our own work in recent years with and for companies of all sizes and shapes, we've personally learned a great deal. We wrote this book because we feel strongly that creating a community of trusted leaders who can then help trust permeate through all levels of an organization—particularly in today's business context—is critical to every company's long-term survival and success.

We wrote this book because even though there has been a great deal published about the role of the leader in creating a successful company, no one has ever given due credit to the important implications of having an organization with a *trusted* leader.

A lot of literature addresses trust in families, between friends, and in society, as well as trust—and the related loyalty—between company and client. But trusted *leadership*—the force that guides and builds trust *inside* companies, between employees, between senior managers, across levels and departments—hasn't received nearly as much attention. Part of the reason is a widespread misconception that trust is trust, and that if you understand the dynamics of trust in one arena, you'll understand them in any other. This is simply not so. Just to cite one example, consider the relationship between company and client. If trust breaks down, one party or another can usually exit the relationship, perhaps not without some difficulty, but with few, if any, long-term aftereffects. "That relationship is over, but no worries; there are other, similar, vendors (or suppliers, or consultants, or what-have-you)." Trust issues inside an organization, however, more closely resemble the relationships in families living under one roof. Individuals usually *can't* just walk away and forget, and every action or reaction has a lasting ripple effect.

Yet trust issues inside organizations don't completely mirror those among family members either. Trust inside has its own unique set of dynamics. They are not widely understood, yet they are vitally important. Today's customer demands, the pressures to succeed competitively, and the new "employment contract" (the reality that there *is* no "employment contract" anymore) mean that trusted leadership is more important now than ever before. We have come to believe that creating organizations that are bound by strong, deep connections between peers, across levels, and across functions may be the only recipe for sustainable success.

Trusted leadership is not a "new economy" versus "old economy" issue. Nor is it an issue that is solely the challenge of running a large company versus a smaller-sized entity. Our background research and review of trust-related episodes at a number of companies (ranging from $20 million technology firms to $20 billion multinationals) demonstrate that trusted leadership is, above all, an issue of human interaction, and, as such, requires constant and vigilant treatment.

Trust is intangible—like culture—but it is useful to think of it as an "outcome" that results from very tangible processes. There arc management tools you can use to become a trusted leader, and established, proven methods for sustaining trust inside and for repairing once-trusting relationships that have broken down.

The Trusted Leader is primarily for people in senior leadership roles. It is presented in five parts. The first part, "An Overview of Trusted Leadership" (Chapters 1 through 4), defines trust inside, the characteristics and competencies of the trusted leader, and the natural enemies of trust, in broad strokes. It also includes a self-assessment drill, to help you define where you are in your efforts to become a trusted leader and build trust inside your organization. (We're list-happy, and we like to put our readers through the occasional exercise.) In Part Two, "Identifying and Applying the Tools of Trusted Leaders" (Chapters 5 and 6), we identify and demonstrate the tools of trust-building on personal relationships inside the organization and relationships between leaders and the organization. Part Three, "How Trusted Leaders Work" (Chapters 7 through 9), drills down into what trust looks like—and how it can be created, reinforced, and strengthened—across levels, functions, and locations. Part Four, "Defining Moments" (Chapters 10 through 12), identifies those critical junctures when trusted leadership is tested, and also pinpoints specific opportunities for building trust inside. In Part Five, "Building Trust in Perspective" (Chapters 13 and 14), we take a longer, more personal view, examining in detail how trust breaks down, what a leader can do in a situation where trust must be rebuilt, and also what it means to build a legacy of trust. Finally, in the Afterword, you will find information about how you can participate in our ongoing research on trust after you have read this book.

All of the advice we offer is "pressure-tested." That is, it comes directly out of our research and work with companies of varying sizes that have experienced the pressures of roller-coaster change, market uncertainties, and strategic and operational turmoil. It comes out of leadership mistakes and successes we have observed. It also comes out of our own personal experiences as top managers working with middle managers and front-line employees. The real case examples we present throughout the book provide a level of detail that paints a clearer picture than a generic description ever could. Some are disguised (to protect both the innocent and the guilty), some are directly reported by the people involved. Some are several cases merged into one to emphasize a particular insight. They're all true, and we hope you think they're as compelling as we do in their illustrations of our theories.

We should note that in the course of our writing this book, the Enron case rose to the fore, calling into question the very essence of trusted leadership. It was followed shortly thereafter by revelations at Global Crossing, Adelphia Communications, Tyco, World-Com, and others. We haven't dwelt on those cases, but we have included examples that are representative of some of the problems that those companies experienced, particularly since, to us, Enron's saga is, for example, the Perfect Storm of how trusted leadership goes awry. One of the most interesting aspects of that debacle has been its effects on Arthur Andersen and many other entities. (To be sure, this book does rest on the premise that the reader is trustworthy. In no way are we attempting to show people how to *feign* trustworthiness!)

September 11, 2001, also hadn't happened when we began to write. That tragic event has had a profound, enduring effect on how employers and employees think about what trust represents within organizations. It has highlighted the responsibilities of leaders and companies regarding the personal safety and emotional well-being of their employees. The influence of that horrific day and the issues it rediscovered are throughout the book, most prominently in the chapter on trust in times of crisis.

The ongoing issues of trust and trusted leadership in organizations have led us to create a Web site, thetrustedleader.com. We invite you to visit us there in order to contribute to the conversation. In the meantime, we hope that this book will help you become a better leader, more capable of building and sustaining trust-based organizations than before. With trusted leadership, organizations are better positioned to weather any crises and to seize any opportunities for success in the marketplace over the long term.

PART ONE

AN OVERVIEW OF TRUSTED LEADERSHIP

1

What Is Trusted Leadership?

THIS IS A TRUE STORY (with the usual disclaimer—only the names and circumstances have been changed). *Dan is the COO of a large public relations firm. A brilliant strategist, he joined the company just six months after its creation, and can truthfully take a great deal of credit for its growth and success. On a personal level, though, he can be difficult to work with. He often doesn't think before speaking; if something displeases him, he doesn't hesitate to berate publicly the person he holds responsible. To his mind, these outbursts are like pressure valves. He recovers quickly, and is happy to have a measured discussion with the person in question soon after. His colleagues and direct reports have generally been tolerant of these unfortunate outbursts; after all, he spares no one, and his talent is great.*

Recently, though, he exploded at Paula, the firm's new executive vice president for marketing, in front of her staff and several other function leaders. Finding fault with her perspective on resource allocation for media buys, Dan told her that she "wasn't ready for prime time," and that she lacked "any sort of professional perspective."

Immediately after the meeting, Paula sought counsel with Michael, the company's head of human resources. Michael was diplomatic—he tried to calm her down by explaining in broad strokes about Dan, and about how the rest of the company generally dealt with him. She said that even if Dan was known for his outbursts, his comments to her, in front of her colleagues and staff, were way out of line. But she asked for confiden-

tiality in her meeting with Michael. After all, she was new to the firm, and she didn't want to make any waves.

Michael wanted to respect her privacy. At the same time, he was worried that Dan was pushing the limits of the company's goodwill. Michael decided to discuss the matter privately with the firm's CEO.

The CEO agreed with Michael; Dan's behavior would have to change. The two talked about what to do. Michael stressed caution; he thought the best course of action was to wait until Dan's next regular performance review, which was coming up in three weeks, and to hit the topic hard then. The CEO said she wasn't sure that was the right path; she told Dan she would think about it and they would talk again.

The next day, however, she went to Dan directly, and brought up the incident with Paula, telling him, in private, that she wanted him to rein in his behavior. Dan asked her how she had heard about what happened; the CEO was vague.

There has been a lot of fallout following that encounter. The atmosphere at the company, for example, has changed entirely, almost overnight. Paula is now virtually silent during senior management meetings. She takes lots of notes, looks angry, but doesn't say anything. It's as if her talent and her drive have dried up. Three other senior vice presidents have started having meetings behind closed doors at least once a day. Those meetings are all centered on rumors—who is saying what about whom, whether Dan is going to quit, that kind of thing—but their staff, for the first time, doesn't know what the meetings are about, and new rumors have started about the company being in trouble. Dan, for his part, seems to have drawn an invisible line through the company. There are some people with whom he is open and friendly (and explosive—his usual self, in other words). And there are other people with whom he won't speak—mostly Paula's staff and Paula herself, but also Michael. He makes no effort to hide the fact that he no longer trusts some of his colleagues.

But that isn't all; the quality of client work has slipped noticeably as well. Several key new clients, in fact, are disappointed with their recent encounters with the firm, and have said so—to the firm, and to colleagues and other stakeholders.

The quality of a company's work and the quality of internal trust are related. Trust is one of the most valuable, and vulnerable, assets of any organization. When people trust one another,

thcy can work through disagreements—both personal and professional—successfully in the context of the greater fabric of the organization. With trust, employees and leaders work with purpose
toward company goals. Over the long term, trust may be the single most significant determinant of a company's success.

But trust can (and does) melt away in an instant. When a confidence is broken, or one member of the senior management team
is excluded from a significant meeting, or employees become aware
that their company leaders are saying one thing but doing another, trust is immediately threatened, and often destroyed.

As a leader, you can actively create and sustain trust. The basic
tenets of trust are universal, but, in the internal context of organizational leadership, trust has a set of characteristics and enablers
that differ substantively from other arenas. In *The Trusted Advisor*,
for example, Rob and his co-authors explored in depth the relationships between company and client, but the realities of building trust with one's colleagues, bosses, boards of directors, and
subordinates require a very different set of tools and techniques
from those used with outside clients or customers.

Inside an organization, there is less of a buffer zone than there
is when you're working with an outside client. Interactions are
more constant and immediate. What's more, the pressure valve in
many relationships with outsiders—that option simply to back
away or terminate a relationship—is virtually nonexistent when
working inside an organization. Inside an organization, little is
forgotten, especially when you are in a highly visible leadership
role. Even less is forgiven.

Inside an organization, your position as a trusted leader can be
built or destroyed on many, many levels. With "trust outside," it's
the advisor and the client, or the advisor and the client's company.
Inside, it's more complicated. You have the relationship between
yourself and other leaders, you have leaders' individual relationships with rank and file, and the leadership team's relationship
with the rest of the organization. You have the relationships between divisions, between locations, and between different groups
therein.

Trusted leadership, in other words, is difficult to map. It's equally difficult to assess where the requisite elements of trust and leadership may be lacking, or threatened. When you're working with a client, it's pretty clear when someone is unhappy, and getting to the "why" is usually a straight path. Inside an organization, it's much more likely that the messages you're receiving are muffled or distorted in some way by the layers of people involved or the politics that go with them. If you're the head of a division, for example, and the people in the front lines of your organization are angry about your actions, you may not hear that anger. Their anger will only reach you by traveling up through the organization if there is trust at every level in between.

People and organizations regularly find ways to compensate for the dysfunction created by a lack of trust. In large part, however, the "quick fixes" are unhealthy and also extremely costly in both financial and human terms. One has only to consider companies such as Sunbeam Corporation in the days of Al Dunlap, or Cendant and Enron in their days of accounting irregularities.

When you get to the heart of the matter as a trusted leader, you deliberately build and sustain trust. This is different from dealing with the periodic outbreaks and repercussions that result from a lack of trust. This is a long-term process that takes time and explicit commitment. But the investment is well worth it.

Three Kinds of Trust

Trust inside organizations falls into three identifiable categories. The first of these categories is the trust that people have in the ability of your organization to be successful. It is trust in the company's mission, and in how you and your organization execute against that mission, both externally and internally. It's *"Our employees trust us as leaders to be correct (or at least directionally correct) in what we do in the marketplace, how we compete, how we price, and how we present ourselves."* Let's shorthand this category as Strategic Trust.

The second category is Organizational Trust. Organizational trust is created through personal trust, but it is something more. It is your employees' trust that the organization you lead is truly

Three Kinds of Trust

Strategic Trust

Trust that *the organization is doing the right things*
• goals and strategies

Organizational Trust

Trust in *the way things are being done*
• processes and decisionmaking

Personal Trust

Trust in *the people leading the organization*
• trust in you, trust in them

---

what it purports to be. Here, the employees as a group, and even the individual leaders, are considered to be separate from the corporate entity. In other words, the company is almost a third party that either does—or does not—make good on its promises. "I don't trust my boss, but the company's compensation policy says X and I believe that the company will make sure that my boss sticks to policy." Here, if the company has a formal way of resolving disputes, you trust that the "system" is aboveboard. Here, if there are layoffs, you trust that the choice of who stays and who goes is made fairly.

The third category is far more personal. It is your employees' trust that you, as an individual and as their leader, will treat them fairly, and that you will extend a level of care for their well-being. Employees believing in this trust, in return, show at least some loyalty to you. It's: "I trust you, whether or not I trust the company." Sometimes it's: "I trust you to protect me from the company!" We call this category, simply, Personal Trust.

You can have personal trust without organizational trust. You need at least *some* personal trust in order to have organizational trust. You *don't* need either personal or organizational trust to have only strategic trust. (The company might be a hotbed of deceit, but it might have a brilliant product, or it might just happen to be sitting on a lot of oil.) But the leader who has strategic trust without the other two is headed rapidly for rough waters. We'll talk least about strategic trust as we go; this book is primarily about building organizational and personal trust.

The Benefits of Trusted Leadership

Trusted leadership looks a little different in every organization, but its benefits are universal. While we've mentioned a few of those benefits early on in the chapter, a careful review of our own and others' experiences gives us nearly a dozen identifiable benefits. Here's our top ten list:

1. Trusted Leadership frees people. With trusted leadership, politics moves to the back seat, freeing people to make decisions based on the market, on your company's capabilities, and on financial considerations.

Lack of trust spawns meetings behind closed doors, private e-mails, and whispered conversations in the parking lot. That isn't a free environment; that's tapping on your cell block walls to communicate what little you know—or think you know—with other prisoners. And the amount of time people spend talking about what was said, and what it might have meant, versus doing any productive work, can be staggering. At one organization we know of, work almost came to a complete standstill for weeks because of rumors that the senior executive overseeing all European operations didn't have a lot of faith in the person who had been newly appointed to head the U.K. office. The very impression of lack of trust at the top caused a ripple effect so extensive—rumors building on rumors—that the organization eventually had to send out a formal communication to the effect that European operations were stable and performance was on track.

Trusted leadership frees people to do their work.

2. Trusted Leadership fuels passion. Have you ever been inside an organization where people work late because they're truly immersed in their jobs? Where they're motivated by whatever challenge the business faces, and they extend themselves to meet that challenge? It's exhilarating. It's contagious. And it's because people trust their leaders and they trust one another.

Tom Valerio, most recently senior vice president of transformation at CIGNA, compared two experiences he had with corporate entities that were each attempting to reposition themselves to improve profitability. In one of them, the CEO leading the effort, Gerry Isom, had established great trust with his peers and staff. Tom told us:

> He went around saying, "The sooner I find out what's wrong, the sooner I can help you fix it." He instituted a feedback system that called for employees at all levels to rate their areas on a scorecard, and then arranged for those assessments to be put on the intranet for the senior management team to see and respond to. At another company, that could have been disastrous, having everyone see everyone else's dirty laundry. Here it caused a snowball effect in a positive way. Suddenly, because people trusted Gerry, they were willing to have everyone see what was broken without fear of personal backlash; they knew that everyone would simply pitch in to fix whatever it was, and you had a lot of dialogue going. Someone way down in the organization could be in touch with someone else on the same day, exchanging useful information. The organization was learning at an incredible rate on the front lines; you don't see that too often.

Tom also recounted a "town meeting" that Isom held at the outset of the overhaul initiative, where people could raise any issue they wanted:

> Someone asked him whether there would be layoffs if the transformation effort didn't make its numbers. And he said honestly that he didn't know; that it was indeed possible; and that that's why he really needed their support for the initiative. He was honest with them; and as a result, people were reaching out to say, "What can I do to help?" The effort became a battle of hearts and minds, not just words, and people had all this energy for their work. We created very aggressive timelines for the organization; we wanted them to move to the top quartile in performance in their area. And we got more than what we asked for.

Earlier in Tom's career (at a different company) he had led an almost identical effort, but under the leadership of someone who didn't inspire trust. Tom reports that that effort "was like night and day" when compared with Gerry's division. "People there were doing the calculations in their heads—you could see it. They were saying 'what's in this for me?' and 'How can I do just enough to stay on the right side of this issue without overextending myself?' And the results were predictably not as good."

3. Trusted Leadership provides focus. When an organization doesn't have trusted leadership, people waste a lot of time trying to figure out where the organization is heading.

In one company we know, the lack of trusted leadership has caused a lack of focus that brought the organization to its knees at a critical strategic juncture. The company—a well-funded, high-profile technology startup—was founded in 1998 to produce a product. Its leaders soon found an opportunity to deliver a host of services around the product as well. Eventually it became clear that in order to pursue services properly, they would need to focus the whole company around service delivery. They needed to decide whether to continue to invest heavily in research and development, thus keeping the product at the center of the organization, or whether to move to a service model and concentrate resources on broadening and deepening the growing array of services the company was providing. As it was, the hybrid business model was straining already scarce resources and hurting overall performance.

Looking at the issue from a purely business standpoint, some leaders admitted that they thought the company should pull back from services and stay product-centered. But because the various senior vice presidents didn't trust one another and felt they needed to look out for themselves before looking out for the interests of the company, the issue was more personal than strategic.

The main problem was that the person heading up the product area was volatile and unpredictable and no one wanted to stick his or her neck out and say, "Look, we think we should stay focused on the product. But if we do, this guy is going to have to take on even more of a leadership role. He can't do that by himself. We can stay focused on product, and he can lead, but only if we bring in someone to work alongside him and handle the people side of the equation. Otherwise, the organization will be pulled apart."

If they had had trust in their leadership, people would also have had the confidence to bring their concerns out into the open, and could even have talked directly to the head of the product area. As it was, political support lined up around the service-focused business model, simply because people couldn't freely discuss the implications of choosing one path over another.

As we write, the verdict is still out; the senior management team has yet to decide whether to focus on its product or continue to try to be a hybrid organization concentrating equally on product and service. As a result, returns are poor and investors are now faced with the unenviable task of having to decide whether to pull the plug or to infuse more capital to keep the company afloat and demand action, in the hopes that it's not too late to reorganize.

4. Trusted Leadership fosters innovation. When people don't feel they have to analyze every last little thing through the lens of distrust, they can spend time, instead, exploring new ways to solve problems or to take the company forward, without fear that their own actions are going to be misperceived as wasteful. At some companies, that kind of exploration is built right into the job descriptions, and trusted leaders allow it to happen. People can tinker; they can say, "I'm going to play with this for a while," and they often emerge with great results. Post-It notes is the classic example of such innovation at 3M. The product was actually the result of an employee "playing" with a new glue that wasn't as binding as it had been expected to be. "Well, this didn't turn out the way we thought it would; but wait, maybe we can do something with it after all."

Forrester Research, based in Cambridge, MA, provided us with another good example. The company is going through a redesign as we write, and has created a new type of internal group dedicated to creating new products and services so that the company can enlarge its offering to each client. The entire premise of the new group is to explore and innovate. Because the organization has a cadre of trusted leaders, the people involved in the project are excited, rather than fearful, about their new task. They know that part of innovation is creating things that *don't* work, and they know that the organization knows it too. Without feeling that they had the trust of their leaders, however, the pressure to produce would be too great to bear, and the group would be doomed to failure before it even began.

Our friend Jim Lawrence, the CFO at General Mills, puts it this way:

> Failing when you're trying to create something isn't the end of your career here at General Mills. It's usually a positive thing because it shows that you're willing to stick your neck out to keep the company moving into the future. In fact, people get to the top here having developed a lot of products that were duds. But you need trust in order to be willing to stick your neck out in the first place.

5. Trusted Leadership gives people the time to get it right. As you can see, all of these benefits of trusted leadership are interwoven; they feed upon and build upon one another. The gift of time is part and parcel of at least two other benefits—the ability to be free to do one's work and the ability to focus. When leaders do not encourage freedom and focus, people tend to make decisions too quickly; they want to produce results so that the spotlight can be off them and on to the next person as quickly as possible. They pass the ball and pass the buck and just get out an answer—any answer—so that they can claim closure.

With trust inside, the pressure is off and people feel free to say "I need more time to get this right." It's OK if the buck stops at you for a while. "Better to have it fast than right" doesn't happen as much in trust-based organizations.

Having trusted leadership *doesn't* mean a lack or reduced sense of urgency. Heaven knows we are all subject to tight deadlines and the need for speed. People in trust-based organizations don't just mosey around, working on pet projects and feeling good about one another. But they do tell one another when they need more time to get things right. They don't just get it done, in other words; they get the *right* thing done.

We'll call on Forrester again for an example of this benefit. The company has a "traditional" way of preparing reports for clients. The style is breezy, and the reports generally utilize a lot of bullet-points, or summary sentences so that readers can get the gist of the research the company has prepared without going into great detail.

For one set of European clients, however, it became clear that adding detail—submitting the supporting data with the summary report—was going to be an important factor in winning more business from those clients. When an organization lacks trusted (and *trusting*) leadership, agreeing to release such supporting data, exposing research methods to scrutiny from colleagues and clients alike, and taking the time to put the data into a form tailored to the client's needs causes a lot of internal turmoil. At Forrester, however, the task was almost a non-event. Forrester's leadership trusted its employees' point of view and allowed the inclusion of supporting data with no questions; more important, Forrester's employees trusted their leaders, and knew that there would be no penalty for taking the extra time to get it right.

6. Trusted Leadership lowers costs. Less wasted time, less cost. It's that simple. Consider what happened when a major media conglomerate introduced a shared-services model in its interactive games business. The parent company made the decision to go to a shared-services approach, thinking that it would be a good way to allow its various businesses (many of them very small organizations creating and producing a single game) to concentrate more fully on their work without having to spend a lot of time and effort on accounting, legal work, human resources, and administrative paperwork. It brought in a consultant, who spent the bulk of its time creating contracts and service agreements, and then traveling around trying to facilitate the transition process.

It seemed like a good idea. Had the process gone smoothly, it would have started saving money for the company right away. But the stark reality of seeing the contracts threw many of the leaders of the smaller businesses into a panic. All of a sudden, they were acutely aware of what their responsibilities were going to be, and what the center would and would not be held accountable for.

There were a lot of new questions: "How are we supposed to track that?" "We've never done this type of administration this way; why do we have to switch when this new process seems more complicated?" And all of a sudden, it became clear—to the company's leaders, and to all those little groups of eight or ten people here and there who had been happily working out of garages, writing games far into the night and ordering take-out pizza— that there was very little trust between them.

Because of that lack of trust, even the wording used in the agreements caused trouble. One business unit head said, "Don't call me a customer; customers have a choice!" However, at the exact same time, another business unit head complained, "You called me a business unit; I thought I was a customer!" As one of the executives told us, "The theoretical savings of a shared services model could very well be eroded by the friction created in the process. Nobody ever quantifies the cost of having to argue about some of these things."

7. Trusted Leadership is contagious. When you have trust inside your organization, everyone knows it, and the internal trust helps build more of it up and down your supply chain, from vendors to customers. Trust inside builds trust outside.

For example, consider the J. Peterman Company, a direct-mail marketer that went bankrupt and was sold at auction, but has since been bought back and rebuilt by founder John Peterman. When the company went bankrupt, Peterman says, most of the vendors got stuck. The printer had the largest claim—over a million dollars. When Peterman bought back his name and relaunched the enterprise, he returned to all of those same vendors with whom he had worked previously. Every one of them, including the printer, returned to the fold. "I did not walk away from the bankruptcy with any money. I got stuck too, and they knew it," he says of his vendors' willingness to renew their relationships with him. "But the main reason they trusted me enough to come back was that I never lied to them. We had a history of fair and straightforward dealings."

Consider, too, L.L. Bean. When one Bean customer received a delivery from L.L. Bean that arrived damaged and with an incorrect monogram, it didn't deter her in the least from her loyalty to the company. "I knew that the person I spoke with when I called to complain would make it right," she said. "He told me exactly what would happen, and I knew he had the authority to do what he said he'd do. With another company, I might have asked to speak to a manager. But I think there they trust their front-line people, and so I didn't have to go that extra step."

8. Trusted Leadership helps recruit people who are on the right wavelength. When people are genuinely enthusiastic about where they work, it's much easier for them (and for the recruiting organization) to engage with prospective employees and convey exactly what the organization is about. When people are genuinely enthusiastic about the person or leadership team they're working for, it's even easier. We asked a wide cross-section of people about the primary influences on their plans and career choices, and we heard countless times "I came here because of the chance to work with (or for) so and so. He [or she] is the reason I'm here."

With trust, in other words, it's a lot easier to get off of someone's paper qualities and get into the more important realm of "fit." Trusted leadership helps make the right match between people with great experience and skill and your organization.

9. Trusted Leadership helps retain great employees. Whenever someone leaves one organization for another or to pursue independent work, the move is usually motivated more by issues of personal and organizational trust than it is by issues of compensation or title.

These implications are enormous. Consider how the average tenure for employees has declined in the past twenty years. From the 1980s through the 1990s, people in every single age group, 25–64, spent less time with the same employer. In some cases, the median tenure with employers dropped by as much as two years per person. If most of the people who shift jobs are doing so because of trust issues, they're naturally moving on more cautiously. They're jaded, suspicious going forward, less likely to extend trust in their next work environment. Lack of trusted leadership has potentially broad societal and cultural, psychological and emotional impacts that are genuinely frightening to consider.

10. Trusted Leadership improves the quality of work. The situations Tom Valerio told us about are also good examples of how trusted leaders improve the quality of work. With trusted leadership, people help one another to do the business of the company; improved quality is a natural byproduct.

Where Do You Stand? Where Could You Stand?

Do you know where trusted leadership strengthens your organization and where is it lacking? Can you envision what your organization would look like with real trust inside?

The exercise that follows here is designed to act as a catalyst, to get you focused on what trust inside really is, and on where trust exists—and doesn't—inside your organization.

Complete the following sentences, being as specific as possible.

1. With real trusted leadership, here's how *relationships across departments in my company* would change:
2. With real trusted leadership, here's how *our ability to keep our best performers* would change:
3. With real trusted leadership, here's how our *senior executives across this organization* would change:
4. With real trusted leadership, here's how *our interactions with customers or clients* would change:
5. With real trusted leadership, here's how *getting our work done* would change:

Now look at each of your responses to the above questions. What changes would have to take place organizationally and structurally, in order to get real trusted leadership? Who would have to change their behaviors? What would communication between individuals and departments look like? Would people interact differently, argue differently, resolve conflicts differently than they do now? How easy or likely would it be for those changes to occur? What role would you or others have to play?

This exercise usually reveals a few painful truths about becoming an organization with trusted leadership at its core. Sure, the long-term goal is positive, and worth pursuing. But the path there can be painful. Think about it. If there were real trusted leadership in your company, senior executives—you—might hear some unvarnished or unwelcome feedback. Customers might find out that your act is not quite as together as you'd like to portray. Episodes in which failure is avoided only by last-minute heroics—and there may be more of them than you realize—would all come to light.

This is not just about you and your leadership style. It is about how you can build a culture of trusted leadership that will become a cornerstone operating principle of your organization.

We like to use that exercise in our client work. Even though it can leave people somewhat deflated for a short time, it also clarifies the importance of becoming a trust-based organization. Maybe you don't want customers to see your underbelly, but if your company becomes a trust-based organization—or even if it already operates with a great deal of internal trust, and you simply improve on what already exists—it's almost certain that your performance will follow suit. So what customers see will reflect an increasingly positive reality.

We usually do this exercise several times. You can change the emphasized phrases to reflect whatever corporate organization units, internal and external relationships, processes, or systems you choose. Once you do the exercise on several levels, and then rank the results in order of potential positive impact, you're facing a pretty compelling set of initiatives to attack.

With an agenda in hand, how do you move forward? While every organization and every set of organizational dynamics is different, we nonetheless think it's possible—and beneficial—to apply a consistent approach to each initiative. (We'll outline that approach in Part Two, "Identifying and Applying the Tools of Trusted Leaders.")

Key Messages, Up Front

In *The Trusted Advisor,* one of the things Rob and his co-authors stressed was the belief that it was not just appropriate, but in fact valuable, to "give away" some of your expertise up-front. For example, when pitching a client, if you know the answer to his problem, it's worth it to say what the answer is, and also to say why. That way, the client gains insight into your understanding of the problem, and also gets a sense of how you would approach it. Armed with that knowledge, he'll have a better sense of whether a future with you will be worth the investment.

So here is our list, up-front and given away, of the major assertions of *The Trusted Leader.* The ensuing chapters will explore each of these in depth, through case studies and exercises. But this list will give you an idea of what you're in for, so you can see if you're on the same wavelength we are, and if these ideas are something you want to invest your time in.

1. *Trusted leadership takes many forms.* From the way the CEO talks to the members of his or her senior management team, to the way front-line employees show how they feel about the company in the way they deal with customers. From the way people get promoted, or passed over for promotion, to the expectations they have when they sign on or leave. In order to get a handle on trust inside, you need to develop some form of 360-degree, multidimensional perspective on the way trust manifests itself in the leadership group. Or doesn't.

2. *Trusted leadership shows itself as the sum total of many interpersonal interactions, all of them extraordinarily fragile.* Even in the best work environments, trust is potentially under attack all the time. Every time one manager says something about another without his or her knowledge; every time two staffers meet at the coffee machine; every e-mail sent, every announcement made; every time a high-profile executive walks down a hall or engages in casual conversation. Trust needs vigilant protectors.

3. *Every day, every organizational juncture provides opportunities for building trusted leadership.* Every instance in which trust might come under attack is also an instance in which trust might be created or strengthened. Every meeting with your employees gives them a chance to see you and other leaders in action, hopefully not posturing or wearing false smiles.

4. *The speed at which trust is destroyed is always faster than the speed at which it is built, but the process of building trust does accumulate deposits in your company's "trust bank."* A major violation of trust can quickly spread and

poison an entire organization if it's not managed properly, however, no matter how strong that organization's "trust account" had been up to that point. A leadership group that works to build trust inside achieves a rhythm that helps it move smoothly through the kinds of business situations that cause other leadership groups to sputter and stall.

Your "account balance" provides a buffer of sorts. Where there is a history of trust, people are more inclined to give the company the benefit of the doubt in tough or questionable situations.

5. *An individual's ability to build and maintain trust with clients correlates with his or her ability to build and maintain trust inside.* Relationships with clients are all about expectations, promises, and delivery. So are relationships inside an organization. You can only set realistic expectations and make good on promises from the inside out if you're sure that the organization behind you can deliver. Your professionalism and certainty requires trust.

6. *Becoming a trusted leader requires both message and medium.* In other words, inspiring language, by itself, won't do the trick. Trust is intangible, but the acts of building, maintaining, and repairing trust require concrete processes. For example, you could easily proclaim, "From now on, the head of marketing will work to build trust with the head of finance!" Heads may nod, people may say "Aye, aye!" But the words by themselves are meaningless. If your head of marketing thinks about his need to build trust, however, and picks up the phone to call the head of finance to discuss a touchy resource allocation issue in advance instead of presenting it as a *fait accompli* a week later, then that's progress.

7. *Trusted leadership is a combination of what you accomplish (outcomes) plus who you are (skills and competencies).* Great outcomes and trustworthiness are often found together.

Hide and Seek

Most of the time, in our teaching and consulting work, we're not called in for trust problems, per se. In fact, what often turns out to be a trust problem is usually cleverly disguised as something else, something less "soft"—a "solid" business problem. At one firm, Rob was retained to help think through and plan how the management structure was going to change and adapt as the company grew. Fine. But three meetings into the work, the CEO (who had founded the company) said quietly to Rob, "Let's take a walk." It turned out that he didn't want to be the CEO anymore. But, as he confessed halfway up a hill overlooking Boston, he didn't know how to tell anyone, and felt that if and when he did tell people, two members of the senior management team would immediately and viciously compete for his job, at the expense of the welfare of the company as a whole. A trust issue. A leadership issue. And one that presented the obvious problem—the challenges of growing the company—in an entirely new light.

At another firm, we were called in to help the senior management team get up to speed on the company's new global strategy. We were to create some processes that the managers could use to improve the way they passed along newfound knowledge about the markets they were entering. As it turned out, the issue wasn't that general. The real problem was that most of the senior managers didn't trust the CEO, and so they avoided contact with her as much as possible.

More often than one might suspect, what presents itself as a business issue is much more organizationally and personally driven. People usually don't open with, "Betsy is a star performer, an industry guru. But internally she drives her colleagues nuts. She has such a big ego and totally personal agenda that no one wants to work with her. Can you help?"

Trust issues hide, and often hide well. That's why we devote one chapter of this book to the enemies of trust. First, though, we'll offer an exercise that may help you define your own starting point on the journey to becoming a trusted leader and on building trust inside your organization, and we'll detail the characteristics and competencies that need to be developed by those charged with meeting those responsibilities.

2

The Trusted Leader
Self-Assessment

FIGURING OUT WHERE YOU ARE, so that you can more thoughtfully plot your course forward, is a useful investment of time. Hence this self-assessment drill, designed to give you a starting point to use in the process of becoming (or remaining) a trusted leader. Some of the questions may seem, at first blush, to have a "right" answer. That's not always the case, however. Many of these questions are designed purely to make you reflect, or to force you to hear the views of those who might be better suited to provide an objective response. Those two activities, reflecting on one's own progress and hearing the objective views of others, are part and parcel of trusted leadership.

The Trusted Leader Self-Assessment

Please indicate your level of agreement or disagreement on the 1 to 5 scale shown underneath the statement. (Circle one)

Section I (Questions I–5)

1. The people I have hired are smarter or more talented than me.

1	2	3	4	5

Disagree Strongly   Neither Agree nor Disagree Agree Strongly

2. The people currently reporting to me are smarter or more talented than me.

1	2	3	4	5

Disagree Strongly   Neither Agree nor Disagree   Agree Strongly

3. I have played a significant role in the development of people in this organization who are outside of my direct area of responsibility.

1	2	3	4	5

Never   Rarely   Sometimes   Usually   Always

4. At least two or three people in the organization would regard me as an active yet informal mentor.

1	2	3	4	5

Disagree Strongly   Neither Agree nor Disagree   Agree Strongly

5. I give people more latitude for error than do most other executives.

1	2	3	4	5

Disagree Strongly   Neither Agree nor Disagree   Agree Strongly

Section I Total (Questions I–5):

Please add the numbers you have circled in your responses to each of the above questions in this section and write the total here:

Section I Total:_____

Section II (Questions 6–II)

6. The people I lead have a clear, explicit understanding of the desired leadership characteristics of the organization.

1	2	. 3	4	5

Disagree Strongly   Neither Agree nor Disagree   Agree Strongly

7. I openly praise the people who work for me.

1	2	3	4	5

Never   Rarely   Sometimes   Usually   Always

8. People working for me feel free to disagree with me publicly.

1	2	3	4	5

Disagree Strongly   Neither Agree nor Disagree   Agree Strongly

9. People understand the evaluation and reward standards I have established, and consider them equitable.

1	2	3	4	5

Disagree Strongly   Neither Agree nor Disagree   Agree Strongly

10. I am considered highly trustworthy by my direct reports.

1	2	3	4	5

Disagree Strongly   Neither Agree nor Disagree   Agree Strongly

11. I trust my direct reports implicitly.

1	2	3	4	5

Disagree Strongly   Neither Agree nor Disagree   Agree Strongly

Section II Total (Questions 6–11):

Please add the numbers you have circled in your responses to each of the above questions in this section and write the total here:

Section II Total:_____

Section III (Questions 12–15)

12. There is a succession plan in place for me, and I have shared it explicitly with someone who could implement it if necessary.

1	2	3	4	5

Disagree Strongly   Kinda Sorta   Agree Strongly

13. I have explicitly told my potential successor how valuable he or she is to the organization, and to me personally as well.

1	2	3	4	5

Disagree Strongly   Kinda Sorta   Agree Strongly

14. I know what my legacy to this organization will be.

1	2	3	4	5
Disagree Strongly		Kinda Sorta		Agree Strongly

15. The individuals in this organization could easily articulate what my legacy to this organization will be.

1	2	3	4	5
Disagree Strongly		Kinda Sorta		Agree Strongly

Section III Total (Questions 12–15):

Please add the numbers you have circled in your responses to each of the above questions in this section and write the total here:

Section III Total:_____

Section IV (Questions 16–20)

16. This organization (or my part of it) would be in fine shape tomorrow if today were suddenly my last day.

1	2	3	4	5
Disagree Strongly	Neither Agree nor Disagree			Agree Strongly

17. This organization (or my part of it) would be in fine shape two years hence if today were suddenly my last day.

1	2	3	4	5
Disagree Strongly	Neither Agree nor Disagree			Agree Strongly

18. Everyone in this organization knows how we make money.

1	2	3	4	5
Disagree Strongly	Neither Agree nor Disagree			Agree Strongly

19. Conflicts are resolved in my organization in a healthy and timely fashion.

1	2	3	4	5
Disagree Strongly	Neither Agree nor Disagree			Agree Strongly

20. I explicitly discuss the importance of trust with the people in the organization.

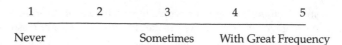

1	2	3	4	5
Never		Sometimes	With Great Frequency	

Section IV Total (Questions 16–20):

Please add the numbers you have circled in your responses to each of the above questions in this section and write the total here:

Section IV Total: _____

Tabulating Your Self-Assessment

The tabulation of this self-assessment is designed to get you to reflect and become more aware of the context in which you work. Armed with that awareness, as you read through the book, we hope you'll find a myriad of useful ways you might take action to improve your score and achieve your goals. If your numbers are low, *please* don't interpret them as indicating you are not cut out to be a trusted leader (not that you would anyway, we hope!). A low score may indicate, however, that you will have to reallocate some of your priorities, your time, or your approach to those activities that can help you generate the form of trusted leadership you seek to achieve. The value of the self-assessment comes in figuring out what comes next for you as you hone the skills of a trusted leader.

Interpreting Your Self-Assessment:

The questions in each of the four sections were designed to highlight the broad steps that leaders can take as they build their careers, and the questions they should continually ask themselves along the way. If you look at them as they are grouped, you might well see that certain areas require more attention from you than others. Take a look, section by section.

Section I (Questions 1–5): Here's what it means:

Section I focuses on the course you are setting for your organization, trust-wise, for the future. While a total of 20 points would mean that you have done a terrific job in this area, having picked up on the importance of hiring people who truly are better than you, and giving them lots of leeway to learn and risk, don't be fooling yourself about this. Do you *really* think they're smarter or better? A lot of people put on the false modesty posture here. But be honest with yourself. If they really are not smarter or better than you, you'll do yourself no favors when the chips are down. Find people who are.

You also can't be complacent about this, either. That's what Question 2 (about those currently reporting to you) is all about. Organizational needs change, and offerings to clients and customers change, too. If your direct reports aren't equipped to meet those changes going forward, just imagine how the people below them will do.

Finally, Question 5 (about giving your people more latitude for error) has a tricky element to it. If you gave yourself a 5 here, make sure it's for the right reasons, and not because you tolerate continued under-performance. It's very, very hard to take people out of their roles, or off assignments, or fire them. People just hate to do it, especially to people on their team who have been loyal, or formerly successful, or have been helpful to one's own career. It almost seems internally inconsistent, trying to be a trusted leader on one hand, and firing people with the other. So if you gave yourself a "5" on this one, be careful.

Section II (Questions 6–11): Here's what it means:

This section examines how well you understand and model the appropriate leadership behaviors for your organization, and for your role. The questions in this area look closely at three particular issues that can affect your success in building trust:

1) the clarity with which you have articulated the behaviors you expect and will reward, and that presumably they are healthy ones;
2) the openness of the work environment, in people feeling that they can disagree with you without onerous consequences; and
3) your ability to be both trusted and trusting.

Pay particular attention to your response to Question 11, regarding your implicit trust of your direct reports. It checks up on you as a *trusting* leader, which is one of the identifying characteristics of *trusted* leaders. If you have scored yourself in the 21–24 point range, then you are truly a role model for others, setting a workplace tone that makes people really want to be there.

Section III (Questions 12–15): Here's what it means:

This section helps you to evaluate your progress in thinking about your legacy. It isn't easy. For many readers, the questions in this section could seem irrelevant, especially in the earlier stages of one's career, or if you have not yet fully settled into your organization or role. You may currently be far more focused on getting it right in the first place than on getting ready to leave it well-tended, or in good order. If you are truly in such a situation, you might be tempted to disregard the section. But don't use it as an excuse. You can (and should) be thinking about this early on in your career.

If you *have* been in place for a while, then Question 13 (about telling your successor how valuable he or she is) can be among the stickiest. If you are uncomfortable about letting someone know prematurely that he's your designated successor, it still doesn't absolve you of the responsibility of being absolutely certain (and therefore explicit) about his importance to you and to the organization. While that may edge too close to the "mushy" or overly affectionate for your taste, please don't make the mistake of assuming he knows it, and just skip this. It's far too easy to take it for granted, and it might be something you could come to regret.

Section IV (Questions 16–20): Here's what it means:

The final section focuses on clarity, trust and sustainability. Pay particular attention to your response to Question 18 (regarding how well people understand the company's basic business and value propositions). Time after time, in company after company, it continues to dismay us how *few* employees really do have a good grip on how their company actually makes money. Finally, take a close look at your response to Question 20 (talking about trust). While trust is shown more through actions than words, there is great value in making sure your people know how important it is to you. Just think what can happen if people understand that deeply. It will bring out the best in your company, your people and in you.

Total Score: What It Means

Where do Trusted Leaders end up in total scores? That is hard to say, as great strengths in one or more areas can help compensate for less-than-perfect scores in others. Here are some very rough guidelines, based upon an as-yet statistically insignificant body of results.

If your total is less than 60, either you are way too self-critical, or you have got some work ahead of you. It makes sense for you to do some close looking at why the numbers are where they are. Are all your subsection averages 3.5 or below? Is it just in one or two particular subsections that they fall into this category?

If your total is between 60 and 80, then you are in a range of where the plurality of people in leadership roles fall. You may be a good performer in a particular environment, thus the question that arises is how easily would you make the transition should that environment or the surrounding circumstances change.

If your total is between 80 and 90, then you are probably working with some clear successes in the realm of trusted leadership. You are probably finding more of your challenges to be specific, identifiable ones rather than general issues of overall effectiveness.

If your total is 90 or above, you are doing very well, and given that, it would be helpful for you to examine how to raise the bar of performance for your entire organization. At the same time, remember that this is a self-assessment. With this high a score, it makes sense for you to have a number of people rate you anonymously on these dimensions. If your self-assessment matches their ratings, then you truly are a trusted leader.

We put this self-assessment early in the book so that you could locate, for yourself, a starting point. But we encourage you to revisit these pages often. We believe that this type of reflection is something that trusted leaders should engage in regularly.

3

The Characteristics and Competencies of the Trusted Leader

For your consideration:

- *Manny is smart but not brilliant. He is not a lightning-fast decision-maker. (In fact, he sometimes takes what could kindly be described as a meandering path towards making decisions.)*
- *Mary is a quick study. Perhaps too quick for some people. She tends to rely much more on instinct than on analysis to make decisions.*
- *Moe is about as dry as dust. He relies heavily on analytical formulas to make decisions. He doesn't have a particularly good sense of humor. He tends to focus even his informal conversations on work.*

What do these three people have in common? They are all trusted leaders.

Trusted leaders come in all shapes, sizes, and personalities. That, at the bare-bones level, is the core message of this chapter. We're not going to fill the next few pages with stories of big-name personalities—those charismatic, larger-than-life celebrities you read about every day in the news—corporate, political, or otherwise. Some of them may even be trusted leaders; their histories might make a good read. But this chapter is not about other people and their stories; it is about you and yours. Why? Because you are (or you will be) your own best role model when it comes to being a trusted leader. The best benchmark you can use on your journey to becoming a trusted leader (or as you work to strengthen that position) is your own best behavior.

What's our rationale here? Put simply, it is that if you strip away all but the essentials, being a trusted leader is about knowing yourself. Knowing your strengths, your shortcomings, what gives you pleasure, what annoys the hell out of you. Knowing why you go to work, why you react as you do under pressure, what scares you, and what makes you proud. The true trusted leaders we know all have one thing in common, if nothing else: they know themselves very well.

Self-knowledge is fundamental to being a trusted leader for a simple reason: trust is built on honesty. If you're to be trusted about matters of strategy, staffing, marketing, mentoring, and so forth, you must first be able to understand what your natural tendencies are, and why, in some situations, those tendencies work for you, and why, in other situations, they work against you. You must first be comfortable in your own skin. *And you must also be able to share your understanding of yourself with others, so that their expectations will be in line with your delivery.*

Above all else, trusted leadership means not faking it.

The Trusted Leader from the Inside Out

Let's dig a little deeper into what we mean by self-knowledge. We mean having the ability to say that you're a people person, or not. That you're tech savvy, or not. That you're a perfectionist, lazy, patient, or impatient. That you avoid conflict whenever possible. Or that you relish a good argument. Once you understand your strengths and weaknesses in some depth, you can step back and consider how your personal makeup works when it is applied in the many roles you take on as a leader. Does your preference to deal with data rather than people work for you or against you when you're analyzing the market? How about when you're facilitating a discussion? Working with a client? Monitoring company performance? Mentoring a direct report?

Once you understand how your own personal makeup works for or against you in your various leadership roles, you can then begin to figure out how to use your strengths—and compensate for your weaknesses—while maintaining your integrity.

Too often, we see people who would otherwise be trustworthy—and who would otherwise be perceived as trusted leaders—run into trouble in trying to overcompensate for a weakness. They put on a "game face" that is all too easy to see through. An awkward personal comment from the manager who is by nature not a people person but who is trying to seem so during a pep talk; a forced tone of gratitude in a speech made by someone who is really not grateful; put-on enthusiasm from someone who is not demonstrative. None of this works. Perhaps the most egregious example we've seen is the corporate executive who was giving the news of layoffs to his employees with a broad smile on his face. (The man was trying to appear grim by gritting his teeth as he spoke, but to those in the back of the room, it really did look as if he was smiling. Truth is, he was greatly disturbed by the layoffs, but he felt that his usual deadpan expression wouldn't go over well with the troops. Little did he know . . .)

It would have been far better in his case, and in the other circumstances we just mentioned, if the people in question had simply been themselves. If their employees, or colleagues, or bosses were already well aware of their own personal styles, and were thus prepared for a response in keeping with those styles. It would have been far better, in other words, if that CEO had delivered his layoff news with no expression, as was the style to which his employees had grown accustomed. It would have been better if the person receiving the pep talk already knew that his or her boss cared, but that he or she would probably show it by writing a sincere note, rather than delivering a perfunctory pat on the back.

Just because you might not be particularly good at one or another style of leadership does not mean you can't be trusted. Just because you have to try harder in certain areas doesn't mean you are not or will not be a trusted leader. Do you by nature avoid conflict? Do you do whatever you can *not* to deliver hard messages? That doesn't mean that you *won't* deliver those messages when you have to. It means you have to work harder at being able to do it with some level of comfort. *Or* it means that you have to find an appropriate delivery mechanism to support or supplement your efforts.

Let people see that some things don't come naturally to you.

Let people see that you're trying to improve in certain areas. Say you're by nature a quiet person. As long as you can even say something like "It's hard for me to be boisterous. I can't froth at the mouth. But I can tell you how pleased or angry something makes me. I can express it. I can demonstrate it in other ways," that's fine. You'll be doing something we call "name it and claim it," which is a big trust-builder. What's critical is that you're not faking a level of comfort you don't feel.

What happens if you do fake it? Eventually you'll be faking it more and more and your fake self will be the person people expect to see. If that's the case—if you're in a role that you really feel calls for the portrayal of a person you're not—doesn't that tell you something about your "fit" at your place of employment? Isn't it telling you something about your life? Isn't that a signal you'd do well to pay attention to? There are numerous ways of developing that self-knowledge, or coming to terms with who you are.

Your Own Motivational Mix

One good way to gain self-knowledge is to spend some time thinking about what motivates you. In the course of our work, we've found that most people's motivation stems from some combination of the following four sources: duty, meaning, accomplishment, and joy.

Motivational Mix

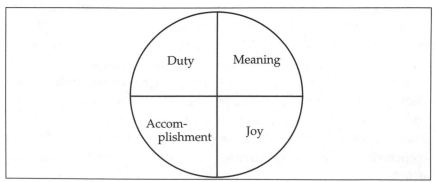

Why do you go to work each day? Is it mostly to put food on the table and pay your car loan? To maintain a certain lifestyle for your family? Do you work in large part because you feel that what you do genuinely makes a positive difference in the world? Because you want to see how far up the ladder you can climb? How much you can achieve before you retire? Do you work because you love what you do? Because it genuinely gives you great pleasure?

The key is being honest with your answers. There is no right or wrong response. There is no right or wrong mix. If duty is your lead motivator—that is, if your reason for doing what you do is rooted in a sense of responsibility—that's fine. You can be a trusted leader through and through—so long as you don't try to fake a level of joy you don't feel.

If your lead motivator is accomplishment, it's important to understand whether or not your sense of achievement comes from within or whether it relies primarily on external cues. We're *not* saying that satisfying your ego is a Bad Thing. Not at all. Imagine how difficult it would be for anyone to be motivated if there were no ego involvement—if you couldn't take pride in your work or receive some recognition for it! A healthy level of pride in your work will motivate you continuously to increase quality. Insufficient pride will reduce your investment and lower the quality of what you produce. An excess of pride may mean that you're overcommitted to a particular outcome, even at the expense of your moral compass, or the longer- (or shorter-) term implications of what you're doing. The writers of headline-grabbing business stories just love a good tale of excess.

Be aware, too, if you find that your mix is dramatically skewed toward one or another of these four elements, with the others registering near zero. If you're motivated entirely by duty, then you may, over time, stick with a particular job for far longer than you should, or stay with a company solely out of a sense of obligation. If you're motivated entirely by joy, more power to you, but it wouldn't hurt to check in with the big picture to ensure that your work is sitting in balance with your life and that your bills are getting paid!

(Just for the record, we are acutely aware that even *having* a motivational mix is a luxury of our time and place. Through significant periods in history, many people couldn't indulge in the thought that work is driven by anything other than duty. In too many parts of the world today, that still holds true. But generally speaking, with the changes in the nature of the workplace that we've seen in the last 30 years, and the evolution of nontraditional families and family roles, factors such as accomplishment have taken on more importance. In periods of economic growth and opportunity, motivators like joy and meaning have had the opportunity to rise to the fore.)

Our point is this: Most any combination of the four elements is OK; extremes can be dangerous; but as long as you know why you're doing what you do, then you stand a fair chance of being able to *carry that honesty through all aspects of your work.*

The Trusted Leader from the Outside In
(What Others See—and Judge)

When you know yourself well—when you understand what drives you to work; when you can acknowledge your strengths and weaknesses; when you can let others know what to expect (and what not to expect) from you in different types of situations; when you seek help from others to handle situations in which your own natural tendencies wouldn't serve you well—then you yourself will feel more like a trusted leader. And others will feel that way about you as well.

In other words, self-knowledge—and the willingness to work with the hand of cards you've been dealt—manifests itself in the kinds of characteristics and competencies that others will subconsciously assess when they're deciding whether or not to put their trust in you.

What are those characteristics and competencies? They are: credibility, reliability, intimacy, and a lack of self-orientation. The idea is to either (a) be strong in all four areas, or (b) be so outstanding in one that you make up for any relative shortcomings in the others. In other words, your credibility, reliability, intimacy, and lack of self-orientation—as perceived by your colleagues and employees—are indicators of your trustworthiness. And the relative strengths or weaknesses of those indicators relate to one another, as the following equation illustrates:

$$T = \frac{C + R + I}{S}$$

Where: T = trustworthiness
C = credibility
R = reliability
I = intimacy
S = self-orientation

Credibility

The shorthand definition is "expertise." Do you know enough about whatever it is you're working on or talking about to warrant others' confidence? But the right trust-building answer doesn't have to be "Yes, I'm an expert." The right answer can be "Yes, I'm an expert," if you do in fact have the knowledge. But it can also be "No, I don't know a lot about this topic but I know exactly where to find the information we need."

What makes someone credible inside an organization? Chances are, it's a combination of experience, the way in which he's handled himself in the past, her track record of tasks accomplished, and how well-known all of those things are throughout the organization. That last is key. Credibility with clients is usually built with one other person (the client). But inside an organization, people cast far larger shadows because they have relationships with many people, and also because those people have relationships with one another. You may be credible, but the internal "spin" on your credibility is of equal—and sometimes greater—importance.

Put another way, credibility in an organization isn't just about how one other person perceives you; it is "What's the take on you?" across the board. Think of the department head who, as he steps to the podium at a company-wide gathering, seems to cue the opening ceremonies of the Eye-Rolling Olympics or trigger a wave of restlessness throughout the audience. The people who don't know him personally see that, and their impressions begin to form. It's as if there is a credibility index of sorts, and the actions of the person in question have some bearing on it, but don't weigh nearly as much as they could, or should.

What can you do to bolster your credibility? First, make it a point to give credit where credit is due. (Does "Don't fake it" sound familiar?) Be up-front about what you know and what you don't know. Be up-front about where you're going to go for the expertise you don't have.

Second, develop a network of people you can go to for the expertise you don't have. Know how to get your hands on the right tools. A note of caution here, though. Make sure that your network is the real thing. Dropping names for the sake of dropping names won't serve you well. (Again, don't fake it.)

We once worked with a guy (we'll use the name Leo here) who we can only describe as the Willy Loman of real estate. Leo used to say, insistently, "I know people. I get answers. I get results." Trouble was, he did, but he didn't, and he didn't. And once, as he was busy presenting his case for why he should become the broker on a particular deal, and he made his "I get answers" speech for the nth time, one of the owners involved said "Yeah, Leo, and the answers you get are 'Go away. Don't bother me.'"

Reliability

Reliability is all about being consistent and dependable. In that way, it sets itself apart from the other variables because reliability is largely about action. But it has an emotional aspect as well. Reliability, as part of the trust equation, also has to do with whether a person is able to deliver their consistency and dependability in a way that makes the receiver comfortable.

Some obvious reliability killers are constantly changing your schedule (and dragging others along on the wild ride). Not showing up for meetings. Showing up late, or ill-prepared. Overpromising what you're able to deliver. And perhaps the biggest one for many leaders: changing focus, apparently on a whim.

Less obvious, but equally poisonous, is using a rote set of phrases. Or having only one set of solutions, regardless of what the problem might be.

Because reliability is such a well-understood term, there's a tendency for leaders to minimize it—or at least to gloss over it, saying "Yeah. I know, I know." A trusted leader's reliability is based on an understanding that people need him or her to be reliable in order to do their work. (Reliability is absolutely critical in times of crisis, where leaders must be the ones to soothe, calm, and inspire.)

Intimacy

Relax. We're not suggesting that you need to share any private details of your life—or ask for the same from others—in order to be a trusted leader. Personal doesn't have to mean private. We're talking about *being intensely personal about the work at hand.* That is, taking to heart issues including compensation, promotion, and hiring and firing people. Think of the number of lives that are affected each day by business issues ranging from one person's small promotion to a major change in organization or ownership. Think of how what you do affects other people, inside the office and in their lives outside of work. Business is personal, and trusted leaders never forget it.

What intimacy really means, in this sense, is the understanding of personal motivations, situations, and sensitivities. It means getting close, emotionally, to the issues you and your employees face as you work.

Here's a story in which intimacy made an enormous difference: Rick was a senior executive. He'd been a manager for a long time, but now, due to a corporate restructuring, the CEO had asked him to take on some client responsibility. Rick hadn't worked directly with clients in years (though he'd been great at client work back when). He delayed, he stalled, he said he didn't have time. Weeks went by. The truth was, Rick was very nervous about re-engaging with clients. He wasn't at all sure he would still be any good at it. But that was something he felt he couldn't say.

The CEO came through. He could see that Rick's excuses were just that, excuses, and he was close enough, emotionally, to sense what the problem was. He went to Rick and said, "Look, I don't know if this is a factor, but if it is, I want you to know that we really need you to do this, but we won't make you go it alone.

We'll ease you back into it. Pair you with someone at first, if you like. Let's talk about it."

A few months later, Rick was handling client relationships with ease, as he used to.

Your ability to be intimate, with regard to your work, not only gives others a clearer picture of where you stand, it can also help you spot others in your organization who might be trying to "fake it" to get by, and help them get back on track.

Lack of Self-Orientation

We were uplifted when we heard Rick's story. Not so with this next one. Sam set up a meeting with his boss, Sarah, to discuss his compensation. He felt that he deserved a raise. He had asked for the meeting specifically to talk about his pay. But in the first seconds of the conversation, Sarah steered the topic to her upcoming client presentation. Could Sam offer any input there? Could he help her prep the presentation?

Sam came away frustrated. Was Sarah giving him some sort of test? Was she showing the classic tendencies of the conflict-avoider? Or was it just all about her, all the time?

The lessons that can be extrapolated from this story link back to honesty and self-knowledge. Could be that Sarah was simply preoccupied with the client presentation. But if that were the case, she should have been honest with Sam. "I know you're here to talk about your compensation. I know I agreed to meet with you now on this. But I have to confess, I'm all tied up in knots about the presentation I have to make today at four. Could we reschedule? (And while I have you here, could I run a few ideas by you?)" Sam might have left her office frustrated, but he wouldn't have been confused, and his trust in Sarah would not have been stressed to the same extent.

Your level of self-orientation has a lot to do with what's motivating you. If your work doesn't interest you—if your motivation is coming mostly from the duty or achievement arenas—chances are that you're going to focus more on yourself when you're interacting with other people. It's a natural fall-back. But if that's the case, it's time to take a hard look about whether or not you belong in your current job. There are so many interesting things to do out there; you owe it to yourself to find something that clicks for you.

The Trusted Leader Survey

We conducted a broad (albeit highly unscientific) survey, specifically for this book, to pinpoint just what characteristics and competencies people think of when they're asked to define a trusted leader. We asked approximately one hundred people across a variety of organizations to identify people they considered to be among the most trusted leaders in their company. Their names, who they actually were, were not terribly important to us. What was important, however, were the criteria the respondents used in making their selections. Rather than giving them a list of descriptions typically associated with trust or leadership, we asked for their opinions. Their responses, strikingly similar, clustered around six criteria in particular: **caring, honesty, reliability, straightforwardness, integrity, and consistency**. The most unexpected of those was caring, which, next to honesty, received the most mentions.

Time

To close this chapter, we'd like to share with you parts of our conversation with Regina M. Pisa, who is now in her second three-year term as chairman and managing partner of Goodwin, Procter LLP, one of the larger and more distinguished law firms on the East Coast, with more than 550 lawyers and offices in Boston, New York, Washington, D.C., and elsewhere. In our experience, Regina Pisa qualifies as one of the real trusted leaders.

Pisa said, "When I first took the job as chairman and managing partner, more than a few people advised me, 'Make all your big changes now, because three years from now it will be too late.' That advice was wrong. If I had tried to propose the most sweeping changes up front, I would not have succeeded. I began to have more power with—and trust from—my partners after they had seen my values in action. Trust and respect of your partners is not something you take; it is earned."

She gave us an example of how building trust over time gave her leverage. As she told us:

One of the more dramatic changes that we accomplished during my term as managing partner—and one that will have real impact on the future strategic direction of the franchise—was changing our partner compensation system. I proposed that change not in my first year as managing partner, but at the end of my third. It had become clear to me after three years of leading the firm and working hard to build a national franchise that our retrospective, individual revenue driven compensation system was holding us back. I didn't need to hire a consultant to tell me that, nor did I believe we had the time to convene another committee to study the proposition.

The train was heading out of the station and we needed to get all of our systems aligned, including our compensation system. So, I turned to two of our partners in whom I had a lot of confidence and said, "Here is the behavior we want to incent. Here are the principles we should follow. Go off and draft a revised compensation system. No consultants. No committees." They produced a new plan within a few weeks, which I then circulated to our partners for discussion at an already scheduled partners' retreat shortly thereafter.

On the first day of the retreat, I spent the entire morning talking about our values as a firm and our strategic direction, how we were going to achieve our goals and in what time frames and, finally, about what I hoped my legacy would be and what I envisioned for our legacy as a partnership. I had done a lot of thinking about this, especially after September 11. I said that I didn't want our legacy to be that we were the most profitable firm in town. It had to be more than that. It had to be that the next generation of partners would look back on us, this generation of partners, and say, "these were men and women of vision." I said, "We need to align the entire organization with our vision and that means we need to change our partnership compensation system. We can't do this without sacrifice."

After some spirited discussion, I called for a straw vote on the proposed changes. Virtually every hand in the room went up. As partners looked to their right and to their left, their surprise and excitement were palpable. People came up to me later and said, "I believed in it, but I had no idea that others would go along with it so readily, too." Within weeks, amendments to the partnership agreement effecting those changes were circulated and formally voted on. If I had tried to do that when I had first taken the position, even if it had been the right thing, I would never have succeeded. When I first took the job, I had their hope, but not their trust. There's a comment you sometimes hear that trust is a "wasting" asset. I actually think it's a growing asset.

Granted, leading a professional services firm can be very different than leading other kinds of companies. For example, you may not have to build partner/owner consensus before taking action. But you still have to gather support, make your case, hear people out, and stay attuned to process. And it all takes time.

Achieving trusted leader status doesn't come easily, naturally, or quickly. But becoming a trusted leader is *not* an impossible quest, and the payoff can be dramatic. It can be dramatic for those we lead, for each of us personally, and for our organizations at large.

4

The Enemies of
Trusted Leadership

ARNIE WAS THE COO of a large, publicly traded company facing tough times in a tumultuous marketplace. He asked Nina and Carlotta, two of his most senior finance people, to figure out just how far below projected earnings the company was going to be at the end of the next quarter, and to estimate how many locations would need to be closed, and how many people would have to be laid off as a result.

They studied the situation intensely, and together agreed that the company would have to close a number of its locations and lay off 15 percent of its workforce. They informed Arnie, who concurred, and began to spread the word to other members of the senior management team. Most understood, and agreed on the planned course of action. But one senior manager, while agreeing with Arnie to his face, privately balked, and within a few days, had leaked a rumor that the "finance group" was "hysterical and out of control," and that they were "gunning to gut the company."

The result was a huge amount of damage to the company, internally and externally, including frenzied gossip behind closed doors, a dramatic drop in productivity, and speculative articles in the press.

To stabilize the situation, Arnie felt he had to take a dramatic stand. He announced that the company had no current plans to close any locations, nor to cut any jobs. But at the end of the following quarter, Nina and Carlotta's projections proved right, and the company was in much worse trouble than it would have been had it cut the 15 percent as originally suggested. Nina and Carlotta justifiably felt wronged. Employee stress levels skyrocketed. Arnie never recovered from the about-face.

You really can't be a trusted leader in your organization, or in your part of a larger organization, unless an environment of trust exists beyond your office walls. Sure, you can be an island of trust in an otherwise untrustworthy world, but what good is that? If you're the last bastion of open, honest communication and the free flow of information, you'll quickly become a target. Your position, while just and heroic, just won't hold. We have all seen individuals fight lonely battles of truth in otherwise corrupt organizations only to leave in disgust (or be fired) when the final cards were being played.

Trusted leadership simply doesn't work in isolation. That's why a large part of becoming a trusted leader means building trust in the organization around you. We'll go into detail about the specifics of how to do that in the chapters that follow. This chapter, though, is devoted to the enemies you'll encounter along the way.

We're putting enemies relatively early in the book to help you build awareness and vigilance. The more sensitive your antennae, the more likely you will be able to protect what you're trying to create. Sometimes trust is affected and eroded in ways that aren't obvious. In fact, most enemies of trust are covert, not overt, and we'll highlight them as such as we go. A verbal exchange you might have thought of as personal, for instance, can have organization-wide implications in terms of trust. A decision that seems small, even inconsequential, can have enormous repercussions in the "trust" department.

We also want to list the enemies of trust early on simply to acknowledge the tendency to discuss breaches of trust, rather than stellar examples, when the topic of trust is raised. "Oh, I can tell you about trust," people say, and they follow, almost inevitably, with a negative story. When we spoke with George Hornig, managing director and chief operating officer of Credit Suisse's Private Equity Group, for example, he said, "In my 20 years on Wall Street, I can think of very few senior people worthy of the kind of trust you are talking about. That in and of itself says something."

By putting the enemies of trust on the table here, we're attempting to give you an opportunity to say, "Been there," and then have a deeper look at what happened, how you might have seen it coming, what you might have done differently in reaction, and to what effect. (We will offer a broad-strokes remedy for each threat we identify. But our intent is to cover as much ground as quickly as possible so that as we get into more detail later on, you'll be able to do a quick mental inventory—a vulnerability spot-check, of sorts—and make what you're reading more action-able for your own situation.)

Mostly, though, we put the "Enemies of Trusted Leadership" chapter here because we wanted to emphasize that *defending trust is, in large part, what building trust is all about.* Trust is fragile, and it's always under attack. So when you set about to build trust, what you're really doing in most cases is setting up a web of catch mechanisms that will identify threats to trust early on. In this manner, you can deal with them promptly and properly before they do substantive damage. If extremely long titles for books were in vogue, in fact, the title of ours would have been *Becoming a Trusted Leader in Spite of People with Personal Agendas, Inconsistent Messaging, the Unintended Consequences of an Event or an Announce-ment, Rapid Change, Elephants Meandering Undisturbed in the Par-lor . . .* (The rest of the title would have been the remaining list of the twenty-plus threats to trust that makes up this chapter.)

One of the people we interviewed for this book likened the process of building and protecting trust to something he'd heard once about twigs in a river. This was the gist: Twig after twig can float down a river without having any effect, and then one catches onto something and holds, and then others catch onto it, and all of a sudden the shape of the river, the depth of the water, and so forth are forever altered. With trust, every threat has the potential to be that one critical twig. Even the seemingly most innocuous vi-olation of trust can bring down the entire organization, if left to fester unattended.

A Rubik's Cube of Enemies

Some enemies of trust are individual—the person whose ambition acts like a steamroller, flattening colleagues or undermining team-work without even slowing down. Some are organizational—cul-tures that punish dissent, or hide conflict, or kowtow to hierarchy.

Some are situational—such as when ill-founded survival instincts cloud someone's better judgment. Some are systemic—for example, if compensation systems inadvertently reward damaging behaviors. Some are overt, and some are covert. In fact, there's a veritable Rubik's Cube of enemies out there.

We're listing 22 of the most onerous threats, and we made no attempt to shorten, or lengthen, the list for cosmetic purposes. (The "Top Twenty" sounds better, but it just didn't serve.) These are the worst enemies we've encountered; they're all potentially equally dangerous, and so each deserves its own spotlight.

We divided them into two groups—overt and covert—mostly because we felt that the covert enemies should be flagged as such. As we said earlier on, a few of them do such a fine job of masquerading as inconsequential tics, or even benevolent behaviors, that they warranted the extra attention.

We'll start with the overt enemies, though. There's comfort in the devils you know.

The Enemies of Trust

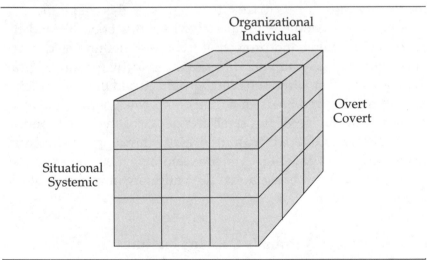

Organizational
Individual

Overt
Covert

Situational
Systemic

The Devils You Know

Building trust can be like hiking a hazard-strewn trail—at least there are some easily recognizable dangers. To wit:

1. People whose needs for promotion, power, and recognition are potentially lethal to the organization. We mentioned a few of these in Chapter 1 (remember "Explosive Dan," the COO?). The people who stomp all over their colleagues in pursuit of their own glory. The competitors whose need for control overrides any moral commitment to fair play. The executives whose need for perks and status outweighs their commitment to the financial health of the firm and its employees.

What can you do when there's someone like that in your midst? First, ask yourself, Is the grief worth the relief? In other words, does this person really contribute so much to the organization that their untrustworthy actions are worth suffering? Is there enough inherent value in this person (or hope for his reformation) to make it worth your while to have to deal with trust violations on a regular basis? If the answer is no, then your path is clear (Get rid of him, for heaven's sake!). If the answer is yes, or even maybe, then you have to think about what can be done to keep the damage (present and future—because there *will* be more) to an absolute minimum. The quick moralistic answer to this question is usually, "Fire him, fast!" But it's not always that easy or cut-and-dried.

Ask yourself, Can this person be isolated from as many other people as possible and still do his or her job? Can he or she be put in charge of a focused, one-person area or project? Minimizing work-related contact with others in the organization, while at the same time increasing responsibility (or at least increasing the perception of responsibility), is one alternative.

Another option is surrounding the person in question with proven commodities, and realigning his or her performance measures to emphasize teamwork. A senior vice president at one company we studied nearly brought down his entire department because his personal need for recognition wouldn't allow him to hire talented people near his own level. He suffered from what we call the Big Daddy syndrome—he was not able to develop a team at the next level down because he perceived anyone with any talent or drive at that level as a threat. As a result, he surrounded himself with a cadre of people who were far too junior to perform in his absence.

The president was in a quandary. If she fired him, she felt, the department would collapse in on itself. "It took me two years to find this guy," she said to us. "I don't know what we'd do without him."

She didn't fire him, in the end. What she did instead was to bring in a group of people at a level between him and his direct reports as he had originally organized them. These new people had proven track records in other parts of the company; they came in as a group, and, having been given specific responsibilities, they were off and running. At the same time, she brought in a coach for the senior vice president to improve his team-building skills, and also reset his goals so that his compensation depended increasingly on the performance of the people under his leadership. She also reserved the option of moving him into more of an individual-contributor role, several months out, if things didn't improve.

Turns out, the guy was coachable. Surrounded with highly talented reports, he was no longer able to say "They're not ready," or, "They can't survive without me," and the coaching helped him realize that his other talents were still very much needed and appreciated elsewhere in the organization.

Not all of these stories end up in such a satisfying manner. Many, maybe even most, others are about someone who is his own worst enemy and who eventually self-destructs.

2. People whose personal agendas are at odds with the organization's strategy. These are people who are thinking, We're going to put this product on the market. I don't care about our other products; this one is my baby. Or, We're going to go into retail, come hell or high water. No matter that our catalogue business has a track record of success and the numbers for retail don't look promising. I want stores. Or I want to open an office in San Diego; I have family there. So what if our business focus is the Northeast?

Do any of these characters populate the top levels of your organization? If their personal agendas are different from the organization's strategy to the point of incompatibility, you'll have to let them go. Why? Because if you don't, you'll end up with a lot of employees thinking, Why are we doing *this* when I thought the company wanted us to do *that?* Why are we doing something that only helps *you?* Their trust in the company as a whole—as a place that is strategically sound, as a place with leaders who are looking out for them, as a place that "walks its talk"—will erode rapidly if they sense that the organization's goals have diverged from the things they're being told to work on.

But first, ask yourself why the person in question is pursuing something that goes against the organization's strategic grain. Does his or her behavior reflect a conflict in your own policies or processes? Also, ask yourself, Is this person's ego irrevocably out of control, or is there something we can do to help this person realign his or her personal agenda with the organization's strategy?

At one firm we know, the top management team decided that it was not economical to serve clients who wanted to contract for less than $50,000 worth of work. They issued an internal statement to that effect, explaining that the company could no longer handle smaller clients because they were losing money on those jobs. Some of the partners were uncomfortable severing personal relationships they had developed with smaller clients, and decided, "I'm going to keep this guy even though it's a direct violation of the new rules, because we've been in this together for so many years. I have numerous $100,000-plus accounts, so why shouldn't I have a few $10,000 accounts?"

The solution was involving a large cross-section of the management group in reworking the compensation system. (The new system would tie compensation more closely to account size and profitability.) The top managers also asked that same group to work together to lower costs so that the company could continue to serve loyal, smaller clients.

As it turned out, even when costs were lowered as much as possible, the organization was still unable to justify serving accounts under $50,000. But at that point, with the numbers out on the table, and all executives having participated in the process, the new rules took hold with little resistance.

3. People with volatile personalities. These are rainmakers who are class A jerks. They are often senior-level high fliers who routinely torment their juniors and the administrative staff. These are often people for whom the words "politically incorrect" have no meaning.

We could say that the best option is to bite the bullet and get rid of them. It probably is, but few leaders do that with alacrity. So here are a few alternative courses to consider:

First, put some walls between your troublemaker and the rest of the organization. Start with real, physical walls. Give the person in question a great big office down the hall or on a different floor in order to minimize the frequency of contact with other people. Also, to the greatest extent possible, isolate him or her organizationally. For example, make him or her a separate profit center; try to have him or her fly solo as often as possible. This is often the optimal course to deal with "individual contributors" in order to minimize the havoc they can wreak when they interact with other parts of the organization.

Second, rearrange your administrative set-up so that staff members serve this person among others, instead of working directly for him or her. If dealing with a bad guy is 10 percent of someone's job, the experience is probably tolerable; if it's everything, they'll quit and may well spread poisonous rumors about your company forever after.

Third, whenever possible, if this individual is in a client-facing role, make sure that the organization has an independent link to the client (outside of your rainmaker) and vice versa. The idea is to ensure that if this person jeopardizes the relationship with his behavior, you'll still have a shot at saving it.

Companies or firms that utilize apprenticeship models should be particularly aware of these personality-based threats to trust. If you have rainmaker/jerks in your ranks and you can't bring yourself to get rid of them, you should certainly opt them out of serving as mentors. Bad behavior is not the kind of precedent you want your apprentices to presume is a role model for success.

4. A corporate history of underperformance. This is also an overt threat. Think of the kid who does badly in elementary school, and (rightly or wrongly) is branded forevermore as someone who is never going to excel. That's what we're talking about here.

There are two ways an organization can fall prey to this enemy of trust. One is indeed through constant underperformance in the marketplace. If a company consistently fails to meet the expectations set by its senior management team (and anticipated by Wall Street), trust, both inside and out, will rapidly erode. Look at Kodak, Polaroid, Xerox in periods of decline, for example. Sure, pockets of trust may continue to linger in these organizations, and sometimes these organizations recover. But in large part, what you'll see is a growing group of employees—at all levels—who fear for themselves on a daily basis, and spend less and less time thinking for the organization, and more and more time seeking their own next move. What can you do? Be as realistic as possible when you set goals. Don't let optimism guide your projections. Communicate to all of your employees as much as possible why you're setting the goals you're setting, and what has to happen in order for the company to meet those goals. The more people understand what lies behind expectations, the more likely they are to continue to trust you and the company as a whole, even in tough times.

The second way an organization can succumb to this enemy is by consistently failing to deliver on internal expectations. When a company promises to revise a bonus system, and then waxes silent on the topic for the next year, trust erodes. When a division head announces a new commitment to regular performance reviews, and then lets the agreed-upon deadline come and go, trust erodes. The old, old saying, "Don't make promises you can't keep," is the answer to this one. Even if those promises are made with the best of intentions.

5. The bait and switch. This enemy is a close cousin of the enemy of consistently failing to deliver. Consider the following example. Cheryl accepted the position as head of compensation and benefits at a publicly traded corporation *on the condition that she be allowed to multiply the size of her department within a year.* At the time she was hired, the company was doing well; her request made sense; the COO said "Sure." But within a month of her hiring, the economy took a dip, and the firm found itself tightening budgets as a precautionary measure.

By many acceptable standards, the COO could have turned around and said, "Sorry, Cheryl, we know we promised, but we just don't have the resources right now; you'll have to go it alone." It would have been a reasonable decision. But think of the effect that kind of backpedaling would have had on Cheryl's trust in the COO and in his decisions regarding her budget going forward, not to mention the effect it would have had on her attitude toward the company.

Instead—and since the option was fiscally possible (although not easy)—the COO stuck to his promise. He let her build her staff. And just a few years later, as the economy once again dictated tough times in the marketplace, he saw what a good decision he had made. Cheryl's department, fully staffed, justified its existence on a daily basis. As it turned out, when the tough times hit, having a department that was able to handle tasks such as the massive amounts of work that go along with reductions in force, severance payments, salary reductions, and the like, has been of significant value to the organization. And Cheryl is a trusted, trusting, member of the management team—making contributions above and beyond what her job description calls for.

At times, a bait-and-switch situation is unavoidable. There are often circumstances under which leaders must rescind on agreements they've made. But the lesson here is this: Bend over backward *not* to do it. Don't encourage people to do things with a promise you're not certain you're going to be able to deliver on. It's easy to get swept up in the enthusiasm of the moment—to let your vision bounce ahead of the realities, or probabilities, of the organization's abilities and the market. At the same time, pulling a bait-and-switch move inevitably puts "ink in the water." The victim's disillusionment will spread until he or she leaves the company.

6. People whose behavior reflects controlled vengeance. These are often folks who have been passed over for promotion. They include people who feel that they've been short-changed on bonuses or raises. They don't do anything outright to sabotage the organization; but they operate as if there's a cloud around them that they can't shake off. Given the choice, they'll see the negative side of everything the company does. Often, their behavior escapes management's attention—they fly under the radar. But the people around them notice; after a time, it becomes a downer to work with them. And the "cloud" is contagious.

What can you do? First you have to identify the source of the contagion. While this isn't easy, it is worth the effort. When you've promoted someone (to the exclusion of others), take some time to consider the also-rans. Then "double back" with them or their direct supervisors a few weeks after the news has sunk in, in an attempt to discover whether any residual anger or disappointment has dissipated.

Assuming you are able to identify them, you then have to try to help them move on. Sometimes it can't be done; the person in question can burn himself out with his own attitude, and it may just be time for him to go. But sometimes taking the time to identify the person's strong points and then tailoring her job to play to those strengths can revitalize her. We know of one person who was demoted from his position as head of sales for his company because he couldn't keep up with the demands of his job as the organization grew. The CEO brought in a new head of sales above him. But instead of allowing the shift to demoralize our guy, the CEO instead put him in charge of creating and running a sales *training* area, a position he held and excelled in for many years.

7. Inconsistent messaging. One of the fastest-moving destroyers of trust, inconsistent messaging can occur anywhere inside the organization, from the broad, strategic level, right on down. It can also occur externally, in the way in which an organization communicates with its customers or any other stakeholder. Either way, at any level, the repercussions are significant.

Consider the company that started out manufacturing a certain product, and then decided that servicing that product, along with others like it, had more potential, and *then* decided to get back to basics and focus on manufacturing the product once more.

Employees in the service area feel they're on shaky ground; so do their colleagues in manufacturing. They're suspicious of one another, and of the company.

Consider the large insurance company that makes repeated forays into the middle market, withdrawing each time after barely a year. At best, customers will be confused; at worst, they'll decide the company is unreliable and take their business elsewhere permanently.

Consider the company that offers, say, four different product lines, and keeps changing its policy about whether each line should have its own dedicated sales force, or whether one sales rep can sell multiple lines. Its customers won't know whether to expect four different sales visits or just one this month. They won't know whom to call if they need more of something or they have a problem with something they've purchased. Internally, account managers won't trust that the time they've invested learning about one or another product, or developing certain customer relationships, has been well spent.

Consider the story recounted to us of a senior executive who announced at an all-staff meeting one month, "This is the year of the customer!" People immediately began to ask each other, in a scene worthy of Dilbert, "Well, if this is the year of the customer, what will next year be?" One can then easily imagine the same executive making a similarly impassioned speech about how the organization should "focus itself around quality" only 11 months later, and the rolling of eyes after that.

Feedback scorecards, CRM, TQM—there's generally at least some potential in any popular management tool or technique. Some even have great potential. But unless the company vets the idea thoroughly before implementing it, and then sticks to the program (whatever it is) for a predetermined length of time, which has been communicated to everyone involved, employees are going to give less of themselves each time they're rallied around a new "cause."

Finally, consider the manager who tells employees in May that he's going to start a weekly brown-bag lunch meeting to discuss relevant issues in the marketplace (and alludes to the notion that somehow, enthusiastic participation is going to have an impact on employees' performance reviews). Then, that same manager cancels the lunch the second, fourth, and fifth weeks because of his own travel schedule. In week seven, he drops the idea entirely because "with the summer here, we really can't count on a good turnout." When he re-introduces the idea in October, do you think his employees are going to believe him when he says, "It will work this time"? Do you think they're going to be at all stressed come their performance reviews, about what they're really being evaluated on?

The antidote to inconsistent messaging is thinking things through as much as possible before implementation. And if you find that you have to change course, tell everyone why and be as forthcoming with information as you can be. Reserve "big bang" announcements for truly major initiatives.

It boils down to this: If you keep changing the music before the song is even half over, your people aren't ever going to learn to dance.

The Devils You Don't Know

If you give our list of covert enemies a quick look, you may find yourself nodding in recognition, but more likely, you'll say, "But what's the trust link? Why would that have repercussions on trust?" Ah, that's why they're covert. These are situations and behaviors that occur naturally in most organizations. They are many times understandable. They are sometimes unavoidable. They are not deliberate or calculated affronts to trust, but they are no less dangerous than their glaringly obvious peers. If trust's overt enemies are the next-door neighbors who scream at one another and regularly receive visits from their local police department, the covert enemies are the ones you hear people talking about in the news after some tragic event, saying things like, "He was always so polite." Or, "We had no idea."

Here they are:

8. Complicated situations. Most covert enemies of trust have their roots in incomplete communication. In fact, incomplete communication is what *turns* some otherwise innocent or innocuous scenarios into trust-breakers. That's the case with complicated sit-uations. Why? In a word: *rumors*. Consider an organization that is trying to decide whether or not to discontinue a certain product line. During the study period, it's understandably hard for top managers to say anything definitive to the rest of the employees. But distrust thrives in a vacuum. Without anything solid to grab onto, employees will over-read into any shard of information they find. If they hear the vice president of marketing sigh, word will get out that he is being let go. If they see outside consultants meet-ing behind closed doors with the CFO, they'll think the worst (even if most of them are well aware that bringing in an outside team to perform an analysis of a business under review is stan-dard practice).

Michael Rice, head of Prudential Financial's Private Client Busi-ness, recounted the following story:

> Recently, in response to a proposal for a set of initiatives, I re-sponded, "Well, the way you've described this, you're scaring me." A strange silence came over the room and the meeting ended shortly thereafter. At that point, one of my lieutenants came up to me and said, "Now everyone is frightened that they're about to lose their jobs!" I was shocked. When I asked him why, he said, "Don't you remember? The last time you said you were scared about something, we had a large round of lay-offs. You used the phrase 'scaring me' again, and people picked up on it."
>
> In complicated situations, the most important thing I've learned is the importance of consistency.

So what can a trusted leader do? Be as up front as he or she can—even if what ends up being said is that he or she really can't say for certain how the situation is going to be resolved. Incomplete in-formation breeds uncertainty and mistrust. So if you're in the midst of a complicated situation like that one, you could say something like, "There are a range of options, and nothing is off the table at this point; I'll tell you more as soon as I know some-thing more definitive." But don't say, "We're probably going to sell this thing," (and leave the possibility hanging). Don't say,

"Nothing unusual is going on," (which will be an obvious lie). And don't say, "We have full faith in the product," (which, although a positive comment, is also an obvious lie, under the circumstances). Anything you say or do during complex times—however minute—will be analyzed at least ten-fold more closely than it is when it's business-as-usual at your company.

9. The unintended consequences of a particular event, announcement, or initiative. There was once a U.S.-based company with an office in Paris, and a European business approaching 20 percent of its overall revenues. The company, in a very aggressive growth move, acquired a London-based competitor. The press gave the acquisition very positive coverage; the acquired company was assimilated as smoothly as these things can go, and in the U.S., management was highly satisfied with the action.

The problem was that, in Paris, what had been a stable, confident crew of managers was suddenly thrown into a panic. The people in the Paris office were convinced that the acquisition meant that European corporate headquarters would be moved to London. They lost faith in their U.S. bosses; they feared for their jobs; and they started making decisions based on that fear, rather than on what was good for the business as a whole.

It took months for the senior managers in the U.S. to figure out what had gone wrong (and by the time they did, the Paris team was in such disarray that the company almost *did* move its European headquarters to London!).

People tend to view changes—any changes—through a very personal lens. So to avoid the surprising breakdown in trust that can follow even a positive change, ask yourself, "How is this action/announcement/initiative going to look to the people in Paris (or in marketing, or sales, or HR, or accounting, and so forth)?"

Keep in mind, too, that going out of your way to provide all the necessary information and reassurance about any given announcement or situation isn't a one-time deal. In another company, senior managers pretty much bent over backwards to ensure that everyone knew exactly what was going on and why, the first time they had to do a round of layoffs. They issued multiple internal memos, freed up their calendars to meet with worried employees, really did everything they could to minimize the inevitable stresses of the situation. It worked, and they took justifiable pride in their efforts. But six months later, when they had to do another (albeit much smaller) round of layoffs, they felt their previous explanations would suffice, and failed all around to provide the same sorts of communications. The ensuing turmoil was worse than they could have imagined (possibly worse than it would have been if they hadn't been so conscientious the first time around because employees felt that since they'd been so up-front the first time, the silence had to mean disaster).

Most organizations run the risk of falling prey to this enemy of trust the first time they make a major announcement, or launch a new initiative. But the risk the second time around is just as great, no matter your track record. Always release and constantly update a set of FAQs and recommend that people go there to learn all you have to offer about whatever is going on. Get them to be wary of complacency in the same way you are.

10. The constancy of corporate reorganizations or management changes. We're not talking about companies that can't provide an updated organization chart. We confess that we know many organizations that do not have up-to-date organization charts. Because most organizations are in a somewhat constant state of flux, what's documented on an organization chart today may well be out of date tomorrow. When folks sense that there isn't any stable ground to walk on, however, they're going to be constantly uneasy.

Change in and of itself has no direct link to the level of trust in an organization, but the way in which change is viewed, handled, communicated, and positioned does. Incomplete communication will be the culprit. (Do you see a trend among covert enemies emerging here? We do.)

11. Rapidly changing situations. Picture a large group of senior executives for whom stock options have become very important. Formerly compensated with cash only, they're now getting a mix of cash and options, as part of a new compensation system designed to fuel growth.

The system was conceived at a time when the marketplace and Wall Street were not only receptive to the company, but in love with it. The move was well-understood; top managers took care to provide detailed guidelines on the new program, all questions were answered honestly and completely, and buy-in on the part of those employees affected was virtually unanimous at the time the system was implemented.

The problem was, in the three months following the implementation of the program, the market turned. The options had been issued, and their value eroded almost immediately. These senior executives, paper-rich only a short time ago, became paper-poor, and their cash flow was much less than it used to be. Are they still the trusting, optimistic group they were when they said "Yeah, great idea!" to the new system? No, of course they're not. And their mounting distrust of their company and their senior peers could pull the company apart at a time when it critically needs to hang together.

This is, sadly, an all-too-familiar scenario in the world of new-economy companies. And in many cases, there is no remedy. The most we can offer here is a word of caution: Be mindful of expectations when you implement a long-term tool in a context where it can have a major impact in both the long and short term. Be careful of designing an apparently long-term solution in the context of what may be a short-term marketplace condition. Do the best you can to communicate thoroughly what you're doing and the logic behind your actions. Options were never supposed to be a ticket to instant riches, but in the excitement of what was a growth boom, many people lost sight of that fact, because options in many cases did create instant—and great—wealth. If they had kept the long-term purpose in mind, would things have turned out differently for any of the new-economy firms that have flamed out and are no more? Probably not. But it is likely that there would be fewer people looking back in bitterness.

12. Benevolence in the wrong place. This enemy could also be called "Reluctance to change difficult situations."

People tend to look for the good in their fellowman, which is, of course, the right thing to do. But there is a fine, blurry line between looking hard for the good and avoiding dealing with the bad.

Here's one example: When a CFO of a major investment firm joined the organization, he inherited two direct reports, one of whom he quickly realized was extremely valuable to the firm (but who was soon to be going on a three-month leave). The other, he felt, was a liability to the firm, but he was reluctant to fire her. His theory was that at least she knew the business inside out; if he let her go while her colleague was on leave, he'd quickly find himself behind the curve in all the things he had to do.

Now, this situation at least had a natural ending-point—the return of the valuable employee. Most do not. And we have never seen an organization in which people have benefited by waiting to rectify a problem later (the firm in this example included). We'll repeat an "ask yourself" question we posed earlier in this chapter: "Is the grief worth the relief?" Be honest about the answer.

13. False feedback. All too often, when an organization tries to get rid of deadwood, or remove under-performers, they find themselves facing wrongful-termination suits. "Look at these performance reviews," the supposed victim says. "They're all great."

And he or she is undeniably right. The performance reviews *are* all great. The problem is, they're all lies.

As hard as it is to be honest about your employees' shortcomings, particularly when you have to talk to them about it in a regular, formal, face-to-face setting, you must, must, *must* do it. False feedback is just another form of benevolence in the wrong place. If you don't honor your own company's systems, you will find yourself facing difficult situations like the one we just detailed. And what's more, your other employees (the ones who are actually worthy of honest praise) will become demoralized. ("Private" information like performance review results spreads; it's a mysterious fact of corporate life.) Why should I work so hard? So-and-so doesn't, and every one knows it, but we got the same bonus, they'll think. Why should I trust this system/these processes/my boss? And you won't have a leg to stand on.

14. Elephants meandering undisturbed in the parlor. As we were putting this chapter to bed, we heard a classic tale of an elephant in the parlor. The division head in a large research company told us about a recent executive committee meeting he had attended. It was the first one conducted by a new president, following the rather abrupt and unexplained departure of his predecessor. Even though this was a senior management group, there was no discussion or acknowledgment by the new president that the prior president was no longer there, or the fact that a new person was now chairing the meeting. "It was as if we were all just supposed to pretend that nothing unusual had taken place."

Another way to describe this enemy of trust is "Failing to name it and claim it." We're talking about when someone has been fired abruptly, and the next day, at the regular staff meeting, no one mentions it. We're talking about when an outrageous internal rumor circulates and finds its way to the CEO's office, yet no one ever discusses it openly, even in a closed-door senior management meeting. While these stories come from our own personal experience, in the course of our work we've heard many similar stories, and we're sure you could add to our collection as well.

Don't ignore things that you know everyone is whispering about behind closed doors. Bring the issue into the open; explain it briefly; answer questions as best you can, and don't be afraid to say, "I'm sorry, I can't offer more detail because that would violate a confidence" if you need to. People will, albeit sometimes grudgingly, respect the fact that they're not privy to all the gory details. But their trust will erode if they know you're trying to slide something by them. And even if the whispering stops after about a week or so, please don't think that the whole thing has blown over. Trust us; it hasn't.

15. Inconsistent reactions or standards. In other words, your employees' perception that you or the company play favorites. Here are just a few examples:

- Does one corporate location have palatial offices, and another have a cramped space? It's possible that local real estate markets drove location decisions; after all, it may be easier to find affordable offices in Albuquerque than it is in New York City. Nonetheless, employees will, at some level, feel slighted if theirs is the smaller warren.

• Is it easier to get promoted in one department than in another? At one advertising company we know of, the creative department seemed to issue a constant stream of happy promotion notices. On the account side, by contrast, people rarely received title changes (let alone pay raises) to reflect their tenure or evolving skills and responsibilities. Remember the teachers who were hard graders in school? You might get A's from everyone else, but from Mr. Kellogg, you'd barely ever score better than a B? This is a similar situation, played out in the world of commerce. And it's no easier to deal with on a personal level here, if you're in the "wrong class," than it was back in the seventh grade.

• Did you take your new vice president of marketing out to lunch when he got promoted two months ago, but fail to respond in kind when you appointed a new head of IT? There are any number of valid reasons for inconsistent behavior along these lines, but that's not the point. One person is going to feel slighted by your actions; their reaction may turn them into an overt enemy.

16. Excessively strict or inflexible standards. Think of this as the flip side to the hard-grader problem. This covert enemy of trust is the organization that fails to adjust sales quotas for its reps even when it's painfully clear that the economy is in a slow-down. The remedy here is *awareness*. When change of any kind affects your business, make an explicit, organized effort to follow it down all possible paths, and see if anything else should be adjusted in its wake. Put together a task force; hold one or more multilevel or multifunctional meetings to do some brainstorming. Your efforts will be worth the investment of time.

17. Scapegoating. "How come Jack got fired when all the other people who have been doing the same thing did not?" "How come we got gypped on our bonuses? Our performance was better than the other divisions!"

Making an individual or a group within a company suffer in order to teach the rest of the organization a lesson might have a good short-term outcome—you might shock people into better behavior, or cause a temporary increase in employee effort. But scapegoating produces motivation through fear, and over the longer term, it's more destructive than productive. Your employees may think, I'm glad it wasn't me, in the immediate aftermath, and they may be more conscientious for a time about doing whatever it was that your action was meant to highlight, but sooner rather than later they're going to start thinking, But it could be me the next time—who knows how "they" decide on these things. The organizational trust they might have had in the company is going to break down, as well as any trust they might have had in the person who pointed the finger.

Sometimes the desire to "teach a lesson" or "set an example" can backfire, or can have derivative consequences that will harm you and the organization in the long run. So before you take action, think twice. You might be better served by resisting the temptation.

18. Taking away part of the everyday. Whenever we're explaining this covert enemy of trust, "the milk story" immediately comes to mind:

A company we know used to stock four varieties of milk in its staff kitchens for its thousand-plus employees to use in their tea, coffee, and cereal. There were sixteen kitchens, two on each floor of the company's building, and every Monday, the milkman would show up and put several large containers in each refrigerator: skim, one percent, two percent, and whole.

Employees liked the perk; many even brought their own breakfast cereal to work because of the milk; it also made for a good snack during the day.

Then one day, a member of the finance department did the math. He realized that the company could save nearly $40,000 a year if it stopped providing four types of milk, in large containers, to each kitchen, and instead offered one type of milk in single-serving sizes (the size used for one cup of coffee). The company made the move, and the following Friday, without any fanfare, the refrigerators were stocked with boxes of single-serving milks.

The reaction? "They took away the milk!" To say people talked about it would be a gross understatement. They bitched about it.

They moaned about it. They used it as an example to illustrate and supplement any other perceived negative actions on the part of management that they could think of. "This place isn't what it used to be." "The good old days are gone around here." Even "Another 'we're all family company' sells out." (Not that it was a family company in the first place!)

Even the smallest change to an individual's environment can, if you're caught unawares, erode trust. To be sure, the age of entitlement is over. (Remember the early days of 2000, when a 23-year-old junior investment banker at Salomon Smith Barney submitted a memo to management that detailed 36 ways to retain young employees such as himself? The list contained, among other things, corporate credit cards "where the analyst never sees the bill, yet accumulates the bonus points or cash back," reimbursement for toothbrushes, underwear, and other personal items bought on business trips, and a concierge service that would pick up dry-cleaning.) Nonetheless, before you make any change, no matter how justified, take the time to think about how it will be received and what its enduring effects will be.

19. Paralysis in the face of difficulty. When leaders "go dark" in the face of a crisis—no matter whether it is at the strategic or marketplace level, or at a very personal internal level—employees start to worry. When they worry—about how the company will survive, about whether the people in a given department will ever be able to work together again, about whatever—it is a sign that trust is evaporating.

Leadership has to have presence; if you're faced with a crisis, and you don't know what to do, don't withdraw. Let it be known publicly (through a memo and an e-mail, in person, and in town meetings—whatever methods you feel are appropriate) that you're aware of the situation, and that you'll keep everyone posted as events unfold, and as decisions are made. Set up an updates schedule and keep to it, even if the update is that there will be no news until next week. (You're no doubt hearing echoes of our "perils of incomplete communications" chorus here, but therein lies the insidiousness of the covert enemy of trust. The same sicknesses can stem from many different sources.)

20. Incompetence, or perceived incompetence. We'll start with straight-out incompetence. Anyone who has spent any time at all in the halls of business has encountered someone along the way who is, simply and sadly, so out of his league that everyone around him is genuinely stupefied that he's in the position at all. Colleagues wonder why management the next level up doesn't do something. Direct reports take deep breaths and try to work around the person in question as best they can. The general consensus is that so-and-so "must have the pictures," or else he or she would have been fired long ago.

The person in question has usually been in his position for a long time; the manager above him is usually reluctant to make a change. (See Enemy No. 12, benevolence in the wrong place.) The remedy, however, is taking action: *Move 'em out!*

Perceived incompetence is another matter. No doubt you've also encountered the person who really does understand the tasks at hand, and who really can demonstrate a credible level of expertise in his or her job. The problem is, for whatever reason, a number of his colleagues and reports think he's a boob. As a result, they don't trust him, and their level of trust in those who hired him is in danger as well.

What can you do in this case? If you really believe in him, go on a subtle campaign to promote his competency. Give him a highly visible, short-term goal, and publicize its successful completion. (Talk to him about what that project might be; let him in on what you're doing and why. It's clear that the person in question isn't very good at presenting himself in the best possible light. Maybe he can't run an efficient meeting to save his life. Maybe he mumbles. Maybe his work-style is unorthodox, or brusque, or confusing, and doesn't translate well to the masses. Maybe he's an introvert, someone who is by nature very quiet, and his colleagues and staff mistake his silence for contempt and decide that he's incompetent as a defensive measure.) Some good coaching, and some hard work on the part of the person in question, can turn these scenarios around.

21. Failing to trust others. Trusting other people can be difficult, especially if you're a perfectionist, or a workaholic, or both!

When you know that you're going to be held responsible for the performance of a group of people or of a department, it's only natural to involve yourself actively in ensuring high standards of performance (by micromanaging, or by failing to delegate critical responsibilities). The problem is, that behavior is also destructive.

One top manager (whose job was simply getting too big to handle) swore that he was going to delegate several important responsibilities. He even brought in a new person at the senior level to take on some of them, but he was simply, ultimately, unable to let go. He made the new person's life miserable by always double-checking her work. After only a few weeks, he began to "manage around" the new person, issuing directives about things he had supposedly delegated, and not even letting his new lieutenant know what he was doing. The new person soon felt unable to make a decision on her own. Then, predictably, she felt unwilling even to try to make decisions. "Why should I bother?" she commented. "The work is going to be done for me anyway, and [the top manager] is really happier doing it himself."

Failing to trust others causes several problems. First, you'll be isolating yourself, so that eventually, when you absolutely *can't* go it alone anymore, you truly won't have anyone to turn to. The folks who might have been willing to pitch in will no longer be waiting for you to come around. You'll be jeopardizing your company's growth prospects. Because if the market is there, but the management isn't, the organization will stumble as it tries to make more products, or service more clients.

Second, if you don't trust others, you won't ever effectively grow future leaders for your organization. If you don't trust other people, you won't create a community in which those potential top managers can learn and prepare for the job. The only kind of community that will form under your guidance is a community of avoidance and resistance. You'll have a group of people at the next level down who have perfected the skill of doing their work without involving *you*. When one or more of them do move into top positions, they'll carry that destructive practice with them.

You may have one or two people on your management team whom you don't entirely trust, but if you see yourself in the above example at all, if you sense that you are the kind of leader who really *doesn't* trust the team around you, you need to take action. This is going to be a slow process, since you can't suddenly throw open your arms and trust everyone. Instead, you have to take baby steps toward building a bridge between you and the folks around you. Here are two ways to start:

Take a vacation. Let someone else run the ship for a week; and don't check in. Make sure he knows how to reach you if really necessary, but leave your contact information with only one person—your assistant.

Want to start even smaller? Instead of checking your e-mail "one more time" at 11 p.m., give it a rest. It will still be there in the morning.

22. Your own sweet self. Do you *really* know how you come across to colleagues, employees, customers? Probably not. At the upper levels of an organization, there are inevitably filters in place that block out true reactions to the things that you say and do in favor of the reactions that people think you want to hear.

It's not likely, for example, that you'll wrap up an executive management meeting, and have your senior vice president of marketing clap you on the back as he leaves and say, "Lousy meeting, Bill. You really can't stay on one subject for more than twenty seconds, can you?"

This problem is like having a sign taped to your back that you're unaware of; you have no idea it's there, so you don't ever go looking for it. The remedy? Get yourself a truth-teller. A *consigliere*. Only occasionally will this person come from inside the organization, unless you can find someone to whom you would never be a threat—someone whose well-being is not affected by you in any potentially significant way. (Doubtful, if you're the top manager.) You could tap a vice-chairman who is close to retirement, and is no longer gunning for a promotion, but more likely, you'll end up engaging someone like your outside counsel. Tell that person what you need him to do and be clear about the fact that you need him to do more than communicate with you through innuendo. You owe it to him and to yourself to make sure that he is explicit in his counsel.

You may not like everything you hear from your truth-teller, but presumably, if you're reading this book, you're serious about building trust, and this is a critical step to achieving that goal.

You can also help yourself by altering your own perspective on the world and your place in it. People in senior leadership roles tend to take on disproportionate amounts of personal responsibility. They tend to hold themselves responsible for ensuring that even things outside of any human control are taken care of. While this level of responsibility is in some ways admirable, it clearly can have a negative effect on your life. You need to remember, even with all your noble aspirations, that you also have limitations. Rob's co-author from *The Trusted Advisor*, Charlie Green, with tongue-in-cheek, often makes this point to those he counsels with the phrase "There is a God. And you're not it."

Here are three ways to gain (or regain) that human perspective, depending upon the situation at hand:

1. Make it a point to expand or alter how you're thinking about the world. Regularly read books or magazines from something outside your normal landscape. The outside stimulus will reduce the free-floating anxiety about your job that has most likely built up around you.

2. Remember the basis of your affiliations. We recently heard this fascinating quote: "Me against my brother. My brother and me against my cousins. My cousins and me against the town. My town and me against the state. My state and me against the country. My country and me against everyone else." The quote went on, step by step, until everyone was on the same side.

Trusted leaders do need to trust others, and you have to be clear about who the enemies really are, and which battles are truly important. Starting at the broadest level, try to think about your management team as being engaged together against the competition. Solicit feedback about one particular issue at that level, and try to be aware, as you engage in discussion, that the people you may view as enemies when you're micromanaging them are in fact allies in a greater battle.

Then give yourself a test. Pick one situation where the stakes are high (but not "bet the company" high), and *make* yourself delegate the responsibility. For example, let a group of senior managers (excluding yourself) decide on the bonus levels for certain executives. Let them make the final call on the timing of promotion for certain key individuals.

3. Whenever you have the opportunity to hire somebody to do something that has, up 'til then, been part of your job, go for it. When Rob was chief people officer for a newly public company, he was charged with doubling the size of the organization within a year. He thought that he should be the person to handle all the senior executive appointments, and he initially resisted the suggestion that he hire someone to take charge of it. He figured that he could work with all of the search firms himself; that he should be the one to get the job done, since he knew best what was needed.

Rob's initial reluctance to delegate probably slowed the company down for a while; when he did acquiesce and hire someone to help, tension (his own and his colleagues) eased considerably, and the pace of progress accelerated dramatically. *Remember, delegating is not the same as abdicating.* Learning to delegate will open the door for you to do other things for you and for your organization that, right now, you can't even conceive of.

"I Wonder What He Meant by That?"

Asking you to memorize 22 discrete enemies of trust, sort them into covert/overt categories, and evaluate your own actions and your colleagues' every move against that master list as you go about your daily work would be slightly unrealistic. In any case, we don't want you to obsess about the enemies of trust or become paranoid. Consider the story of the centipede who was marching merrily along until another bug stopped him and said, "However do you manage to coordinate all those legs?" As the tale goes, the centipede immediately began to try to figure out how in fact he *did* manage to coordinate his legs as he walked. He became quickly confused, fell over, and never walked again.

Or think about that even older joke about the two psychiatrists passing one another on the street. "How are you?" one of them asks. And the other one thinks, "I wonder what he meant by that?"

You get the point. If you don't memorize each of the 22 enemies, it won't get in the way of building trust inside. But we don't want you to forget them entirely, either. So in that spirit, here are three general categories of enemies to keep in mind: Inadequate Communication; Misbehavior; Situations Not Remedied or Addressed.

Each and every one of the enemies we've identified in this chapter can be grouped under one (or more) of those headings. Enough said. Now that your antennae are up, we'll turn to Part Two: "Identifying and Applying the Tools of Trusted Leaders."

Three Overarching Categories, But (at Last Count) Twenty-Two Actual Enemies of Trusted Leaders

Inadequate Communication	• People with unhealthy levels of need for promotion, power, or recognition • People whose personal agendas are at odds with those the organization • Volatile personalities and/or class A Jerks • A corporate history of underperformance • Pulling a "bait and switch" • Behavior of "controlled vengeance" • Inconsistent messaging • Complicated situations
Misbehavior	• Unintended consequences • Endless management reorganizations • Rapidly changing situations • Misplaced benevolence • False feedback • Elephants meandering undisturbed in the parlor • Inconsistent reactions or standards • Excessively strict or inflexible standards
Situations Not Remedied or Addressed	• Scapegoating • Taking away part of the everyday • Paralysis in the face of difficulty • Incompetence, perceived or actual • Failing to trust others • **Your own sweet self!**

IDENTIFYING AND APPLYING THE TOOLS OF TRUSTED LEADERS

5

The Tools of
Building Personal Trust

WELCOME TO PART TWO of *The Trusted Leader*. In Part One, we covered a lot of ground rather quickly, introducing our broad-strokes views about building trust inside organizations, and offering you a few exercises to jump-start your own trust-building efforts. Here in Part Two, we're going to slow down, step back, and review the fundamentals.

To begin, we'll offer an overview model we created to help people codify the elements of both personal and organizational trust. The SEEKER model, as it is called, is not the Cliffs Notes of building personal and organizational trust; it is not a summary. Instead, it is a way to prioritize the critical elements of trust-building, and also give you a 360-degree sense of what trust inside looks like. It is, in other words (we hope), a potential "copy this page and pin it to your bulletin board" kind of thing. We also hope that as you read through this chapter and the next, the SEEKER model will keep you grounded. There are, as we've noted, many, many ways to consider how trust can grow; the SEEKER model captures the essentials.

(In pulling together the common, most critical points of trust-building, we hadn't set out to create an acronym, but the result was very close to SEEKER, a term we felt apt. So we changed "Set out" to "Establish" and "Stick to" to "Keep to" to create it. SEEKER, to us, has a great ring of *optimism*, which you need in abundance to build and maintain trust inside, and it also seems to connote *perseverance*, also critical.)

Here it is:

S—*Show that you understand the needs of the person and group.* A long-ago cartoon said, "I know you understand what you think I said, but I am not sure you realize that what you heard is not what I meant." Does "what you heard" accurately reflect the reality of the situation? Are you able to home in on the real issues at hand (even if those issues are not the ones the other person has identified), and talk about them in language that everyone understands?

E—*Establish the guiding principles of how you'll operate.* By this we mean setting clear tenets for how you work and what you expect of others. What are the values you want to instill throughout the organization? What are the accepted, and encouraged, norms of behavior? What goals are you setting? Are they reasonable? Can you explain how they will be achieved?

E—*Explain the resources you'll be using.* Try to put yourself on the receiving end of your own words; do you make sense to the people you're addressing? Is the organization set up to handle what you propose? Is the ability there? And the willingness to proceed?

K—*Keep to the principles you've elaborated.* Stop-starting and changing course in midstream causes confusion, which erodes trust. Yes, it is important to be flexible, market-savvy, adaptable. It is equally important to adhere to a higher purpose. Deciding to enter a new market, or exit an old one, will be received with trust if the principles guiding the decision are consistent and well-understood.

E—*Engage in constant, honest, two-way communication.* This step is ultimately about commitment. Constant honest, two-way communication is a powerful weapon against resistance (to change, to trust, to new ideas). It is also an incredibly useful way to monitor your progress, and a great indicator of new issues coming down the pike. One good conversation won't do the trick. You have to keep at it.

R—*Reinforce your words through consistent behaviors.* Think back to the enemies of trust. Trust doesn't do well when people are confused. Give people confidence by providing a positive "constant" they can depend on.

That's it. As close as we can come to a nutshell description of what it takes to build trust inside without oversimplifying things. Six "buckets" into which the elements of building personal and organizational trust can be ultimately sorted and stored. (You don't need to do so explicitly as you read on; in most cases we've found that this sorting and storing is an organic process. You'll do more or less depending on the points you find most relevant to your own situation.) We hope that the SEEKER model will jog your memory when you need it the most.

The Steps for Building Trust Anew: The Seeker Model

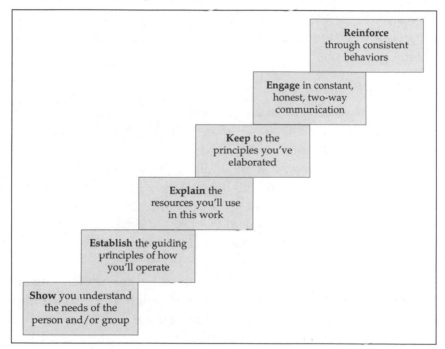

Reinforce through consistent behaviors

Engage in constant, honest, two-way communication

Keep to the principles you've elaborated

Explain the resources you'll use in this work

Establish the guiding principles of how you'll operate

Show you understand the needs of the person and/or group

On to the basics of building personal trust.

The Five Stages of Building Personal Trust

Building personal trust means moving through five stages, from engaging (the point at which you first establish a connection with someone else) to committing (the point at which both sides are ready and willing to act in concert to achieve a goal.) The stages are, for the most part, sequential. But they are not entirely without overlap. You may be doing a fair amount of listening (stage two) even as you search for a point on which to engage. What's more, you may be starting to enter stage five with someone around one particular issue, and, at the same time, entering stage one with that same person on another topic. Trust, as we have said, is not built once and then set for life. It must be constantly reinforced in order to gain strength. Of course, if you have reached stage five with someone, and you find yourself tackling a new issue with that same person, it's likely you'll move more quickly through the stages that next time around. Your collective expectations—coupled with the knowledge of past success—will adjust to facilitate the new challenge.

Stage One: Engaging

Picture yourself at a large function where you're required to make small talk with people you don't know. It can be difficult—even if the function is part of a professional conference, which presumably has attracted people with similar interests and levels of expertise. You move around, talking briefly with one person, and then another, and then suddenly something clicks, and you find yourself having an animated discussion. Maybe the topic is related to the conference; maybe not. But you've found common ground with another person; you've *engaged.*

Engaging, as a stage in building personal trust, then, means reaching the point where the person you're talking with decides that the subject is of interest, and that you are the person to talk with about that subject. It is the point at which that other person "clicks" with you, regardless of your assigned roles, and regardless of the context, political or otherwise, that surrounds you. Put another way, it's the point at which you achieve syzygy (pronounced siz-uh-jee), which is really a scientific term for when the sun, moon, and earth are configured along a straight line. Here, we use it to mean when you and the person you're trying to engage with are able to put aside political distractions, conflicts born of level differences, departmental tensions and anything else that would typically come between you. Then you concentrate, together, on the issue at hand. In a new client relationship, syzygy is already present when you first meet: you're both optimistic; you're both willing to be open and up front, at least to an extent, to explore the possibilities at hand; and you probably are not bringing a whole lot of baggage to the table. In a relationship inside, more often than not, syzygy must be created.

How can you create syzygy? If there is existing tension in the organization, or in this person's department, it's critical to address it up front, before moving to the issue at hand. "I know that we've each been affected by the recent layoffs in different ways, and that there's a lot of concern about what's going to happen as we continue to restructure. We've got to put that aside for now, and come up with a good campaign for this potential client . . ."

Syzygy also means putting yourself in the other person's shoes, as much as you possibly can. What might that person be feeling, sitting there across the desk from you? What is his or her job? Have you ever been in that position? What does he or she know about you? Is it enough? Would it help to know more?

Consider the director of a college public relations department, who was having a difficult time connecting with a group of relatively new hires until she realized that they had never seen her in anything other than a supervisory role.

They didn't know that she had great skill as a copywriter and editor—that, in fact, she knew how to do their jobs very well because she had, at one time in the not-too-distant-past, *performed* those very jobs. The rest of the people in her department, by contrast, had worked with her as a peer before her promotion; they had come to respect her skill before she became a manager. But to the new folks, she was simply someone who emerged from her office, gave a few directives, and retreated to her administrative duties. (Her quiet style, due to shyness, was also a factor. Those who had worked with her in the past understood her delivery; the new folks thought her aloof and condescending.)

The solution? The director made room in her schedule to take on one particular campaign personally, for a limited time. The ruse was that she was demonstrating a preferred work-flow process. But the project involved the whole range of skills required to excel in the department, and within two weeks, the new staff members had seen her in action, writing, editing, designing, and so forth.

Once they were able to see her work, they were much more willing to engage. In this manager's case, a little demonstration of proficiency went a long way to create the common ground that is the basis for syzygy.

Another way to think about syzygy and engaging is to adhere to a directive that Charlie Green, one of Rob's co-authors for *The Trusted Advisor*, coined as the "contact contract." Put simply, the contact contract means that as part of being a leader (and employee) of your company, you have an obligation to keep in touch and on point with the kinds of things that concern the people you work with. Don't lose contact. Beware distance. Check in—often enough so that you can put your finger on the two or three issues that the other person would consider most relevant to his job and workplace. Try to meet people where they live, while opening yourself up, at least enough so that they can see where you live. You don't *have* to know how to do their jobs. But you have to know enough about it to understand how difficult it is. And you have to be able to demonstrate that understanding. Because if you can't engage with the person you're trying to work with, that person is not going to be receptive to the idea of being open with you—*connecting with you*—about anything.

Stage Two: Listening

Listening is an essential part of building a trusting relationship for a very simple reason: it shows that you care about the person you're listening to, that you are willing to invest of yourself and your time, that you think the other person has something to offer you, and the organization. Listening is about more than being quiet while the other person speaks. It's about hearing what is being said, *and also what is not being said.*

Think back to Enemy of Trust No. 14, elephants meandering undisturbed in the parlor. When someone is sitting in your office, venting about something (or being reticent), what are they really talking about? If Elise says, "Paula steam-rolls everyone at our all-staff meetings," does that mean you should tell Paula to pipe down? Or might that also mean that Elise is feeling underappreciated, or maybe needs some help codifying her thoughts before meetings so that she feels confident about jumping into the fray?

Here are the steps we've come to believe are most useful for people who are trying to improve their listening skills:

1. *Be patient.* It's natural to try to plug gaps in a conversation, but when you're trying to understand what's important and real, "giving it a minute" will serve you better than unloading a lot of verbiage. Ask open-ended questions, and if the room falls silent for a few moments, just wait.

    Along those same lines, *don't jump the gun on pinpointing the critical issue.* Often, what comes out in the first part of a meeting (or even the first entire meeting!) isn't the whole story. If you identify and solve the problem very quickly, you might just be solving the wrong problem.

2. *Let the other person tell her story in her own words, and respect the way in which the story unfolds, but don't be afraid to try to clarify what you hear.* That is, try *not* to direct the sequence of the story ("Wait a minute. Tell me first about *this,* before you get to *that.*"). But if you're not sure you understand what the other person is saying, by all means break in, tell her what you think you heard, and ask if you have it right.

3. *Try not to use stock phrases to excess.* We all have our own quirks of speech, but try not to employ them when you're listening to someone. ("I feel your pain," comes to mind. Effective once or twice, maybe, but word gets around if you use the same script too many times, and your returns on the phrase will quickly diminish.)

4. *When you're listening to someone, behave like you're listening to them!* Of all of our bits of advice here, this one may seem the most obvious, but perception is important, and in this world of e-mail and Internet, it's easy to look (and be) distracted even if you think you're not. Consider Peg, a senior leader in a relatively large organization. The people who worked with Peg all knew of the perils of trying to deal with her over the phone; even when they were talking about the most important of issues, they could all hear the pings and rings and tappings of her computer and keyboard in the background. It was obvious that she was multitasking. Her colleagues and direct reports constantly felt that she was dissing them. Eventually they got bold enough to say, *"Peg, turn off your computer,"* when initiating a call with her.

We'll give you another extreme example just to make you feel good because rarely have we encountered anyone who is as bad a listener as this man, a television executive who had five (albeit small-screen) televisions mounted on the wall opposite his desk, tuned to five different channels. The televisions were always on, and inevitably, in the course of a meeting, the executive's eyes would wander up, above the head of the person earnestly trying to be heard, and focus for a few seconds on one or another screen.

There are certainly going to be times when you can't be the best listener. If someone buttonholes you in the cafeteria, or in the parking lot, or just before you have an important presentation, you're going to be distracted. But if that's the case, acknowledge the context. Say, "This isn't a great time to talk. But we've got to figure this out. Call me at three o'clock, and we'll work on it then." When you do meet with that person, turn off your computer, shut the door, look alert, and look him in the eye (but don't be afraid to blink!). And try to hear what's really going on.

A friend of ours, going on the radio for the first time, asked for some advice from a veteran newscaster. "Sit up straight and smile," he said. "But it's *radio*," she said, disbelieving. "No one is going to see me!" His response: "They'll hear it in your voice if you're not. They'll know you're not really 'on.' And they'll turn you off."

Same deal.

Stage Three: Framing

You've found, or created, at least temporarily, common ground. The person sitting opposite you is willing to invest some time and effort—with you—on whatever issue you are facing. You've listened and tried to understand what it is that other person is trying to say, whether or not he's been able to put it into words.

Now it's your turn to prove that you've been listening. Part of what you're trying to accomplish at this stage is making sure that you understand what you've heard, and that the other person knows you understand. So part of what you're going to *do* is to restate the issue, as you understand it from your listening. But at this point, you're also going to be trying *to infuse what you've heard with your own perspective and insights.*

This is a treacherous step. This is the point where, depending on what you say, you'll either create a strong connection, which you can then use as a basis to proceed, or you'll lose your audience, and you'll feel the syzygy drain right out of the room.

Why is this moment so critical? Because this is the moment when you're obliged to let the other person know that you have stood in his shoes, that you see the issue, whatever it is, from his perspective, and that you are confident that there *can and will be a meeting of the minds between his perspective and yours.*

That other person wants your views, your input, your counsel. That's why he's sitting there. But he needs to know that, whatever your views are, you truly understand and care about what he's been saying.

This story was told to Rob by a friend, and attributed to Garrison Keillor. Apparently at the end of one summer, Keillor's mother sent him (then a young boy) and his sister out to the yard to pick the tomatoes that were ready to fall off the vine. The overripe, squishy ones. The sister bent over, picking them. Keillor looked over and saw her backside. He looked at the tomato in his hand. He looked at his sister's rear end. He knew that if he threw the tomato, his sister would cry, tell their mother, and she would send him to his room. Then he'd get a licking when his father came home.

You know what he did. And you know he was pretty miserable when his father came home.

The moral is: *Knowledge of the consequences is not enough.* Understanding what's going on isn't enough. Knowing inside yourself that the issue, whatever it is, can be worked out, is not enough. What's important about framing is being able to restate the issue so that there's no misunderstanding about whether or not you understand what matters most to the other person and why.

When you frame the issue—when you say, "Here's the real problem, as I see it, based on my information and on what you've been telling me"—you must hit the other person's taproot.

When Rob was a boy, he often got called on to weed the garden. You may have suffered the same fate. He remembers being criticized, gently, when he didn't get the weeds' taproots because if you didn't pull out the taproots, they would all grow right back.

The person on the other side of the desk from you has to be able to see that you have reached the taproot—the central core of what he's dealing with. That person has to be able to say to himself about you, "Yes, she understands me, and understands how things are with my office, or department—with my part of the organization. She may not have done my job, but that's OK. She knows enough about it to understand where I'm coming from."

When people believe that you have a firm grasp on the taproot, you truly have a chance to build trust and make a positive difference in your organization.

Probably the biggest hurdle in framing is addressing and working through the emotional issues that may go along with whatever it is you're talking about. As Reverend Gary Smith, senior minister of First Parish Church in Concord, MA, says, you can be truthful and trustworthy without being hurtful.

And think also about how unpredictable reactions can be when emotions are running high. It's the straw that breaks the camel's back, not the larger load. Consider one company we know of that, for a long time, paid its employees above-average salaries for the industry. Its salaries were in the 75th percentile. Then it hit some rocky times, and as a result, laid off about 20 percent of its staff and reduced its average annual pay raises from the historical 9, 10, or 11 percent to 4, 5, or 6 percent.

Now comes year two of the troubled times. The CEO, the director of human resources, and the COO are once again facing some tough decisions. The notion of reducing the head count even further is on the table. But then the head of HR suggests that they restructure compensation packages across the board instead. No one will lose a job. Base salaries won't even be touched. They'll target bonuses instead; cut them in half.

The managers are happy with the idea. So imagine their reactions when they roll out their plan and they're met with resentful stares and a lot of negative buzz.

What went wrong? The answer lies in the framing. The managers did not realize that, to their employees, bonuses weren't something extra. Since they had always been in place, employees had come to regard them as part and parcel of their compensation. They felt entitled to their bonuses, and the managers had not clearly made the case that it was either bonuses or whole jobs. The CEO and his colleagues were thinking, Hey people, you're lucky to have a job. But from the other point of view, the deal was, Less pay, and we're already doing so much more work than we used to.

Part of the challenge of framing is gathering all the emotions related to the issue at hand and weaving them into a tapestry that makes sense to as many people as possible. Framing an issue isn't like writing a broad mission statement, where a lot of information is expected to be understood in order for the broad, often blurry, mission to resonate. (We'll resist the temptation to go off on a tirade about mission statements.) When you're framing something, you need to limit the time you spend on the "big picture" point of view and concentrate on recognizing the threads that make up the tapestry. Acknowledge what people are feeling, even if you believe their emotions to be rooted in side issues.

Stage Four: Envisioning

Envisioning is all about looking forward. Your objective in this stage is to create an image, for yourself and the person you're working with, of what will be. What can be accomplished. What positive thing is going to come out of whatever situation you've been dealing with.

It could be that you're resolving bad feelings about a recent layoff; what you're envisioning is the actions you, and the other person, are going to take to make the company strong again. It could be that you're dealing with the other person's conflict with a third party; what you're envisioning is resolution of that conflict. It could be that you've been discussing a marketing issue, or a distribution problem, or a conflict with a client. In any scenario, this is the point in the process where you turn from the past to the future—where you set a course of action—where you determine how you're going to get from where you are to where you want to be.

Envisioning is positive. Depending on the situation, it can even be exhilarating. At this stage of building personal trust, you are embarking on a journey with the other person, where both of you agree on a desired outcome.

Here's perhaps the most straightforward example of envisioning in action: it's in the last twenty minutes of a performance review that you're conducting, when you turn your sights from the past year to the year to come. You've identified (and framed) problems and challenges in such a way that the person you're talking to is still in the room with you, mentally as well as physically. Now it's time to paint a picture of the future that is both optimistic and realistic. Attainable, but with a stretch. Interesting, dynamic, and reasonable, given the constraints of the market, or the organization at large.

Here's an actual example that faced a company we know, involving someone who was responsible for a major account that he had run essentially by himself. While he had done an excellent job, he had not developed relationships with trusted lieutenants, nor had he engaged key colleagues in the running of the account. The task was to get him to expand the management team on that account. Rather than simply asking him to grow that relationship 20 percent in the next year by adding people to the account team at the senior level, the top manager had to help him envision it. This required using phrases such as "What would it be like for you if you could still control the XYZ account, but not have to spend four days a week traveling there?" Or, "How would it be if we assigned a partner to help you increase your account size by 20 percent or to spend time helping you build a new account?"

Envisioning is helping people see that you are working in their best interests in very tangible ways. This is the point at which what you say can change the atmosphere from passive to purposeful.

Another way to use envisioning is to consider the future as an alternate, achievable reality. You're not giving a pep talk about a pipe dream. You're outlining what can happen, if you and the other party commit to making it happen.

Which leads us to the final stage of building personal trust:

Stage Five: Committing

You've agreed on a desired outcome. Now it's time to agree to *pursue* that desired outcome. It's also time to agree on the method of pursuit.

Committing is about moving toward—and taking—constructive action. This is where you set goals, points at which you'll check in. This is where you make promises about what you'll do on your end, and where you exact promises from the other person about what she'll do, for her part. Committing isn't a one-off deal. You don't agree, shake hands, and part, never to cross paths again. Committing is the beginning of a looping process that requires discipline and constant reinforcement.

If you're committing to help someone attain the level of expertise he needs to be promoted nine months hence, that means you're going to follow through, make time in your and his schedules for the requisite training. You'll take him off the travel circuit, or put him on the travel circuit, as needed. You'll connect him with the appropriate mentors, re-set his performance expectations to dovetail with his goal, and ensure that his compensation and bonus measures reflect the schedule you've set.

If you're committing to a new product introduction by May, that means you're committing to creating a viable schedule, making the right connections with the folks from research and development, ensuring an open channel of communication with marketing, and dedicating the resources necessary to get the job done.

Committing is where you live out the promises you've made or implied at every other stage of building personal trust. It's where the rubber meets the road. Without it, the first four stages are useless.

It can be daunting. On the other hand, it's not as if you have much of a choice if you want results. One of our colleagues described a sense of serenity that occurred when he finally reached the commitment stage, saying something to the effect that "You know it has to be done, and it may have taken a long while to get there. But now it's finally time and you come to terms with that."

Being Easy to Work With.
A Clarification on Building Personal Trust

When we talk about the stages of personal trust, and the kinds of things we believe leaders should try to do—the ways in which they should behave, the things they might consider saying—in order to create and strengthen that trust, we're not talking about forcing unnatural change onto your basic personality.

Being a trusted leader doesn't necessarily mean that you are easy to work with.

There are two different "opposites" of being easy to work with. The first is being hard to work with, in the sense that people don't trust that you're looking out for them. That no matter what they do with you or for you, they're going to view you with suspicion. The second is being a challenge to work with, in the sense that you may be brusque, or reticent, or given to sudden outbursts, or whatever, but that the people you work with understand that you have their best interests at heart.

Building personal trust does not mean, necessarily, that you are totally in sync with the other person's preferred work style. Some of your employees will by nature be more comfortable working with a boss who is more of a micro-manager (or macro-manager), more gregarious (or quiet), or more hands-on (or hands-off) than you are. *That doesn't matter.* What matters is that you are treating your employees fairly, and that they know you are doing so. What matters is that you are managing with integrity. That at the end of the day, you can say with confidence that you did the best you could, and that you didn't mislead, across the board.

The movie is *Annie Hall.* Woody Allen, in character, is doing a voice-over in the very last scene, recalling a story he heard about a guy talking to a psychiatrist: "'Doc,' he says, 'My brother's crazy. He thinks he's a chicken.' And the doctor says, 'Well, why don't you turn him in?' And the guy says, 'I would, but I need the eggs.'"

Then, still in character, Woody Allen says, "I guess that's pretty much now how I feel about relationships. You know they're totally irrational and crazy and absurd, but I guess we keep going through it because most of us need the eggs."

We agree. Our point is that we're all willing to tolerate odd, uncomfortable, sometimes even absurd circumstances as long as we have no doubt about the value of the experience. Don't worry if you don't fit your own mental image of what a "trusted leader" looks like. Your own mirror image can do quite nicely.

The Ordinary Versus the Extraordinary

One final note about the five stages of building personal trust. It may seem as though we're framing the issue as if you need some sort of monumental problem to solve in order to move from stage one through stage five. Generally, your biggest opportunities to build or strengthen trust do arise when another person needs your help to sort something out, or is in a vulnerable spot. It's easier to describe the stages if you couch them in a scenario where there's some sort of problem to be resolved. (We'll talk more about trust-building under stress in Part Four.) But trust doesn't always have to be built on conflict with a capital C. The five stages of building personal trust play out in the same way when you're simply establishing a working relationship with a new colleague or direct report. Or when you're talking about one small project or deadline. Personal trust is, more often than not, built and reinforced in the course of day-to-day interaction. It's true that your deposits in the "trust bank" will be significant when you deal well with an employee in crisis. But the cumulative gain resulting from moving through the five stages on whatever issue is at hand, no matter how mundane, is no less important.

6

The Tools of Building
Organizational Trust

ORGANIZATIONAL TRUST IS BELIEF IN *the way things are being done.*
It's faith in how policies are set (or changed) and whether they're
respected; how processes are determined, and whether they're
fair; how dilemmas of any kind are considered, and how the ensuing decisions are made.

You can have personal trust without organizational trust. ("I
trust you, my friend, but I don't trust this company.") And you can
have organizational trust without personal trust ("I trust the company to do what's right, even though my immediate boss is a
jerk.") But you can't have organizational trust without a critical
mass of personal trust. And you can't have organizational trust
without a framework of sorts that exists independently of the
people in the organization.

Put another way, organizational trust derives from an amal-
gam of lots of personal trust, plus something more. It's not just the
extent of trust that an employee has in the members of senior leadership, although that may be a part of it. It's not just the trust that
you have in your immediate superior, although that is clearly a
part of it as well. (We all pay attention to hierarchy, but looking for
signs of trustworthiness in the person above us on the org chart is
but one part of the mix.) Organizational trust is truly a composite.
It's the trust that develops in a wide range of individuals throughout the organization. *And* it is the processes and traditions to
which those individuals adhere.

Bizarro © 2002 by Dan Piraro. Reprinted with permission of the
Universal Press Syndicate. All rights reserved.

You *could* think about building organizational trust as building personal trust in multiple—that is, over and over again with,
and between, each and every individual in your company. But
that approach (depending on the size and scope of your enterprise) might very well send you whimpering under a bed. And
who could blame you? Think of a car or an airplane (or a cruise
ship; all sorts of analogies work here) that drives or flies (or floats)
because all the critical pieces are in place and functioning correctly. But not every single component has to be in perfect sync at
all times for it to maneuver safely. We've driven cars with broken
radios, broken odometers, broken gas gauges. A friend of ours
drove (for a very long time) a 1978 pickup truck that wouldn't
start unless one person held open the choke with a long plastic
pole while the other person turned the key in the ignition and vig-
orously pumped the gas pedal. We've all flown on jet planes where

the air conditioning was down, bathrooms were blocked off with duct tape, or some or all of the appliances needed to prepare the food were on the fritz. But the critical components were in order, and there was also a series of checks and balances in place to ensure that enough was going right to be able to move ahead.

It's the same with building organizational trust. Organizational policies and processes change to remain relevant and effective. Not everyone trusts everyone else all the time—relationships in and among departments, from the top to the bottom, don't always hum on and on peacefully with no interruption or irritation. It just doesn't happen.

Nonetheless, to meet the challenges of change and conflict, there are certain critical variables you can monitor and work on to ensure that, on the whole, your organization is a trusted one.

Consider the following equation; it's the best way we've come up with to illustrate those critical variables of trust-building at the organizational level.

The Organizational Trust Equation

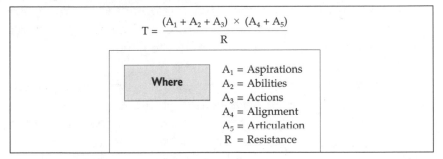

$$T = \frac{(A_1 + A_2 + A_3) \times (A_4 + A_5)}{R}$$

Where

A_1 = Aspirations
A_2 = Abilities
A_3 = Actions
A_4 = Alignment
A_5 = Articulation
R = Resistance

We'll take each variable in turn:

Aspirations

"We *want* to do great things."

What does your organization believe in? What does it stand for?

Aspirations give the people of an organization a reason to *want* to trust one another. Think of the person who is just learning how to swim. The thought progression could be something like this: I want to learn to swim, so I need to work with this teacher. If I don't trust the teacher, I'll never be able to reach my goal.

It's the same deal no matter the situation. If you have aspirations, most likely, you need to be able to trust someone in order to fulfill that aspiration. If you share an aspiration with another person, or a group of people, you need to trust others to do their part to get you all there. And they need to trust you.

If your organization doesn't have aspirations, what is it that keeps people working? We can safely say that the answer won't be anything positive. And we can also safely project that in a few years—probably sooner—there won't be an organization to work for anyway.

How can you focus your organization's aspirations? How can you ensure that they accurately reflect consensus? And, subsequently, how do you go about pinpointing answers for all of the questions that cascade from that resolution? (Such as "What does the aspiration promise to its employees regarding how success will be measured?" And "What are the promised rewards or consequences of those measures?")

One way is to develop your own version of the Hertz Never-Lost® system. No matter where you are, and even if you don't know where you are, this system can locate you, inform you, and direct you back to where you want to be.

Hertz and other similar systems use global positioning satellites. In the context of an organization, though, you won't need tools as much as you'll need people who have a good sense of the pulse of the organization and whether that pulse is in tune with what's going on outside. Keeping aspirations on track is, in part, about being able to put your hands on data that informs, but it also has a lot to do with the hearts and minds of the people who get up every day and come in to work. It also has to do with being able to look up and out at the same time as you're meeting Monday-morning demands.

Alan Colsey has been a police chief in Rockland County, NY, for more than 20 years. One of the youngest chiefs in the country (he was first appointed chief when he was 27), he has been involved in more than his share of headline cases. Most notable of these was the capture of Kathy Boudin (of Weather Underground and the Brinks murder-robbery fame) and her group of self-proclaimed revolutionaries. He spoke to us about the importance of having a shared set of aspirations:

> So much of what we do has to be reactive. It's not like people schedule an appointment for a rape, robbery, medical emergency, or house fire. We're always in a state of acute management. I've always considered our service as a business, and part of making it work as a business is getting people to agree about our mission and our direction. The quality of our efforts are judged less in dollars awarded to us, and more in the way people feel about paying for what we do, even if it's indirectly. But we do have customers. And you can't serve your customers well if you're not all agreed on how you're going to serve them, and what you're going to concentrate on.

Colsey also talked to us about the need to see the big picture at the same time as you're dealing with the day-to-day:

> There can be such a great level of detail in police work. It's not always easy to look up and around as much as we should. But you need to get the big picture perspective right if you have any hope of building consensus about what you stand for, and where you're going. For me, tapping someone to look up while I'm looking down is a good way to stay on track.

In some companies, the "never lost" system is made up solely of the people in the CEO's inner circle. While that's probably the norm, it's not right for everyone. At other organizations we know of, the system includes people on the board, people in similar industries, analysts, retirees, and people far down in the organization. (Some of the most effective members of a never-lost system are people who work directly with clients or customers.) At one publishing company, the members of the CEO's never–lost system all have their own rudders: each has identified (and notified) a group of colleagues throughout the organization and also experts on the outside—academics, analysts—to whom he can turn at any time for counsel.

Some top managers call these people members of their "kitchen cabinets." Some call them "the other folks in the foxhole." Some people prefer "vision" to "aspirations." Pick the words or phrases that suit you, so long as the meaning is clear.

Abilities

"We *can* do great things."

Can your company execute its stated aspirations? Does it have the resources available? Does it empower or impede individuals as they attempt to put life into their vision?

Match your organization's abilities to its aspirations. Locate (within the company) or acquire the right skills or tools you need. It sounds so simple, but given the array of possible combinations of skills, tools, and possible aspirations, it's one of the most difficult of management challenges.

Think of a big-box store, a giant building-and-hardware emporium. You have a week's vacation, and you want to build a small stone patio off of a new exterior sliding door you've installed in your family room. If you go to the emporium, chances are you'll see exactly the kinds of stones you have in mind, but you'll also see other stones. And maybe a model of a deck that would look just terrific. With a deck, you could build a riser and install a hot tub. And look, the hot tubs are on sale right now. You decide to buy a hot tub because it's such a good deal. But now you don't have quite enough money left to buy the lumber. That's OK. You'll get the lumber soon, you think. You go home, happy. But a few weeks later you realize that you have no patio or deck, just a hot tub that you can't use because it can't be installed.

We like to use the West Concord, MA, Five and Dime as an example for understanding what abilities (or tools) are required to solve a problem or reach a goal. A strong survivor of a dying breed, the West Concord Five and Dime has an inventory of 40,000-plus items, and a staff that seems to know where each item is, and what each item does. If you go in to buy something and you explain to Maynard Forbes, the owner, what it is you're trying to do, he won't hesitate to talk you out of your intended purchase—to say, "You don't need *that*, but you will need *this*. "But he's also not averse to exploring, from a solid starting point, a few ancillary avenues, just to make sure you're not missing out on something you might not have thought of. The ultimate goal, though, is to know that at the end of the day, you accomplished maybe just what you set out to do, maybe more, but that whatever it was, you did it well and didn't get hurt in the process.

Actions

"We *are* doing great things."

Inevitably, organizations get distracted from their aspirations. Crusades begin, people get excited, a crisis hits, and the company's purposeful activity—those actions that use the organization's abilities to achieve its aspirations—loses its momentum, stalls out, or gets put on a back burner.

This "A" is about (1) Getting down to it, and (2) Getting it done right. How can you go about it? We like to say that you have to find (or be) your own Doug Baker.

"Excuse me?" you ask politely. "Who is Doug Baker?"

Doug Baker is the curator and sexton of the historic First Parish Church in Concord, MA. (Established in 1636, it is one of the older churches in America—Paul Revere's grandfather made the Communion silver, and it is the original home to Emerson, Thoreau, Hawthorne, and the Alcotts, among others.)

As curator and sexton, Baker is the official who ensures that the various church buildings are maintained in good order. But he does, and is, so much more. He has a master's degree in fine arts, for example, but if there's an electrical problem anywhere on the church campus (and keep in mind, the First Parish electrical system had its origins in the time of Edison), Doug knows what to do. And he's an expert on bonsai, herb gardening, and Buddhism, but if the historic clock in the steeple is broken, Doug is the one to call to figure out that if you just bend that little piece of wire *that much*, it will work again.

Doug Baker, in other words, allows First Parish to do its work uninterrupted and unencumbered by the challenges and digressions of day-to-day operations. He's the next best thing to a quick-start manual the First Parish of Concord has. Think "operational handyman." If you don't have a Doug Baker—a jack-of-all-trades, or a "fixer"—in your company, you need to find one.

Critical point, this. We mean *find*, not *cultivate*. To the best of our knowledge, these folks are born, not made. (That's why if you're *not* a jack-of-all-trades, don't go out and sign up for a bunch of self-improvement or handyman classes. But don't despair, either.)

Chances are good you already have a Doug or a Jack in your company. You might just not be using him or her to full potential.

How do you find him? First look among your never-lost group. Not there? Try middle management. And here's a clue. These folks (Doug is an exception) are not usually well-rounded individuals. Think diamond in the rough. They may be completely lacking in the kinds of social or managerial skills that would normally put them front and center on a top manager's radar. They are not usually the people you would think of to succeed you. They may lack finesse in dealing with the public or the patience to wait for process to play its role, or to mentor someone. They may not suffer fools gladly. But what they do, they do extremely well. And if you find them, and you create the kind of atmosphere for them in which they can excel, you've got a powerful secret weapon that can free other people to do their own jobs to the fullest.

When we talked about Doug Baker types with George Hornig, who is currently the COO of the private equity division at Credit Suisse, he pointed unhesitatingly to one of the four CEOs he had worked with in his days at Deutsche Bank:

> Other CEOs I've observed managed by "mood," or used some tactic like "last person in loses" to motivate their people. Still others had too grandiose a vision—anyone with a sense of reality could look at it and know it would blow up. But this person had no personal agenda for the job at hand, other than getting it done. He didn't seek publicity; he didn't value showmanship. Getting glory on the backs of others was not his way.
>
> You know, a lot of people thought he was an odd choice for CEO, since he had started working with Deutsche Bank as a consultant, but the thing is, the German board members trusted him

right away. And they were correct in their assessment. He was detail-oriented; he got into the numbers himself. And he was consistent. He didn't practice situational decision-making or politics. Instead, he was the kind of guy who would look at you and say, "You're working at a rate above what your contract calls for, and you deserve more money. I'll get it for you." And then he would. He was a true "Doug Baker" for the bank.

Here's an example of a Doug Baker in a media company. At first, this "fixer" was head of the company's online creative capabilities in New York. Then he became head of all creative online operations. Then, head of all creative online and offline; then, head of all capabilities. Then he did a stint in Hong Kong; currently, he's at the helm of the company's European operations. His great skill is versatility. The company sends him wherever there's a problem and he solves it. Not without pain—he is not a managerial mastermind and a therapist all rolled into one. But he gets the job done, and he doesn't make many enemies or burn bridges in his wake. As a Doug Baker, he's ideal.

(The luckiest companies have Doug Bakers, "fixers," at the leadership level and also at the technology help desk. They're few and far between, but even a Doug Baker in distribution can work wonders if allowed to flourish. Begin your search today.)

Alignment

"We're all moving in the same direction."

It would be very difficult to be the lowest-cost producer and also customize products for different clients. It would be very difficult to pursue a global expansion at the same time as you're trying to change from a product-centric company to one with service at its core.

This "A" is, at bottom, about consistency: consistency in your aspirations; consistency between your aspirations and your abilities, your aspirations and your actions, your abilities and your actions. You get the idea.

Some things are inconsistent because they don't make sense. Is it consistent to proclaim to your people that they should run after new customers when they can't keep up with the current ones? Achieving alignment can be particularly frustrating because an organization can be doing all the right things and still not achieve it. The company can have great aspirations, great abilities, and even take great actions, but if they're not consistent, then it is all for naught.

Other things are inconsistent because they're not achievable. For example, if you're operating a chain of high-volume super-markets, is it really feasible to push the company to expand geo-graphically if it will tax your overall QC capabilities?

What's the best way to monitor alignment? Always use a stone wall plumb bob. When professionals build a stone wall, they don't simply eyeball it as they go to ensure that it's the same height at any given point. They use a tool called a stone wall plumb bob, which is the vertical equivalent of a level.

You should do the same. Don't rely on your own perspective—or even a cadre of trusted cronies—to inform you here. You need independent verification across each area in your organization.

Who or what are your stone wall plumb bobs? They could be traditional employee surveys or feedback mechanisms. They could be people who are not part of your inner circle, but whom you feel confident in approaching with a question about what's going on inside the organization that might be escaping your radar. Maybe someone who isn't terribly senior—say a vice president of employee relations. There's someone who might be able to serve as a plumb bob on aspirations and actions. Maybe someone who is retiring—someone who has seen a great deal and can point to differences between the "then" and the "now" (though it will be up to you to interpret those differences). A retiring head of sales will often be a good plumb bob with regard to the organization and the marketplace.

We know of two CEOs, each with very different styles, who rely on people who are relatively old-timers in their respective or-ganizations. In one case, David, the CEO, gets a sounding from Sandra on something-or-other every few weeks. In the other case, George tends to rotate around his organization, taking soundings on a regular basis from a wide variety of staffers.

Articulation

"Everyone knows all of the above."

Suppose we visited your organization today. Suppose we randomly stopped people in the hallways, and asked them the following questions: "What does this company aspire to do? How well suited are the abilities of the company to its aspirations, and what does the company do to ensure a match? Does the real work of the company focus on achieving its aspirations? How does your work fit in?"

What would they say? Would they say what *you* would say? Would their answers even sound remotely similar? Or would it be like the case of the three blind men describing the elephant—each giving a totally different description of the same animal? You don't want to be like the poor traveler in a foreign land who consults his language book and asks for a green bowl filled with crankshafts instead of a room with a view. You don't want to risk that kind of misunderstanding in your organization.

To avoid this, you have to communicate. But how much? How often? What form?

Chief Colsey weighed in for us on this topic:

> In police work, we have lots of ways of communicating information. We have to, because the work is 24/7 and I can't be there all the time with just the right words to motivate someone, or answer a question. There are policies and procedures, written guidelines, memos, bulletins, all sorts of things that you might need to pass along information or to document something. For me, face-to-face beats all. I believe in as much face-to-face communication as possible. But you have to get it right for the person you're trying to reach at the other end. The "how" makes all the difference.

Diane Hessan, a well-known expert on the internal transfer of intellectual capital, and, most recently, president and CEO of Communispace Corporation, offered her view as well. She stressed the importance of keeping a channel of choice open and well-oiled at all times:

Every leader has to find some particular, reliable way or ways of communicating, whether it's voice messaging, weekly staff meetings, or all-hands meetings in the company cafeteria. Maybe I'm a hyper-communicator, but I leave a company-wide voice message every weekend. I have for years. Sometimes it's just a progress report. Sometimes it's upbeat. Sometimes it's celebratory. Sometimes it's not. It's not a vehicle to use for talking about something horrible inside the company, of course. And maybe it's only once a quarter that I say anything of the quality worthy of what you'd want to put in this book. (The other 11 weeks it may not be anything profound.) But the value of the continuity is huge.

To ensure that what you're saying is translating well, think about it as music. Think about how a melody sounds when it is played with two fingers on a piano, and then think about how that same melody sounds when it is fleshed out by an orchestra. Communicate with your peers, your reports, your company at large, as if you *have* an orchestra and you can use every instrument in turn, or in groups, or en masse, whatever your choice. (If you simply can't conceive of having an orchestra, at least communicate as if you have a decent synthesizer!)

Vary the medium, vary the tone, but make sure that the message—a consistent message, customized to resonate with the audience it is reaching—is continuously being delivered.

We have tried to stay away from sports analogies, but being baseball fans, we could not resist this one. It comes from Paul Clark, a senior executive of National City Corporation, a multi-billion dollar bank and financial services company. His way of framing the issue of how to communicate was to say that, as a trusted leader, you need to be like a great pitcher. You need lots of pitches. You need a strategic pitch, an organizational pitch, an operations pitch, a management pitch, and a customer pitch. "You need them all," he said. "And you need them big time."

Resistance

It's natural. It's inevitable. It's perennial. In the course of building—and maintaining—a trusting organization, you're going to meet with resistance. And it's going to stem from one (or more) of the following four sources: skepticism, fear, frustration, and an embedded we-they mindset.

Skepticism . . . That Your Statements or Actions Are Sincere or Realistic

It's highly unlikely that the people who make up your organization have never been hoodwinked, that they've only ever worked in trusted and trusting environments, that they're going to take whatever you say, and whatever you do, at face value. You may be the one-in-a-million, extraordinarily lucky leader whose troops are 100 percent ready to commit to your plan. More likely, though, you're going to be facing at least some people who are "twice shy."

How can you overcome skepticism? Think *stray cat* or *stray dog*. Think *animal at the shelter*. Really! When you bring home an animal from a shelter, it's with the understanding that you have a long road ahead of you, and that only consistently kind, honest behavior is going to yield a loving, trusting relationship. Dealing with resistance borne of skepticism requires the same approach. Time—time that you fill with consistent trustworthy behavior—is the initial answer.

And, since you're not really dealing with stray cats or dogs here, you have another highly effective action at your disposal as well. It's called frankness. You can talk about the roots of the skepticism you're facing. If you're the new kid on the block at an organization that has gone through several rounds of layoffs, acknowledge what has gone on before, and be as straightforward as you can be about what you think is going to happen in the future. If you yourself have made an error, admit it. Come clean.

Diane Hessan told us that admitting mistakes, for her, is just a part of her policy to be "totally straightforward" with her employees, and that that policy has served her well:

> For example, I signed a lease for our corporate offices at a time when rents were at the top of the market. Even though we had board approval for the lease, I still felt responsible as the person who had signed it, and we just couldn't stay there. That space had multi-million dollar implications for us. And we ended up

moving our headquarters to cheaper space soon after we moved in. The thing is, by having done all the disclosure earlier on about what a mistake I had made, we avoided—virtually eliminated—all of the complaining that would have otherwise accompanied our people having to move offices twice in a short time frame.

Fear . . . of Negative Consequences

If it looks like an apple, and smells like an apple, and you bought it at a fruit stand, can you be 100 percent positive that when you bite into it, it won't taste nasty? Not really. It may have worms, or it might have just been sprayed with some toxic bug-killer, or the person who visited the stand before you did might have sneezed on it, dropped it on the ground, and put it back. Chances are the apple is fine, but it's a rare scenario that is utterly immune to the question "But what if . . . ?"

Minimize the opportunity for those what-ifs by allowing people to become part of the trust-building process. Ask for their advice. Use their responses. Show them that their input is valuable. Paul Clark told us that for him, one of the absolutely fundamental tools of trust-building is getting people engaged by *inviting them into the process* rather than mandating their participation. Such an invitation could be a request for suggestions through e-mail. It could be bi-weekly face-to-face meetings between small groups of people, their bosses, and their bosses' bosses:

> Personally, I'm a big believer in meals. Sharing the commonality of a meal—even if you're not talking about anything to do with the business—opens things up. It gives people the chance to offer input or feedback on their own terms. Trust is so much about knowledge, and the way to gain knowledge is to invite people to share what they know and to share of yourself in return.
>
> You can't force people onto your side. They have to come over of their own free will. If you force participation, you're not going to get their hearts and minds. You're not going to give them any encouragement to drop their guard.

Frustration . . . from Being Micro- or Macro-Managed. From Being Underutilized, Undervalued, or Under-leveraged

It's demoralizing, to say the least, trying to do your best under one of those conditions. As one person, now president of her own business, told us:

> Before I founded my own business, I worked as a senior-level manager at a communications company. I knew I was talented. I knew that I had a lot to contribute. But my direct superior could not keep herself from redoing everything I did. After a while, I stopped working so hard. I played the role. I looked busy. But I really didn't try. What was the point? If I did my best work, it would be totally redone. If I did my worst work, same deal. It got so that I hated getting new assignments, new clients. New projects are supposed to be exciting. For me they were torture.

To overcome resistance born of frustration, take a good look at how closely—or loosely—your employees are managed, department by department, manager by manager. What are the parameters? Can you identify areas where you think your employees are either feeling suffocated or lost? Do you have a rainmaker manager whose department's accomplishments always look as though they've been penned by the same hand? Do you have a department whose projects are always a little late, or good-but-never excellent? Do you sense any resentment? Talk to the managers in question about trying to establish a different style. Invite their thoughts (see above). Invite input from your rank and file. The resistance you see could be coming from people who have a lot to contribute, *if allowed to do so.* Or from people who might have a lot to contribute, *if only they had a little guidance.*

Interestingly, sometimes this source of resistance has roots in the *perception* of being under- or over-managed rather than the reality of the situation. When National City Corporation acquired Integra Bank, a Pittsburgh-based bank with about 120 branches, the people from the newly acquired company were at first uncomfortable working in the more autonomous NCC culture. As Paul Clark told us:

The Integra people kept asking me, "Where are the binders?" And when I asked them what they meant, they pointed to a shelf in their office with a dozen or so binders in which were contained the rules and regulations of their bank—the manuals that told them what to do and when. I said that NCC didn't have those types of binders. I said, "We hire people and give them some guidelines, but in most situations, we fundamentally rely on them to exercise their own judgment." They weren't happy with that. So finally, I actually had 120 binders made up, one for each branch, and I filled them with some canned stuff and brochures that we had around the office, and we delivered them. And even though the binders really had nothing of value in them, the people all said, "Great!" The sense that there was a very firm hand on them seemed to bring a kind of common sense to their work. It was like when a kid still has training wheels on his bike, even though everyone—the kid included— knows that he really doesn't need them anymore. Those binders helped us build trust across the organization. They helped the people at Integra make the move to our way of doing things.

Embedded We-They Mindsets

Sometimes these mindsets are generations old, with no bearing in reality in the current scenario. It doesn't matter. They are to resistance as fatwood is to a campfire.

Consider this example of the "class struggle"-mindset. Several years ago, Annie had a direct report with considerable raw talent and potential; in fact he was one of the brightest young associates she had encountered. She was surprised to find, though, that he had—and couldn't or wouldn't shake—a fundamental distrust of managers and management in the organization. She couldn't understand why; the company seemed to be doing everything right with him. The other members of the team were trusting of her and of the company, but he just didn't buy it.

The team had spent several weeks of their summer in Peoria working for a major client. One evening during that stint on location, when Annie and this young man were having dinner, she asked about his first job in high school. He spoke about his first work experience (which he held through high school and college), which was as a member of a union that his father had been a part of for 30 years. Now, we're not making blanket statements about unions; many serve an important purpose for their members. This particular union, though, had an extremely contentious relationship with management and it had been that way for years. He had been indoctrinated into corporate life in a contentious "we vs. they" environment. He had, as a result, an embedded we-they mentality that he couldn't shed, no matter how fair, honest, or inclusive the environment.

There's another kind of we-they mindset of which to be wary. We call it narcissistic egoism. When you hear the phrase "It's not my problem," you know you're dealing with narcissistic egoism. That short sentence speaks volumes about a person's natural tendency to back away from any kind of commitment to the organization-at-large, and in particular to building trust in the organization. These individuals tend to shy away from accountability, perhaps from a fear of punishment or a desire to protect their own turf or their own standing.

What can you do? Facing down either kind of we-they mindset requires the same approach: *Encourage your resisters to behave like owners and reward them when they do.* If people feel as though they truly have a stake in the organization, if they believe that the organization's welfare is connected to their own, they are more likely to overcome their own resistance and allow themselves to become vested members of the organization. You can use financial and other tangible incentives that link individual well-being with corporate well-being; they are among the more obvious tools. At the same time, however, be aware that such tools can treat the symptom without addressing the cause. Invest the time to investigate what lies behind the behavior you're trying to change.

Chief Colsey, by the way, told us that he believes the biggest challenge in leading any group of people is what he calls the push-pull. "How do you pull your people along with you as you move in a particular direction, and push them to be stakeholders at the same time?" It's a difficult balance to achieve. Encouraging and rewarding ownership behavior is the answer.

Over-Deliver, Over Time

All four sources of resistance—fear, skepticism, frustration, and embedded we-they mindsets—can be conquered, but only if you're willing to stick your own neck out in the process. There are no subtle ways to overcome resistance. You have to meet the force of resistance with equal or greater strength. You also have to be willing to commit to a long-term effort. One flashy presentation isn't going to cut it. *You have to be willing and able to over-deliver, over time.*

One mid-level manager—whom we'll call James—told us of the time his then newly appointed CEO took him to lunch. The company had gone through a tremendous upheaval; James had worked long, stressful hours with his boss and a skeleton staff to keep things going in his division. There had been a succession of changes in the top management team; finally, this particular CEO had been brought in, and, under his guidance, the company had managed to pull things under control in relatively short order.

James was gratified when he received an e-mail from the CEO inviting him to lunch to "thank him for all of his efforts on the company's behalf." What a class act, James remembers thinking. This guy is taking the time to recognize the work that a middle manager did to keep one division afloat. This is clearly a sign that this company is going to be a much different, better place to work from here on out.

The lunch went well. The CEO invited James to offer his take on the hows and whys of the company's troubles, and said that he truly valued James's opinions. He also invited James to e-mail or call him if ever he had anything to say about the company's course in the future. James told us:

> The thing is, that was the last time I heard from the guy. I followed up with an e-mail, thanking him for lunch. And a few weeks later, I had a thought about our customer service process, and I sent him an e-mail. I got a boilerplate kind of reply from his assistant saying that my comments were important and of course the CEO would look at them. But I never heard personally from him again. And at our all-staff meeting, three months

later, when I went up to him to say hello, it was almost as if he didn't remember the lunch at all. That was three years ago. To this day I wonder if he was really interested in me at all, or if he just thought that taking me out to lunch was going to make him look good.

If you're not willing to commit to a long-term trust-building effort, it's not worth your while to start. The first step is always important. But without follow-through, it will look hollow and insincere to your employees in hindsight. There's great value in giving of your personal time, and in repetition. Paul Clark told us:

> Being there makes all the difference. I remember visiting the Peoria branch of a bank we acquired. The folks there were friendly, and gave me a warm reception. But when I went back a few months later, I got this wonderful, over-the-top welcome. It was truly unusual. I told them so, and you know what they said? They said, "You're the first person [from top management] who has ever come back a second time! The fact that you cared enough to come back really means a lot to us."

Getting past resistance in order to build trust isn't like crossing something off of a list and saying "OK, I've done it." We can't emphasize enough the importance of follow-through.

We can't resist the temptation to include one more example of over-delivering, over time. This one shows that, sometimes, it takes just such a long-term effort to learn how to do things right by your people. It also shows that, even if you make a mistake in your first trust-building efforts, you can redeem yourself if your intentions are honorable and you're willing to put in the sweat to keep trying until you nail it. More than a dozen years ago, just after Deloitte & Touche was formed in a merger of predecessor firms, the firm found itself in a recessionary economy facing a series of layoffs. As Bob Garland, who is now head of the Assurance, Accounting, and Advisory practice there, said to us, "We weren't good at it. But then we finally realized that what we had to do to minimize the pain of the process was to ask ourselves 'If we were being laid off, how would we want to be treated?' And we finally got it right."

What did "getting it right" mean? For one thing, the people administering the layoff actually went out and assembled a list of 250 available jobs, tailored to fit their employees' skill sets. They called clients, competitors, any and all contacts to identify those potential new opportunities. They also followed through with recommendations and counseling for everyone affected.

The proof came in the numbers. Within 60 days of that round of layoffs, one third of the affected employees had accepted new jobs and one third had had at least one job offer. The rest were either still looking, or had gone back to school, or changed professions.

The proof also came in the form of a phone call from a grateful father, who called Bob to say, essentially, "Thank you for helping my son find his next job." The young man's job at Deloitte & Touche had been his first position out of college. His experience had been good, even with the layoff. The father wanted Bob Garland to know that he and his family would always think of (and speak of) Deloitte & Touche in a positive way.

When a Variable Is Missing . . .

Organizations lacking *aspirations* are often characterized as aimless or "lost in the desert." ("We don't know where we're going, but we're making good time!")

Organizations lacking *abilities* are often characterized as ineffective and weak. This can be an issue for young companies, often full of enthusiasm for their mission. Yet even established entities can find themselves hurt by a lack of ability. They may feel it in market conditions, or changes in a prevailing technology. For example certain retailers have struggled with taking on new customer information systems and translating the information it provides into merchandising strategies. Their inability to do so, especially when compared to competitors, can lead to their demise.

Organizations lacking *actions* are often characterized as either lazy or dishonest. While either or both of these might be true, there might be other legitimate explanations as well. We have seen organizations whose leaders are so demanding of perfect analyses that their actions are postponed endlessly. In other situations, debate is such a part of the culture that nothing is ever resolved.

Organizations lacking *alignment* are less than the sum of their parts. Even if your aspirations, abilities, and actions are not all they could be, if you have alignment you have a far greater chance of success than if you have the greatest abilities, actions, and aspirations in the world and no alignment. The obvious analogy would be the 2002 Superbowl Champs, the New England Patriots, versus any other group of stars—a few past Yankee teams come to mind—that can't gel into a team.

Organizations lacking *articulation* are perhaps the saddest of all because they are seen as lacking all five A's. And indeed, without articulation, the other four are not sustainable. If you can't explain what you have, your people will think you have nothing. And if they think you have nothing—notwithstanding their own understanding of their own particular area—they will leave.

Organizations that possess and manage all five variables, but are not prepared to meet and deal with resistance are similarly vulnerable. *Resistance is the trump card—if you haven't overcome resistance, nothing else will work.*

Using the Formula

Our belief is that organizational trust exists in organizations when:

1. Each of the A's we've outlined above is present in good measure.
2. Each A plays off of the others as the equation implies.
3. The A's, as a unit, are united against the R, resistance, which is, itself, inevitable, natural, and perennial.

But the best test of the veracity of an equation or formula such as this one is to see what happens when true numbers are loaded in. If, in fact, you do this with the organizational trust formula, the results actually correlate with the relative valuation of successful and unsuccessful companies, or even in the same company between those times when trust may vary from high to low.

Start with the basic Organizational Trust formula shown in the figure on p. 91. Now, if you use a 1–10 (low-to-high) scale with the equation, just take a look at the minimum and maximum results:

Worst Case (Lowest Level of Organizational Trust Possible):

Assume that each positive attribute (or A) in the numerator gets rated only a 1, and resistance gets rated a 10. In that case, organizational trust would come out as follows:

$$T = \frac{(1+1+1) \times (1+1)}{10} = 0.6$$

Best Case (Highest Level of Organizational Trust Possible):

By contrast, assume that you're in a great situation, and each positive attribute in the numerator gets rated a 10, and resistance gets rated a 1. In that case, organizational trust would be:

$$T = \frac{(10+10+10) \times (10+10)}{1} = 600$$

It's less important what the absolute scores are, in that a 0.6 or a 600 by itself is meaningless. More significant, however, is the relationship between the two scores. In the above situation, contrasting a best case and a worst case, there is a $1000\times$ relative impact on organizational trust. Could this really mean that an organization in great shape is worth a thousand times more than one with minimal trust? Is it practically (or even theoretically) possible that there is a thousand times greater performance coming from a high trust organization? The answer, in more than theoretical terms, is yes.

For proof, just take a look at share prices. Take Enron, for example. At its high, Enron traded at about $90 per share. Look at the dot-coms. Spans of a thousand times, from $100/share to $.10/share, actually did occur. This range is not necessarily a measure of the loss of organizational trust. A lot more went on with these companies than the loss of organizational trust, but with even the modest assertion of a strong correlation between organizational trust and marketplace performance, a difference of this magnitude is not unreasonable.

One can even make the case by contrasting two separate companies, each of which may be operating in circumstances far less dramatic than a best case/worst case secenario, or even an Enron. If you pick a "higher organizational trust" company and a "lower organizational trust" company, then the gap may not be one thousand times, but it will still demonstrate a directionally accurate relationship with the organization's performance, whether it is measured externally (such as on the basis of stock price, profitability, or market share, for example), or whether it is measured internally (such as on the basis of employee satisfaction or morale, or on employee retention). We can leave the precise analysis to the academics for study, but the obvious correlation of organizational trust with organizational performance can be established without a lot of intellectual gymnastics.

The "Game Face"

It strikes us that this would be a good point to remind you of why you're expending all of this effort to build trusted leadership. Please read the following story, told to us by a now-senior-level manager at a service organization, about trust (and lack of trust) at her former employer:

> About five years ago, my brother suffered a heart attack. I was a wreck. I took the day off when I found out that he had been admitted to the hospital—I went to see him, talked to the doctors, made sure his wife and family—and my parents—were OK. The next day, I went back to work. I remember how glad I was to be there. Work was somewhere where I felt I had some control over what was going on. I knew that I was appreciated; that my efforts were appreciated. I also knew that if my performance was "off" for a bit, it would be OK. I told my boss and some of my colleagues what had happened; I didn't have any reservations about letting them know what was going on in my life. And my performance didn't suffer; in fact, I was so glad to immerse myself in my work that I caught up within a few days, and, I think, produced at a level that surpassed my usual output.

A few years after that, my son was hospitalized; it was an emergency medical situation, and it threw our whole family into some turmoil for a few days, until we knew that he would be OK. By this time, my former boss had left the company; there was a new hierarchy in place by then, and a number of my former colleagues had also moved on. There was very little trust in this "new" organization. I remember calling my new boss and a few colleagues to let them know that I wouldn't be in—that I was at the hospital with my son. But I also remember how I dreaded making that call. It was as if I was giving them some sort of ammo they could—and might—use against me later on. Not that they didn't say all the right things. They asked if there were anything they could do, but somehow, none of it rang true. It wasn't real. It didn't feel more than skin deep. And when I went back to work two days later, I remember how reluctant I was to walk back into that office building. I just put on my "game face," and went in. But I didn't want to field personal questions that I knew weren't sincere. And I felt defensive about having slipped behind in my work even though I made it up within the next few days, at the expense of staying home while my son recovered. You know, that's something I'll always hold against that company—that I wasn't there to offer the "Mom's touch" while he was on the mend.

Is it any wonder that this person left that company shortly thereafter? Would you really need to ask which boss got the best work out of her while she was there? For whom did she extend herself? When you've experienced work in a trust-based organization, you have little tolerance for a workplace without trust.

Do you ever wear a game face at work? Do your employees? (Keep in mind that by "game face," we're not talking about people who are, by nature, private individuals. We're talking about people who have one persona at work and another when they leave the building.)

If you can identify areas in your organization where people feel reluctant to be themselves, then you've identified areas that need "first strike" trust-building attention.

Swimming Against the Tide

There are, unfortunately, organizations in which trust has eroded to the point where one senior manager, or even a small group of managers working together, cannot effect positive change. We mention that worst-case scenario here, very briefly, just to acknowledge that there is a point at which, in some situations, you can and should draw the line to save your own career and your own sanity.

You can't build organizational trust in a vacuum. If you are a senior manager in an organization where the majority of senior managers are not at least interested in building trusted leadership, you should think seriously about whether you might be better off making a job change. The organization may right itself down the road; it may not. Our point is that you should trust yourself to know when even your best efforts aren't creating the environment in which you want to work. If that is the case, then it is time to say "enough" and move on. Try as hard as you can to make things better, of course. But we've seen managers drive themselves to the personal breaking-point swimming against the tide. Building trust inside is such a worthy cause. But don't lose yourself in the process.

Trust-Building in Specific Venues

In Part Three, we'll continue to zoom in and tighten our focus on how and when trust is created (or destroyed) as we consider the trusted leader's workplace. What does trust look like from the top? Inside and across your company's teams, departments, and offices? How does it differ from venue to venue, and why are those differences important to understand?

HOW TRUSTED LEADERS WORK

7

From the Top

Trust men, and they will be true to you; treat them greatly, and they will show themselves great. —Ralph Waldo Emerson (1803–1892)

SAM NOLAN *(not his real name) is not a trusted leader. He does a great job with clients. His strategy is right on target. But his employees do not trust him to represent accurately what the company can deliver in terms of quality, time, and content. Nor do they trust him personally or think that his actions are truly motivated by the best interests of his employees and not by his own personal gain. In fact, if you ask them, they'll tell you that Sam can be trusted to do some of what a CEO is supposed to do brilliantly, but that they put their faith in the COO of the organization. In fact, there are times when Sam will make some sort of announcement to his senior management team, or offer a confidence to one of his inner circle, and later, those folks will go behind his back to the COO to get the "real story."*

We know Sam. We think he's an upright guy. We think he does indeed have his employees' best interests at heart, and we've worked with him to mend his image. But he's at the top, and it's tough to build trust from the top.

Being "Whelmed"

A few years ago, a comedy called *Ten Things I Hate About You,* which was very loosely based on Shakespeare's *Taming of the Shrew,* was released on film.

In it, one of the characters, a young lady with the inappropriate name of Chastity, asks her friend Bianca, "I know you can be overwhelmed, and you can be underwhelmed, but can you ever just be *whelmed?*"

That question, only mildly amended, is the essence of our chapter on working from the top as a trusted leader.

To our thinking, "whelmed" means perfectly pitched and calibrated—getting the pitch and the balance just right. That's something the person at the top of the organization is constantly striving to do. (We say constantly striving because we don't believe anyone ever gets there, hangs up their coat and says, "All done." You may be there for a day with some people, but not with others. You may be there on a certain project, but not there on another.) For example, you want to calibrate, constantly, the right balance between the yin and yang (or, as Chief Colsey says, the push-pull) of managing employees. You want to push them to move in the direction of your choosing, yet you want them to pull as stakeholders in their own right. You want to be punitive when it's called for, but you don't want to be excessively restrictive. You want to inspire, but you don't want to be overly directive.

What's the best way to go about it? You could tackle one person, one issue, one decision at a time, in a solitary way. One-one-one is a great way to build and reinforce trust, but we'd venture that that approach will leave you at the end of the day feeling as fragmented as your actions. Instead (and this will certainly come as no surprise), we think that the best way to approach everything you do is from a broader base—a desire to build and strengthen trust throughout your organization, using tools and approaches and mechanisms that extend your reach. *Constant calibration is a natural tendency of trusted leaders.*

Having said that, we would assert again that building trust from the top is harder than doing so from other venues because you have no fall-back position. You know that if your attempts to build trust backfire, you are, ultimately, the responsible party. At the end of the day, it's just you, up there, or out there, by yourself.

The stakes are simply greater when you're the top manager. When you do something—whether it's delegating authority over a certain project, or deciding to promote one person over another, or making the call about whether to change the compensation structure, or choosing not to enter a new market—the entire company is watching, or at least trying to. Whatever they see—whatever they take away from your actions—will not only go into their mental folder about you, it will also go into their mental folder marked "the organization." You are not simply "you" when you're at the top. You are "the company" as well, more so than any other single person in the organization. What's more, no matter how large and influential your inner circle, you are, at the end of the day, where the buck stops. It's up to you whether to accept or reject their counsel. No wonder the pressure is great.

That pressure—and the inability to pass the buck any further— reminds Rob of the first time he went on the Internet, back in 1992 or so. All of a sudden he was there, but the browsers weren't anything like they are today (there actually *was* a time before Netscape or Internet Explorer!) and he had more than a moment of thinking, Now what? Now what do I do? It also brings to mind the following take-off on the radio's emergency-broadcast-system announcement: "This life is a test. It is only a test. If it had been an actual life, you would have received further instructions on where to go and what to do." That's what being a leader can be like.

The "tabula" at the top is about as "rasa" as you can get.

We wish we could offer "further instructions on where to go and what to do" of a highly specific nature for you at the top. We can't. We can, however, offer the cumulative wisdom of our own experience and our clients' efforts at calibration, through the lens of building trust from the top. It's a two-parter: (1) Major Calibration Targets, and (2) Setting the Stage for Trust from the Top.

Major Calibration Targets

There are any number of things a leader has to calibrate, each day. But if you stop long enough to think "balance" or "What is the right mix of yin and yang?" in every instance, you'll quickly lose traction. You're the leader; you don't have time to wallow in minute detail on every issue.

Time and again, we have identified with our clients six major areas that do require attention to calibration. These are the ones that matter, and if you concentrate on them (barring unforeseen disaster) you will find that everything else you must attend to generally falls in line.

Calibrate Your Time

When you're at the top, the scope of your responsibilities is simply greater than it would be in any other position in the organization. There are more things to worry about, and more things to dream about. At the risk of sounding like a schoolmarm, our advice here is brusque, counseling you to budget your time so that you minimize instances in which you find yourself way behind the curve, rushing to catch up. Set an agenda for what you can and can't do on any given day. Build exercise into that agenda, or at least some form of down-time or personal time, and honor it as you do any other commitment. If you are in the middle of working through a complex issue with one person, and you're backing up into another scheduled appointment, either make a clean break and schedule time to continue, or cancel that next appointment. Excessive speed begets clumsy speech, misguided cues, poor listening, *trust erosion.*

Calibrate Your Authority

You don't have the time (see above) to oversee personally everything that's going on in your organization. (Entrepreneurs take note—among all of the people we've worked with and interviewed for this book, the "older but wiser" entrepreneurs were most vehement on this topic. That same "finger in every pie" approach that serves so well in a start-up most often *doesn't* serve beyond the start-up stage.) Think back to the responsibilities of the trusted leader. Map out your universe. Think about what you can reasonably control given the number of hours in a day. Retain control over those things you feel you must, and find or cultivate the people you need to help you, and force yourself to delegate the rest.

Calibrate Your Personal Involvement

How much hands-on work versus how much hands-off work should you do? There are going to be times when your own personal touch is critical to the success of a transaction, a client sale, the implementation of a new process, but if you try to keep your hand in every aspect of your business (if it's more than a one- or two-person show), you'll exhaust yourself and burn out. Building trust requires that you also put your trust in others.

Calibrating your personal involvement does not mean that you have to deal exclusively with the big issues, and never sneak an enjoyable interlude doing hands-on or front-line work. On the contrary. We'd be the first to acknowledge the importance of staying in touch with your employees at every level by spending time with them and reminding yourself of what they do and how they do it. Likewise, we're great advocates of the notion that it's important for the CEO to experience front-line contact with customers regularly. But try to keep the big picture in mind. Look at your schedule for last month. How much time did you spend on whatever you did? Did it feel right? Were there areas you concentrated on to the detriment of others (including your personal life)? Did you find yourself playing catch-up?

One of the great benefits of calibrating your personal involvement is that it frees you to become a more well-rounded person, both on the job and off.

Calibrate Performance Standards

Naturally, you have high aspirations for yourself and for your organization. What would be the point if you didn't? No leader of a successful enterprise is ever quoted in *The Wall Street Journal* as saying, "Well, we really relaxed, and aimed for mediocrity, and that's why we're so successful." But it's also important to be realistic. Think back to the five A's of organizational trust. If your aspirations far outreach your organization's abilities, the entire place will quickly bog down in frustration and a feeling of futility.

Yes, seek to inspire and motivate by setting stretch goals. Yes, by all means, make it clear that you expect excellence. But understand what you're working with. We're reminded of the story of the customer service center that had been fielding 5,000 calls a week. The head of the department felt that there was tremendous room for improvement and set a goal for his people to increase the number of calls handled by 20 percent. He built in incentives to support the new standard. And lo and behold, the numbers changed just as he wanted them to. The problem? Customer satisfaction rates plummeted. Why? Because in order to meet the new standard, his reps were rushing people off the phone. Not listening to the customers' full stories. Prescribing solutions that didn't work, just so they could hang up quickly and "serve" someone else. Enough said.

Calibrate Personal Standards

If you're a perfectionist, this one is going to cause you some pain. The fact is, there are only 24 hours in a day, and you've got to do the best you can with what you've got and then move on. We know of a fire chief who has been "working on" a guidebook for new members of the department for at least five years now. Why? Because he keeps refining it and refining it, wanting it to be perfect. His goal is admirable. But meantime, people who join his department have to learn department rules and regs by the seat of their pants because the book isn't done.

Your own personal standards affect others. If you allow only perfection from yourself, you'll unwittingly cause other people to lose confidence in their own work. They'll be ready to hand something to you for approval, and then they'll hesitate. "She won't like it; she never likes anything." What's worse is when that hesitation and loss of confidence turns into "She won't like it; she never likes anything; why try in the first place?"

Do you want people in your organization to take risks? To be creative? To stick their necks out and try to conquer new markets, invent new products, win new clients? Calibrating your own personal standards is a great way to start.

We would all like things to be perfect. But we also don't want the world to stall out while waiting for perfection to happen.

Calibrate Resistance

Unless you're announcing to the organization at large that you are giving everyone a 100 percent bonus because the company struck oil, you're likely to meet with some resistance on any decision you make. Resistance to anything new is to be expected, and if your organization is trying to thrive in a tumultuous market—or is going through rapid and disruptive change for any other reason—you can expect resistance on a grand scale. What you have to do, as a leader, is consider the level of resistance you're facing, and decide whether it tips the balance on whatever decision you're making.

Put another way, setting out on a day hike with a group of 15 friends can be a fine thing to do. And if one or two of them are apprehensive about the path you've chosen, that's OK. You can be extra supportive and encouraging and still make the hike. But if it starts to rain as you leave the house, and one friend sprains an ankle in the parking lot before you even start out, and you discover that the backpacks holding everyone's lunch and water are back home on your kitchen table, it might be a good idea to modify your plans.

Be as alert and responsive to resistance as you can be. You may have the right plan and the wrong people. You may have the wrong plan and the right people. You may not have worked hard enough on articulation. Resistance is normal and you're bound to have to tolerate (and address) a certain amount, each and every day. But it can also be a good barometer of whether you're setting yourself—and your organization—up for a fall.

Setting the Stage for Trust from the Top

History—and Why It Matters

Emily was the newly named section editor of a large regional weekly newspaper. She had long been the senior writer for the section and had a good relationship with her fellow writers and the people in the production department. No one doubted her ability to do the job. Sure, she was green when it came to the intricacies of production, but she had taken on the role of acting section editor several times in her four-year tenure at the paper, and under her direction, the section had met its deadline—with a minimum of stress—each time.

The problem was Frank, the chief copy editor. Up until last week, when Emily was still the senior writer, she and Frank had gotten along well. But, as Emily put it, "You could feel the frost building up around him," as soon as her title had changed.

For several weeks, Emily took note of Frank's deliberate—and very thinly veiled—attempts to undermine her new authority. The stories that were routed directly into production without her signoff. The ads he "forgot" to tell her had changed the layouts of several pages. Finally, she confronted him.

What he said, when she literally backed him into her office and demanded to know why he was treating her so badly, shocked her. It wasn't that he had wanted the job. It wasn't that he thought Emily didn't deserve the job, or that she wasn't up to it.

"I miss Patricia."

Patricia had been the section editor before Emily.

"But I didn't kick Patricia out of the job," Emily remembers saying to Frank. "You know as well as I do that she decided not to return from maternity leave and that's why I got the job."

It didn't matter. As Emily told us, months later, still shaking her head, "Frank missed Patricia and that's why he treated me badly. After we had that talk, things got better. We went for drinks after work that evening, and talked some more about Patricia, and over the next couple of weeks, he started working with me instead of against me. It still boggles me that his behavior toward me literally had nothing to do with me directly."

History. What happened in the top job before you took it on. What happened to other people before you became their boss. Where you came from (outside the organization, up through the ranks, across from another division). It all matters, and it all has a direct effect on your ability to build trust from the top. In fact, the better you understand what led up to you becoming the top dog, the better sense you'll have of where you're starting from, and the less the likelihood that you'll stumble out of the gate.

We thought of listing history as one of the areas that needs calibration. But history can't be calibrated. It's the trickle effects of history that need calibration. Hence, history has its own section.

History has a great deal to do with how people perceive you as a leader. Whether they feel you have the right to lead them. Whether they are more—or less—willing to connect with you, commit to you, shoulder responsibility on your behalf.

You can't change history, of course. But whether you have history on your side or not, there is one thing you can do to hasten everyone's willingness to look forward and not back: *Show your humanity.* Be a person. Let people know that you have a home life, that you have hobbies, certain tastes in foods, design, music, art.

Opening up in that way isn't always easy. You might by nature be a very private person. Or you might just be insanely busy. If you're deeply immersed in work, or you travel a lot, or you have growing children at home, chances are you just don't really have the time for the kind of conversations that naturally lend themselves to sharing information of a more personal nature. One of the people we interviewed for this book commented on how easy, relatively, it is to build personal trust with others when you're all twenty-something and single, working in the same company. She said:

> You're all socializing together, and work and play become different parts of the same ball of wax. Your work problems are your life problems and your life problems are your work problems. And since you work with your friends, everyone knows everything. That kind of openness is just harder to achieve when more people are married with kids, and have full lives outside of the office walls. It takes an extra effort.

Nonetheless, there are some things you can do to compensate. Decorate your office, in minute ways, with things that reveal something about you personally. Display pictures of your loved ones. Make it a point to tell people where you're going and why when you take a vacation.

The more you let people see the whole you, the less remote you will seem, the less isolated you will be, the more willing people will be to let you into their lives in return.

The Parsing of Trust

Is building trust from the top an all-or-nothing proposition? No. It can't be. We wish we could give people the confidence to say that if they trust someone in one area, they can freely trust them across the board. But that's just too high a hurdle—because it would require a total, surrendering faith, such that many people don't even give to their spouses.

It would be a wonderful world if we could have complete, unerring, unending trust in everyone we like, or respect for their knowledge. But it ain't gonna happen. At least not in our lifetimes.

What's our point? That as a leader, you're likely never going to find yourself in the position of having everyone in your organization trust you on every front. Similarly, you're never going to trust everyone else on every front. You may trust one direct report completely when it comes to accounting, but not trust his ability to tell a good ad campaign from a dog. You might trust your head of marketing to have a solo meeting with your biggest and most important client, but not trust her with information about a pending merger. Paul Clark said to us, of Jim Bell, a senior-level colleague, "He and I share certain values. If anything happened to my wife and me, we'd want him to take care of the kids." That kind of trust in the workplace is very personal and very rare. And we don't know if Paul trusts Jim that completely on every single aspect of the work they do together. It would be nice. But it might not be so. Different people have different strengths. And that's OK.

You get the picture. So total trust isn't viable. Here's a more realistic ideal: Aim for having a fair idea of where you stand, a "minimum requirement" for yourself and for those around you, and a desire to push out, or "improve" in all directions as time goes on.

Picture, if you will, a simple X–Y Cartesian grid. Along the X axis, you've got all the different ways in which people trust you (or in which you trust in them): financial savvy, motives, and so on. The Y axis represents area. Set a minimum acceptable starting point. The threshold of trust. Sort of the point at which you will—even in the face of potentially contradictory or incomplete information—make the leap of faith and trust someone on a particular issue or with a particular task, or even trust that person to work

Parsing Trust

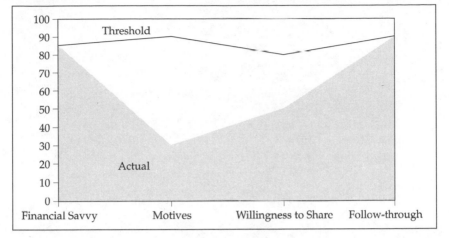

with you. (If you're using this chart to plot your own trustworthiness, flip that.) If 100 percent is optimal, but therefore unrealistic, maybe your threshold is 85 percent. If you're by nature a trusting person, maybe the number is 80 percent. If you're less trusting, it might go up to 92. Your goal, of course, is to be able to fill in the area, as much as you can.

The way kids learn is by taking risks. The only way they take risks is if they feel safe enough to extend themselves. And if they do it once, and don't get burned, they'll do it again, and again. That's how they grow. The same is true with trust. It's not a black-and-white issue. But there's a minimum requirement of taking that first step—and after you take the first step, the going gets easier.

8

Inside Teams, Departments, Offices

BRYANT (not his real name) was hired to lead a new business development team for a medium-sized consumer business that had recently been
acquired by a private equity firm. Prior to the acquisition, the firm had
been family owned and operated, and had experienced steady growth (albeit without any sort of deliberate planning or investment). The company had a strong brand and a strong trade customer base; the new
investors' goal was to take it public within two or three years, which
meant that they needed to tap into steady sources of growth.

Bryant's role was to find ways to tap that growth potential through
new product development or through partnerships to leverage the brand
and the existing customer relationships. He felt well-prepared for the
challenge, had many years of experience as a strategy consultant to high-
growth consumer businesses, and had also done a respectable stint managing the business development function in a consumer products
company. He decided to assemble a team of both new hires—mostly new
MBAs or MBAs with solid strategy and/or marketing experience—and
people with proven operating experience from within the organization.
He thought that the mix would be a powerful combination of strategic
skill and practical know-how.

Several months in, though, he was forced to acknowledge the fact
that the team hadn't jelled and things weren't going smoothly at all,
despite the high level of talent he knew the group possessed. And the
problem boiled down to this: Those with significantly more operating experience were skeptical of the MBAs. They characterized them as "empty

suits" who didn't understand anything about actually running a business. Even worse, Bryant was being accused of showing favoritism to the MBAs. He acknowledged that he felt that he had more in common with this group—they had come from the same schools, had had similar work experience, and tended to use similar frameworks when approaching a problem. At the same time, though, Bryant knew that he couldn't succeed without the deep operational experience of the team members who had long histories with the company.

Unfortunately, the conflict was aggravated by a significant pay discrepancy between the two groups. Bryant had had to pay very high salaries to the MBAs to sign them, and the tenured employees, whose salaries were much lower, took that as a signal that their experience, in Bryant's eyes, really didn't matter. The issues in this team didn't even stop there. Bryant liked to give open, honest feedback in real time. He often gave feedback very publicly, though he was careful not to be too brutal. But he had never explicitly explained his style to anyone on the team. If someone received constructive feedback, did that mean they were at risk? The consequences were entirely unclear to everyone, except Bryant.

The team was going through some intense times; deadlines were fast approaching and the group was working 12–14 hour days to develop their first round of proposals for partnerships and new products. People were starting to wonder what the rewards might be for all of this effort, and Bryant realized that he hadn't had the opportunity to learn about the organization's reward and recognition processes and policies. The company had a "work hard, play hard" culture and the team members were living it during this stressful time. Cliques had formed, however, and the group wasn't "playing" as a whole; they separated based on their backgrounds. Bryant did not know how to bring the two factions together.

Annie selected this example to start off this chapter on building trust inside teams because she has lived through several variations of that situation in a number of different organizations. She experienced pieces of the story, for example, as an MBA working at Pepsi, where the issues were resolved in a way that built trust among the team members. In that case, people from "both sides" admitted to the team leader that they felt the breach, and wanted to do something about it. The MBAs, for example, knew that they needed to earn the respect of their colleagues, and so they asked to be allowed the time to truly understand the experiences of those people. Annie, for one, took a temporary assignment in a distribution facility and got on the truck at 5:30 every morning for nine months. Pepsi, in fact, sponsored her for a series of assignments along those lines. She remembers:

> The people I had been advising—the people who were running the regional operations—didn't initially think that I knew what it took to get things done. At one level, they were right. But by the end of that nine months, I had earned their trust. What's more, I had a greater understanding of how the company really worked than I ever could have gotten from the vantage point of the position I held when I started.
>
> When I was out there every day really understanding what the trade partners needed, I was able to see much more clearly where the directives that came down from "management" worked and where they were lacking. We had been creating initiatives for the people in the field. Once I was out there—doing a stint as a manager of a sales territory—I had to implement some of my own initiatives—and I found that I couldn't. No one could. They were insane.
>
> Spending time in the field was the best thing I could have done.

Not everyone on the team at Pepsi was able to complete a rotation, as Annie did. Her experience was tailored to fit her individual career goals at the time. But everyone on that initial team did spend some time learning the work of the company by standing in someone else's shoes. (Sometimes literally. Annie recalls the good-natured ribbing that a few MBAs received when they showed up for a day out on a truck wearing dress shoes that were destined for ruin by the end of the shift.) And the benefits—the resulting new network that reached across departments and functions—were lasting.

We chose to lead with Bryant's story because it lays out a fairly representative mix of the kinds of trust issues that teams deal with all the time. It emphasizes something important about building and maintaining trust inside teams: more often than not, you'll find yourself dealing with several issues at once. Rarely, if ever, do team leaders find themselves facing a "fix one thing and you're all set" situation.

What Can Bryant Do?

There are a number of steps Bryant can take immediately to begin to close the distance between the two factions in his team.

First, he can clear up the questions everyone has about the criteria for success. Maybe the answers are more important, right now, to the operations folks than they are to the other team members, but that doesn't matter. Without clarification, everyone on the team would eventually find this issue a sticking point. (It's admirable that Bryant jumped right into the tasks at hand, but he was irresponsible not to learn the organization's policies on rewards and such up front.)

He needs to reassure the tenured employees that their skills are indeed valuable, even though they are receiving less pay than their fellow team members (and even though he is less comfortable dealing with them). He should clarify what the team as a group is expected to deliver, and identify explicitly how he expects the various members to contribute their expertise and why he needs that expertise. How should he do this? In a group meeting? In individual meetings? Via e-mail messages? Through a broadcast voice mail? The answer to all of them is yes. This one needs multiple forms of communication and reinforcement.

Judy Jackson, the New York head of human resources for Digitas, is one of our favorite HR executives. She has a mantra: "No surprises." While Bryant is explaining the criteria for success, he should also have a go at clarifying his decision-making process. How will he approach decisions regarding rewards? How will he measure the criteria? "Here are the things I'm going to look at when I consider someone for promotion. Here's how decisions about raises will be made. Here's who's in the room. Here's how the process works." If Bryant says those things to his team members, and follows up each "lead sentence" with a robust explanation, his team members will begin to feel more grounded and secure, and will be able to focus more productively on work (and less on distracting doubts).

Second, he can invest the time to allow his team members to get to know one another. People have been working so intensely and quickly that they haven't had a chance to look up. For all they know, they're rowing furiously toward a waterfall. Some of them maybe even think that's what's happening, because they've been forced to rely on one another before allowing even the smallest amounts of trust between them to develop.

Many leaders resist taking this step. Why? It seems touchy-feely, for one. The investment returns no tangible reward in and of itself. Yet those managers who do invest the time are inevitably glad that they did. Many trusted leaders we've spoken to have suggested that this is one of the most important investments to be made.

This late in the game, Bryant probably can't afford to stop everyone in their tracks and take a half-day offsite. (If he can, he should. A half-day spent in a somewhat less hectic environment, reflecting on progress thus far and the challenges ahead, would certainly be a good start. At the same time, it would present an un-avoidable "chance" for people to interact with each other.)

What if he had thought to invest the time up-front? He could have conducted a short, relatively simple exercise, and asked each team member to write up a list of questions about the project and about the team itself. If doing that felt awkward to him, or if time was indeed too tight, he could have covered the same ground by creating a "playbook" of sorts, a "Here's our team; here's what we're here to do" guide. Upon distribution, he could have made it clear that people were welcome to come and talk to him about what they read.

The important "broad lesson" is that setting up expectations before launching a group of people into a project is always a good idea, and so is sharing information up-front about what each person on the team is bringing to the table. If others know explicitly why their new peers are there, the level of suspicion drops immediately.

Finally, Bryant can create opportunities for team members to learn from one another. This one could be dicey, because despite his apparent strategic expertise, he doesn't seem to have a good radar when it comes to interpersonal relations. However, one of the best ways to breach the gaps between diverse members of a team is to have them introduce one another to their own individual skills and areas of expertise. "I never knew how much was involved in doing what you do!" That's the response you're looking for. A little knowledge here makes it easier for people to communicate.

Some General "Do's"

Beyond our specific advice for Bryant's triage efforts, we also have some general "do's" to offer (which he'd do well to take note of). To wit:

Allow, where possible, inclusion in visioning and goal-setting. Jon Skinner, a former boss of Annie's, was great at this. As he told her once, the first step is building a team whose input you really want (we hope you have that luxury). The next step is facilitating the process. Annie recalls that Jon was thoughtful about gathering input from members of his team, and bringing the team to a solution that they all bought into. "We always felt incredibly valued during the process, even when the outcome wasn't exactly what we had suggested."

The trick, according to Jon, is knowing how to balance the need to be inclusive with the need for quick decision-making. As Jon told Annie, it was important for him, always, to have at least a loose idea of where he wanted to go, knowing at the same time that he shouldn't gather feedback if he didn't have the ability to be open-minded about whatever he received.

We've seen managers become paralyzed by their consensus-driven styles. We've seen the marketplace pass them by as a result. We're not advocating across-the-board inclusive decision-making. There are times when you need to make a firm autonomous decision, and when those times arise, that's what you have to do. Make the decision, in those cases, but also take the time afterward to explain why you needed to go it alone (speed concerns, confidentiality, etc.) Remember, you *are* the leader; it's not like this would be unusual or unexpected in many management circumstances.

Be consistent about public recognition. We've known a lot of managers who tend to recognize people—and team effort—publicly only in times of organizational stress. Public recognition shouldn't be situational. It shouldn't only happen when you think it would be "good for the company" to get a pep talk. If you treat it in that way, you'll look defensive and you'll make the company look defensive.

Instead, recognition for good work should be a regular (but not necessarily regularly scheduled) event. It should be consistent with your organization's aspirations. And it should reflect a consistently high standard. (In other words, there's a flip side; don't begin to recognize everyone, all the time. You'll dilute the effect.)

Many hotels and supermarkets have "employees of the month." It's a big deal—and, if the organization does it right, it truly underscores the company's criteria for success. (Too often, we've seen recognition programs like these dissolve into situations in which "everyone gets a turn, so what's the point in trying.")

We've also seen recognition programs turn into love-fests for a few stellar performers. What if you have one star, or a small number of stars, and you're at risk of recognizing the same people over and over again? We'll talk about that risk later on in this chapter, but here, suffice it to say that one way to get around it is to vary the quality or skill that you're recognizing. You don't always have to focus on the "best in show." You can recognize improvement in one or another areas. You can recognize the mastery of a particular skill. A risk taken wisely. If you vary the "why" and also explain it, you'll not only reinforce your company's aspirations, but you'll also reaffirm for employees that the team (or organization at large) has the abilities it needs to excel.

The precise hotel/supermarket model is, of course, not appropriate for everyone—but the theory behind it is.

Foster alternative viewpoints. Don't sit at the head of the table and say that everything is fine when you know that people have differing opinions. If everyone thinks that they're supposed to behave in a certain way and agree blindly with what you say because that's the message you've put out there, take it back!

Encourage people to speak their mind (that is, if you are secure in the knowledge that you have a conflict-resolution mechanism in place if things escalate). Actually, it's not just enough to have them speak their mind——the issue is how to get the most value out of it, if their point of view is valid and in the minority. We learned one exercise which people refer to as "the big bad idea." When someone had an alternate view, he could raise his hand and say, "big bad idea" and state his thought. Before permitting everyone to exercise the natural human tendency to rip it apart, people had to give thirty seconds stating something, anything, that they liked about the idea. Finding even the slightest bit of value or goodness in it. By engaging in that exercise, the valuable points in the "alternate view" were permitted a hearing, which otherwise would not have occurred.

We said early on in this book that trust frees people. This is where it happens.

Create healthy competition. This is classic, basic stuff, but important, and very easy to gloss over when you're faced with marketplace pressures and internal deadlines. There is healthy internal competition, and unhealthy internal competition. The unhealthy kind breaks down trust faster than you can say "He won because he cheated." The healthy kind engages people, makes them stay involved, makes them want to do it again, makes them want to win.

When Annie worked at Pepsi, the company used to run contests with both individual and team components. For example, she recalls, there was one contest in which three teams in a plant would compete for prizes. The *team* that was ranked the highest (on whatever the measurement was), was awarded the "top tier" of prizes. So if you, as an individual, got the nod for "highest sales" or "most new accounts opened," and you were on the "top" team, you received the top tier prize for that category. If your team was ranked third, you would get the third-in-line prize for that category—even if you were ranked the best individually.

"It was a common incentive set-up. There was nothing new about it," Annie remembers. "But it worked so well. It really did foster healthy competition."

Sometimes big contests aren't the way to go. Sometimes they can provide too great a distraction from the broader range of priorities a team should be focused on. And you don't need to run contests to foster healthy competition. Instead, you might think about publicly highlighting the achievements or behaviors of someone you'd like your team to emulate. Be explicit about the kind of behavior they should strive for.

To Have on Your Radar . . .

Whether you're in the process of selecting team members, or well into a project, there are a few variables that you should keep on your radar screen. They could spell trouble. Pay attention to:

The type and intensity of interaction that the work requires. When people work together intensely for a long time, emotions often start to run high. This can be a great trust-builder: when people feel more open to share of themselves, and receptive to others as well, they can create strong, lasting bonds. But such closeness can also make even minor conflicts seem more personal than business-related. Something as seemingly innocuous as a disagreement over who will introduce the pitch to a client or how an e-mail should be phrased, can quickly escalate into a full-fledged, hurtful exchange that truly exceeds the bounds of reasonable response.

In many cases, team members spend more time with one another than they do with their immediate family (waking time, anyway!). Which means that emotion is always going to enter into the equation at some point. While not every situation requires deep emotional processing, the bigger ones do, and it is in those situations where the "emotional debriefing or discussion" needs to take place. Bear in mind, though, that managers who spend time dissecting and processing every single emotional episode in the workplace would probably find themselves with no time for anything else. This is an issue to be calibrated.

The reputation or baggage that groups or individuals bring with them to the team. For example, the notion that "the accountants are just bean counters." Labels such as those can be demoralizing. They can make individuals or groups on a team feel undervalued.

And although the team as a whole may not seem inclined to give credence to such baggage, beware: one perceived stumble on the part of a team member, and their past reputation will be brought into play, however unintentionally. Baggage and reputation are defaults; if you're unsure about someone, it's all too easy to doubt your own intuition and view and fall back instead on a perception that was formed long ago.

Bryant's MBAs are a good example of this barrier to building trust inside teams. Rob still remembers in his very first job after college, when he was told by an old-timer in the purchasing department in all seriousness "I'm not working with you. You're college." (It took an excessive amount of effort to work with—if not around—this particular individual, and the battle was never really won.)

Cultural and "translation" issues. Worth a mention here, though we will go into detail on them in the next chapter when we talk about building trust across teams, departments, offices, and the like. When you bring people together from different parts of the organization—with different backgrounds, different ways of working, different customers—there are going to be language barriers. You can say the words "application," "architecture," and "platform," and for most people they'll mean "what you fill out to get a job," "what it takes to design a building," and "where you board a train." In the software world, the words have entirely different meanings. Believe it or not (for you software junkies), most of the world doesn't consider "application," "architecture," and "platform" to be software-related terms.

People will approach problem-solving differently. They'll have different work habits. Different definitions of success. Those differences, if not explored and understood, will create a breeding ground for mistrust. (Conversely, if you take the time to demystify the individual characteristics of your team members to their new colleagues, you're more likely to find yourself in that rich, rich land where the whole is indeed greater than the sum of its parts.)

There is a global dimension to all this as well. A representative example comes from the work of Fons Trompenaars in his book *Riding the Waves of Culture*. The book focuses on how different cultures respond to various management issues and approaches. For instance, Trompenaars surveyed employees in dozens of countries on a number of topics. He asked such questions as, "If you are feeling upset at work, would you express it openly?" In Italy, fully 70 percent of individuals would express it, in the U.S., 60 percent would express it, in the U.K., barely 30 percent would express it, and in Japan, less than 20 percent would admit it. It serves as a reminder that building trust and trusted leadership must always be expressed or translated into the language and the customs of the population with whom you are dealing.

Favoritism. How do you reward stars without being accused of favoritism? This is a tough one. First you have to make sure that you are indeed being objective. Everyone is guilty of favoritism at some point in his or her career. Maybe this person is just on your wavelength. Maybe he or she reminds you of yourself ten years ago. Be thorough in your examination, and be honest with yourself when you ask yourself if you have favorite team members. (And be aware that even if you are certain that you are not playing favorites, it is easy for people to misinterpret, or read into, the personal friendships you may have with some team members—or even the fact that you have mutual friends in common with some team members. If anyone on your team tries to take advantage of such a connection, you must encourage them not to. You can first set an example by not discussing these connections in front of other team members. But if the person doesn't follow your lead, you can address it directly and gently.)

As a general rule, the best way to approach rewards inside a team is to make sure that the criteria do not favor one type of team member over another, and also to be abundantly clear about the criteria. Everyone on the team should know exactly what it takes to qualify for a reward.

What about if you have a true star in your midst—someone who consistently exceeds expectations and constantly merits the rewards? Go ahead and give him his due. But at the same time, understand that his constant success might get old, at some point, for the other team members. One thing you can do to minimize any resentment is to make it a point to recognize others on the team, publicly, if not formally, for their own particular accomplishments. Maybe "Tom" isn't your star—but maybe he did a fine job on his most recent presentation to the sales department.

You might also consider giving your star a chance to coach others. On the theory that a rising tide does indeed lift all boats, you can pursue a "share the expertise" tack. But be careful about this one—you don't want to inadvertently foster more resentment. Is your star the kind of person who would make a good mentor? Is he or she in fact a good team player? If the answer is yes, go ahead. But if the answer is no, then you might want to consider moving towards the other extreme and putting some distance between the person in question from the others in the group. Thrusting someone into a situation that doesn't suit them will only put you two steps back.

Incentive programs that overvalue individual contribution. While you're examining your rewards criteria to see if they inadvertently favor one or another team member, take a hard look at whether the rewards are too oriented toward individual performance, and not enough toward the success of the team.

Most organizations claim to have incentives that balance individual performance with team performance. But most managers would also admit that the programs that focus on individual merit are easier to administer. Why? The reality of it is that the contributions made by the various members of a team are rarely equal.

The problem is that if you focus purely on individual contribution, you're bound to foster unhealthy competition within the team. Grading on a curve doesn't work. People understand that in order to win, someone else has to lose. They know that you've got a finite amount of money to distribute and that if you bestow something on one person, you are taking away from someone else. And they may begin to undermine their peers to guarantee themselves a place at the top of the curve. That's not to say that they will turn into deceitful back-stabbers. (We have *some* faith!) But when they're given the chance to offer some constructive input, or if they're asked to help out with a phase of the project in which they have particular expertise, they may just hold back. Just a little. Just enough.

Special deals that have no logical, clear, open, defensible rationalization. In many organizations—in many teams within organizations—customizing jobs has gotten easier to do, largely because of the technology available to us today. But too much customization—or customizing jobs on a case-by-case basis, without thinking through an entire game plan—can be risky. We know of one person who asked her team leader if she could work at home four out of five days, and was given the nod because of the nature of her role on the team and her solid performance track record. Soon another team member requested the same perk, received the go-ahead, and happily began telecommuting. But when a third person asked, a few months later, her request was denied—in part because the manager felt that she needed more direct supervision than the other two, but also because the manager felt that the office was in danger of losing critical mass. With two people out, the place seemed almost too quiet; the manager felt certain that the level of synergy among employees in the group was dropping. Understandably, the third person was annoyed. So was the rest of the team. So were other company employees who were not on the team, but were watching with interest the company's first genuine foray into flextime.

The people who had begun working from home were immediately put on the defensive. And other managers from other areas in the company began to voice their concerns. "We can't let our people do this; why are you letting yours?" "We never talked about this beforehand; now we've got people coming to us with all sorts of crazy ideas for when and how they're going to get their work done, and we can't address them all." "This might have been a good idea if we had thought it out beforehand. We might have been able to construct some sort of universal flextime or telecommuting policy—now all we have is a hodge-podge of behaviors and a growing number of irritated employees."

There's a school of thought that suggests that you should be able to customize the employment contract for each individual. But that's not realistic. You have to accommodate people, certainly, but you also have to have some guidelines shaping your employment value propositions. If you have, say, eight variables—such as flextime, or individual training opportunities— that you can play with, you have to bound each one in some way.

If you don't, you'll end up creating deals that ultimately destroy trust within your team—even if they initially make one person very happy. This is especially true when your team or company is put on the defensive. You may be forced to pay someone much more than you think you should in order to get them to join the company. You may face an extremely valuable producer who wants to do all of his or her work on Tuesdays and Thursdays, and is threatening to leave if you don't acquiesce. Set bounds can protect you—and protect the trust you've worked so hard to establish.

We'd also recommend setting guidelines rather than setting a policy. Policies can come back to bite you because they're too black and white. (Many old-school HR people will disagree here. And in a large-scale, complex organization, our "guidelines over policy" preference might seem too costly to implement and oversee. But we hope that over time, the notion will spread even to the largest and most complex companies. The potential upside is too great to ignore.)

A brief word on setting those guidelines. These things usually evolve in a clunky way, as people—leaders and employees alike— begin to consider what variables are the most important to them and why. If you have a responsible team, you might consider involving them in creating the guidelines; their input will be invaluable. And if you don't, then, sadly, you probably have much more pressing matters to attend to.

Bureaucracy. Companies say that they want to reward people on performance. So they have to put in place measurements of performance. Sometimes they end up spending so much time on process that they lose sight of the reason they wanted to reward people on performance in the first place. (Does "So that they'll understand that we care about them personally and that we have a vested interest in their development" ring a bell?)

When performance measures—or any equitable decision-making mechanisms—become so complex that the word "bureaucracy" doesn't sound far off the mark as a descriptor, team members are at great risk of losing trust in their leader and in the organization. Simplify. Simplify. Simplify.

With regard to performance reviews, for example, you might start with the following two questions: How are you doing so far this year? What do you need to do the balance of the year? You can build on that, of course, but keep this in mind: The more complex things get, the more confusing they can be, the more political they can seem. The more political they seem, the less trust people will have.

An excessively internal focus. We've mentioned this one before; we'll no doubt do so again. Creating identity and building a sense of shared purpose are good things to do. But if you spend too much time focusing on them you run the risk of losing perspective on the world outside the team.

We know of a manager who instilled in his team something we call the victim mentality. "We're the underdogs. No one else in the organization understands us or the value we add." In the short term, his approach actually generated a lot of goodwill inside his team. People became cheerleaders for themselves and their fellow team members. The team culture was highly supportive. Bonds formed. Trust bloomed.

The problem was, the team members became increasingly suspicious of the rest of the company. And when they eventually spent time in the "greater organization"—away from their team leader—they realized that they had built for themselves quite a reputation as being loners, prima donnas, people who were unwilling to give of themselves beyond their own clique.

They knew, then, that their manager had done them a disservice. They started to resent him. And suddenly here was this group of highly talented people with no "home." They felt betrayed inside their team; they felt misunderstood and unwelcome outside their team. Ultimately, the group was significantly downsized and folded into another department. Those who remain are thriving under leadership that is more connected with the rest of the organization.

Another team leader led his group down a similarly dangerous path by encouraging them to be too entrepreneurial in the interests of the team's success. As a result, they put the success of the company as a whole on a back burner. This was a manufacturing company; the team in question was an obscure, technical product group that had only a small amount of customer overlap with other groups. At first, just as in the other example, the inward focus bred goodwill. The leader fostered the mentality that the team was a "scrappy little underdog that could hold its own without help." They started selling products themselves—bypassing the organization's sales arm. They started entering into smaller client relationships, tailoring their products for those customers, celebrating their own increased revenues without regard for the rest of the company.

Eventually the approach backfired. People in the group realized, after a time, that their leader wasn't encouraging behavior that would help them progress through the organization. They weren't getting promoted as quickly as their peers from other areas. What's more, as the organization as a whole became more focused, top managers realized that this small product group had developed itself almost to the point where it no longer had a place in the company's overall strategy.

However important you know your team is, don't underestimate the importance of the greater whole.

9

Across Teams, Departments, Offices

"We have met the enemy, and he is us."—Walt Kelly, *Pogo*.

INKBLOT CORP. *was a mid-sized printing company that made calendars and maps tailored to the academic market. For its first fourteen years of existence—when its business had been concentrated primarily in one region, serving a stable set of schools and colleges—the company had been relatively free of turf wars. Sure, there had been some natural rivalry between the sales and products groups, but as a general rule, people had respected one another across the company's various departments.*

Then Inkblot started on a steep growth trajectory. Its expansion into new, larger markets brought a whole host of changes. The company opened two new regional offices. Salespeople were added to serve previously untapped urban markets that had great potential. There were new faces in product design and in manufacturing. There were even two entirely new product groups, one based in each of the new offices.

Inkblot's top managers—the president, the COO, and the CFO— knew that the expansion had changed the dynamics of the company in some significant ways. They recognized, for example, that some markets now "owned" certain products, by virtue of the volume of demand in that particular geography. So they decided to reorganize the company into a completely regional structure.

The logic behind the idea was sound. The company could be "closer" to its customers if it decentralized. The three regional businesses were big enough to support their own infrastructures. Talented senior managers could now be rewarded with increased responsibility as regional leaders.

The president, COO, and CFO were confident that they had thought through—and addressed—all possible ramifications of the move. For example, they worked hard to create an equitable transfer pricing process so that the various regions could supply one another without undue tension over costs and customization. Cognizant of how quickly a rapidly scaling company can lose focus, they also spent time brainstorming about the company's vision and communicating their thoughts throughout the organization so that everyone would have a clear understanding of the company's overall purpose and goals.

What they didn't do sufficiently was anticipate the effect of their new compensation system. Previously, that system had been consistent across the organization, with all bonuses based upon total organizational performance. Now bonuses were linked only in part to overall company performance; they were tied more directly to regional numbers. And when the economy slowed, the problems began.

The regional managers (no fools, they) realized that if they could supply their customers with products from their own areas—even if those products were not exactly perfect for those customers—they could capture more margin, which, in turn, would affect regional profitability and translate into bigger bonuses.

Inkblot had long enjoyed an "all for one, one for all" kind of work environment. But suddenly it was a numbers game. People began to hoard clients. And clients, in turn, weren't getting what they wanted; they weren't getting what the company as a whole could offer them. Instead, they were being talked into buying products that would improve profits for the region in which they resided.

Managers who had long been friends were suddenly suspicious of one another. Salespeople were hostile. Dissatisfied customers wrote letters. Over the course of a year, the company's culture crumbled, and although profits were up, Inkblot did not meet its internal revenues forecast.

Inkblot's leadership team called a meeting with the three regional managers to talk about the issues and see what could be done. At the event, a simple, one-hour affair that seemed to everyone to last far longer than that, one manager (the head of the most profitable region) minimized the issue, making only generic, broad-based contributions to the discussion. "We're all just getting used to the new system. I think you'll see, if you really study things, that our customers are getting what they want, and that we're all doing our jobs." The second regional leader spent the entire meeting whining. "We're not getting any support. Our customers have the most varied demands. We get no help from anyone. We have the toughest markets." The third was, in large part, uncommunicative. On his way out of the office, though, he was heard to mutter something to the effect of, "Don't get mad, get even."

The situation we've just described is pretty much a worst-case scenario for the distrust that can come between teams (or divisions, or departments) that ostensibly are working on the same side. As a lead-in to this chapter, it illustrates just how damaging a lack of trust across parts of an organization can be.

But we also used it to get you to let down your guard a bit, and give you some confidence about building trust across teams before we get into the details of just how difficult it can be. At least the problems at Inkblot stemmed from a tangible source: a compensation system that was skewed to reward selfish regional behavior. The problem was relatively easy to diagnose (even if the obvious remedy would take a longer time to have an effect).

More common, and insidious, are scenarios in which trust between departments or divisions either dissolves or is never built, and no one can quite put his finger on why that is so. If that's the case in your organization, consider this: In any enterprise—even in the smallest of enterprises—there is a very real possibility that the members of one area won't cross paths very often with the members of another area. In organizations whose various departments reside in their own silos, there's a very good chance that "trust silos" exist as well.

That doesn't necessarily mean that the people in finance think that the people in sales are thieves, or that the people on the production line think that the people in research and development do nothing all day but eat and play games. What it does mean, however, is that the tight-knit (or otherwise) group in one department may not know very much about how the group "across the way" operates, what their incentives are and why, what their cultural peculiarities are, and what value they add to the organization. Where such a knowledge vacuum exists, building trust is difficult, and when small bits of information do manage to make their way from one locale to another, they are subject to gross misinterpretation with enormous implications.

In March of 2000, Little, Brown and Company published the now-bestselling book by Malcolm Gladwell called *The Tipping Point: How Little Things Can Make a Big Difference*. Essentially, as its subtitle suggests, the book explores the phenomenon of how seemingly small events can have large-scale and immediate implications. Gladwell wrote:

> Ideas and products and messages and behavior spread just like viruses do . . . When a virus spreads through a population, it doubles and doubles again. . . . As human beings, we have a hard time with this kind of progression because the end result— the effect—seems far out of proportion to the cause. To appreciate the power of epidemics, we have to abandon this expectation about proportionality. We need to prepare ourselves for the possibility that sometimes big changes follow from small events, and that sometimes these changes can happen very quickly.

Gladwell's message helps describe the problems with trust silos, in which people are not willing to grant one another the benefit of the doubt. Any small piece of negative information can and often will have consequences well beyond what might be deserved. And then you're really in the stew.

Stress, Squared

Building trust across teams, departments, offices, and the like begins with two mandates. First, seek out and correct obvious ways in which the corporation is undermining trust (as in the printing company's compensation system). Second, try to provide as complete a picture as possible to everyone of what the various groups do to keep the company moving so that you avoid the trust silos.

Those are just the first steps, of course. "Building trust across" (we'll shorthand it as that, so we don't have to keep repeating "departments," "functions," and "offices") also requires juggling and balancing increasing numbers of people who may or may not be trusted or trusting members of their own particular team to begin with. Picture a trusting relationship between two people in the same department. Now picture that relationship under some stress that originates from another member of that same department. Now picture those three people trying to build a trusting relationship with the department across the way, in which several internal conflicts are festering. Keep in mind that that department across the way is also a direct competitor for company resources, which have been scarce lately.

You understand the scope of the task. And our words of comfort won't exactly warm the cockles of your heart either: This is not something that you're ever going to be able to say is "done." The best you can hope for is to be secure in the knowledge that: (1) you've made the playing field as level as possible by trying to provide as much information as possible to all parties; (2) you've set up honest, wide open, multi-way communication channels as best you can; and 3) you are constantly on the lookout for situations or circumstances in which trust across teams can melt down.

Danger Signals

What kinds of circumstances or trigger points spell danger to trust between teams?

Parochialism

There are pockets in any organization where parochialism is a natural phenomenon, and where a certain amount of conflict between teams can be expected.

At a newspaper, for example, the editorial and production departments are constantly in conflict—regardless of compensation, incentives, and the like. It's the nature of the game. There's a deadline, and the more time editorial takes, the less time production has. But the more time editorial takes, the better, in theory, the product that goes to production.

Think sales and marketing. Manufacturing and distribution. Purchasing and production. There's a natural tension between these groups simply by virtue of the kind of work they do.

What can *you* do? Create checking mechanisms to see that

there are no obvious barriers to trust across the teams. Think about Inkblot. Is your compensation system fair and equitable? What about the time you afford each team to carry out its appointed tasks—does anyone feel constant pressure to produce under deadlines that are too tight? What about your incentive and measurement systems? Does one department get credit for new clients who are in turn served by the entire organization? (What if those new clients are very difficult to serve? What if the organization isn't equipped to handle them?)

Resource allocation is another hot spot. If you've asked for sacrifices for the greater good, are those requests well understood? (What if you ask part of your organization to cede or migrate some of their clients to another group that can better handle them? What if you ask people to take a back seat in a production or delivery schedule for the benefit of another part of the organization or some other customer? What if you instruct a department to change the design of a particular product in order to give it a consistent "look and feel" with other products under the same corporate brand?) Check also on the attitudes of the leaders of the respective teams or areas. If you're endorsing a bond between teams, but one of those team leaders is reluctant, you won't get there.

Michael Welles, who held the position of general manager at Lotus in that company's early days, and is now an executive in the technology industry, had this to say to us about breaching parochialism:

> Communications mechanisms are so important. And when you think about the kinds of channels you need, they seem so obvious. But they're just not always in place. Common platforms, for example. Using the same e-mail system or meeting scheduler in each office. A way for everyone to access the same information— Notes, or some other program. Those are such small things in a technical sense, but it's easy not to get them right.

Welles also stressed the importance of having top managers travel to other offices. Of ensuring that they spend time with people from all over the company. "Sometimes you have to force people from headquarters to get out there. They think they're doing it enough, but usually they're not. You have to put in the face time."

He told us of a time when he had people in Asia, Europe, and North America reporting to him. It's no secret that building trust across diverse groups like that is a real cultural as well as geographic challenge. Consider the effect that the time differences alone have on efforts to improve communication. There are no "normal" overlapping business hours between Hong Kong and New York. And although e-mail and voice-mail help, the distance means that in order to maintain close ties, someone in one city or the other is going to lose sleep on a regular basis. (Interestingly, former Fed chairman Paul Volcker, working on the reorganization of Arthur Andersen in the difficult days following the Enron scandal, began a restructuring of Andersen to centralize the leadership in its Chicago headquarters. He had quickly come to the conclusion that the overly decentralized nature of the leadership ranks was a significant impediment to the kind of coordinated effort that he felt was desirable, particularly at that juncture.)

Now, layer on the logistics of travel. Welles told us:

> I put off an Asia trip for nearly a year because of scheduling difficulties. That was a mistake. Asia in particular is very people-oriented. It really matters to people that you take the time to be with them—and not just for regular meetings. They need you, particularly if there's a problem. Nowadays, if there's a manufacturing glitch, not only am I made aware of it, but also I'm pushing to help them out so they don't feel they're out there alone. They feel that the people in the other parts of the company really care about the process as well as the product.

Ultimately, Welles said, building trust across teams comes down to strengthening relationships between people, whatever the method:

> You need to build relationships, or your systems won't work. Here's an example. At a former employer, I was deeply involved when we changed our sales compensation system. I wanted to back-load it, to reward people when the effort was complete, while the sales folks (naturally) wanted their compensation to match the timing of their efforts more closely. We reached a com-

promise solution, which never would have happened if the personal relationships with those people hadn't been in place first,
no matter what the right answer was. I had to work closely with
our sales people. I lived or died with them. I needed to take the
arrows they took.

Here's an interesting aside that shows the value in a counterintu-
itive approach to staying in touch.

Ephraim Brecher, the recently retired AT&T vice president
who ran that corporation's tax department, had an innovative
way of handling the numerous (and typically time-sensitive, high-
stakes) demands on his time and attention that came from his direct reports and the roughly one hundred people in the tax area.
He permitted no regular update–type meetings with the people
from his department to be scheduled with him in advance. Meetings could only be scheduled on a same-day, that-day basis. This
ensured that those matters seriously requiring his input could be
heard, that he wouldn't be tied up in an endless sequence of meetings with little result, and that his people knew that at times they
would be forced to use their own good judgment. Brecher says
that while it took a while for people to adjust to his approach, it
became a successful way for him to handle the volume of requests.
It might work for you if you are attuned to the rhythm of your environment, and willing to stick to your guns when introducing a
new way of doing things.

Baggage

Almost everyone flies with baggage of some kind.

Maybe one team or department has traditionally been thought
of as a weak sister. "But that was when it was sorely underfunded,
and under the leadership of someone who has long since moved
on!" No matter. It's baggage, and it will be taken into consideration.

Maybe the teams in question have tried to work together before, with poor results. "But that was ten years ago, with completely different managers in charge, on a completely different
type of project!" No matter. It's history and it will be counted.

Consider one marketing agency that had spent years perfecting its mail and telemarketing businesses. Like so many of its competitors, it created an Internet marketing division in the 1990s. Like so many of its competitors, the company had to pay dearly to attract people with the online marketing expertise it wanted. Did these online folks make a lot more than their paper and phone-based colleagues? You bet. Yet that discrepancy wasn't the problem, in and of itself. People all over the company seemed to recognize the competitive mores of the day, and, if they weren't happy about it, at least they were tolerant. After all, online expertise was a specialization. Over the next few years, though, it became apparent that the company would soon have to reorganize itself around clients and integrate its Internet activities with the other parts of the organization. Clients wanted their online campaigns to work with their direct mail and telemarketing campaigns. They wanted a seamless marketing presentation.

At the same time, the folks from the print and telemarketing sides were becoming increasingly tech savvy. Initially, the skill sets needed to create a commercial Web site had been very different from those needed for other types of marketing. Now, not so much. More people were comfortable with the technology, and the technology itself was easier to work with. Suddenly the compensation discrepancy was a glaring issue. Some 80 percent of employees were on one salary track; the other 20 percent—now working right alongside their colleagues, doing much of the same stuff—were making a great deal more. The former online specialists also had different performance measures in place. Different evaluation systems. And an occasional "spot bonus" program whereby managers could say, "Wow. What a project! Here's an extra $500." The "offline" people had never heard of such a thing.

It would be a gross understatement to say that this company had little trust across its teams, but the top managers didn't throw up their hands in despair. First, they acknowledged to the company at large that they were well aware of the problem. (They "named it and claimed it.") They made it clear that they would be moving to equalize the compensation across the company. They asked for input from representatives of each of the formerly separate departments. What elements of the existing compensation packages were most onerous? What type of compensation system would align best with the new approach to client service?

One of the first steps taken was the virtual elimination of the spot bonuses. The top managers then introduced a new compensation system that made a larger part of the total package variable across the board. It took almost two years to equalize salaries, and the company is still dealing with some residual friction caused by the "baggage" from the days before the merger. But there is a growing sense of unity among employees. And every satisfied client strengthens that unity.

What can you do about baggage in your organization? Part of the answer lies in recognizing the baggage before you attempt to pave over the existing tension. Naming it and claiming it, as the managers at the direct marketing company did. One of the reasons that company didn't implode was that its managers were able to say straight out, "We know that there is a serious compensation discrepancy between the online division and the other parts of the organization. We're going to be working to rectify the situation. But we need all of you to understand that this isn't something that can happen overnight. We can't simply raise salaries across the board in the rest of the company. Nor can we cut salaries across the board for the people who initially joined the online group. We want and need your input; we hope for your cooperation and patience."

The other part of the answer lies in creating new situations that pave over the old baggage. Situations in which people can have a positive experience working with one another. You want the needle to move from, "Those people are getting much more than they're worth so why should I give them the time of day?" to "We know the company is working on this, and in the meantime, I've been getting to know George. He just helped me solve a problem I'd been hashing around for a few days."

And if the issue isn't compensation? If the baggage is about past mistakes, or an old reputation? You want the needle to move from, "Those people are idiots; if you have to work with them, work around them," to "Hey, that wasn't so bad; one or two of them have something to offer," to "Let's ask someone from that department for their input on this project."

Translation Problems

Sometimes a process that worked well in one team just won't fly in another. Why not? Could be that the process was tailored too specifically to the needs of the first team. Could be that the second team isn't familiar with the terminology the first team uses; the problem could literally be a language barrier. Could be that the process shouldn't be forced on the second team; maybe they're doing just fine without it, thank you very much.

Translation problems manifest themselves in a variety of ways. We're reminded of the company that had completed two rounds of layoffs under the purview of a close-knit group of top managers, who then decided to bring in an outside, senior-level expert to handle the third round. The logic seemed sound: The company was undergoing all sorts of changes in its processes; the senior managers were concentrating on too many different issues at once; an outside expert would surely be able to step in and handle what looked to be the final round.

What happened? The expert brought with her a host of tried-and-true processes of her own, most of which did not dovetail with the way in which the company's top managers had previously handled their reductions in staff. They had forged an approach to the process, but hadn't even realized that they were wedded to that approach until the new person showed up. She was smart and well-regarded, but they felt that the steps and stages and checks that she wanted to introduce were process-oriented, not content-driven. They didn't give her time to learn what they had done; she didn't even realize they wanted her to learn the previous method. (She thought she was being brought in because the previous method had been unsatisfactory.)

"She lost credibility in her attempts to add value," says one senior manager, looking back. "She just never got any traction. It was partly our fault, for not being clear about what we really wanted and needed. It was partly her fault, too. She didn't try to understand the situation, and she was trying to over-engineer things."

How can you avoid translation problems? Keep an eye on the pace and the rhythms of each team. Will either be disrupted if you impose a new process, or a universal process? What about the language? Does Team A use jargon that is going to seem foreign to Team B? We know of one company that tried to impose a simple approval system on a department that had long operated without any formal system. The approval process in question had worked well in two other areas in the company; no one expected any additional problems in its adoption. Indeed, the people who were supposed to start using the system for the first time were receptive. But when they tried to follow the process, they got bogged down in the language. The organizational structure in this department was different than in the other departments, and because of the wording differences, approvals were handed off to the wrong people. The system bogged down within a day, and even though the company's managers rectified the problem immediately, the initiative failed. Fearing more wasted time, people simply ignored the forms and went about their business in the old way.

Don't be afraid to ask all involved parties for their input. Don't be afraid to take time up-front to get things right. The idea is to adapt what you think is the preferred approach to current realities. And to establish a common language. We're well aware that in many situations, he who hesitates is lost. But in this case, "Wait a minute" can save you a lot of grief.

Egos, Eccentricities, and Excesses

Think back to the enemies of trusted leadership we described in Chapter 4. The people who stomp all over their colleagues in pursuit of their own glory. The people whose need for control overrides any moral commitment to fair play. That's who we're talking about here.

Beware the outright or unresolved issues of certain individuals' needs for power and control. It's hard enough managing the behavior (or minimizing the damage created by the behavior) of a rainmaker who is great with clients but horrible with direct reports when you've got that person contained in a team or in a department. But when this person crosses departmental borders, the situation can get out of hand very quickly. If so-and-so from Department A suddenly has under his control several people at a lower level in Department B, and he's wreaking havoc with their work lives, you can imagine how hard it becomes to sort out who's responsible for what and how to untangle the mess.

An attorney who headed up a specialty department of a sizable law firm in New York City, we'll call him Strickland, had been a boy genius type—making partner after only six years, which, in New York, was almost unheard-of. He was also difficult, contentious, opinionated, and very self-protective. His zeal for structuring aggressive solutions for clients occasionally brought his ethics into question. Yet he was a client magnet. Clients loved him. Even when he wasn't the person whose expertise they needed, they wanted him front and center on their jobs. For example, he became the quarterback for leveraged buyout (LBO) deals, though he had little experience in the area. The transactions would turn on the work of another partner. Yet clients inevitably wanted to talk to Strickland, work through Strickand, congratulate and thank Strickland when the job was complete, and he would play into their desires. He would have closed-door meetings with clients, excluding other attorneys whose work was important to the tasks at hand.

After a while, several corporate partners flat-out refused to work with the guy. So Strickland began to reach across departments and grab associates to support him. He eventually made those associates miserable, but they couldn't turn to their seniors for help because those partners had distanced themselves.

Ultimately, the senior partners of the firm isolated Strickland to the point where they minimized the damage he caused. They weighed the grief and the relief. They identified people who could tolerate the guy, and they stood behind those who didn't want to work with him. They kept him on because he really was a tremendous rainmaker. The situation was never totally resolved; Strickland's nature didn't permit that kind of closure, but the firm found a tolerable way of balancing his ego with the welfare of the rest of the people there.

If you have a Strickland in your midst, make it clear to him what his behavior is doing to the organization. Isolate him as much as possible. Force him to take some counsel; make it a requisite part of his job, and a factor in how his performance is measured. Monitor the balance of grief and relief, and take the necessary action if the scale tips the wrong way.

A "Building Trust Across" Checklist

Here are some ways to draw a bead on whether you are attuned to the trust issues that can crop up between parts of a company. Ask yourself:

1. *Are you involved, in an ongoing way, with each constituency in your organization?* Do they have unfiltered (we stress unfiltered, *not* unlimited!) access to you? There are legendary stories of executive assistants who were almost rabid guardians of their bosses. There's one (OK, possibly apocryphal) story of an assistant whose business card read "Fender," and when asked why, she would say that her job was to "keep the crap off the big wheel." If you're too isolated, you'll quickly lose perspective on what makes your organization work—and on what makes it stumble. What evidence do your employees have that if they extend their trust to you—and to other teams—it won't come back to bite them?

2. *Can you name and discuss the operational and cultural differences between the various groups under your corporate umbrella?* Do you recognize the realities of distance, differing systems, cultures, hierarchies, motives, possible old-wounds-as-yet-unhealed? Is each team aware of the breadth and depth of your knowledge?

3. *When you're talking to members of two or more teams at the same time, are you using a language that everyone understands?* When members of various teams are meeting together, are they able to understand one another? If not, do you provide a "translator" in the form of someone who understands the nuances of each team? Remember, a common language can mean not just the words or jargon people use, but also having common priorities, common experiences, or common challenges. For example, if one group deals with large clients, and another group deals with the middle market, using only examples from the *Fortune* 500 might not be such a good idea. And keep in mind, you don't need a single language—or a single culture—to have trust between teams. You just have to have the understanding that the differences are OK.

4. *Do you check in with each group regularly?* Not just when there's some transaction to be done? How does that check-in take place?

5. *Do you have an agreed-upon conflict resolution mechanism?* One that has no sanctions for raising issues?

6. *Does the conflict resolution mechanism contain an agreed-upon escalation process?* Sometimes you'll need to be a mediator, sometimes an arbitrator, sometimes a parent, sometimes a dictator. When faced with conflict, are

you confident that you know which role is needed? Communispace's Diane Hessan had an interesting comment about escalation processes. She agreed that the buck has to stop somewhere, but added these cautionary words for the last person on the trail:

> When two people come to you with an issue they can't resolve, I do think it's too paternalistic to put them in a room and say, "You go work it out." But at the same time, if you solve the problem for them, then the next time it happens, you'll have to go and solve it again. I try to coach them through it—especially if we're talking about a conflict between two managers. I try to talk to them about why they're better off if they solve it. I've even said to a manager, "If you can't work it out, would you like me to have someone else direct your group?" I didn't mean it as a threat. What I was trying to do was to have that person recognize the possibility that many people aren't happy in leadership roles. Leadership is about creating current leaders, not just future ones. And helping people learn to resolve conflicts—or helping them realize that they don't want to be in the position of resolving a conflict beyond a certain level—is part of being a leader. I say to people, "You have to help me lead." This is not about me as Mommy coming into the office. It's what I need from people if the organization is going to move forward.

7. *Do the members of each team understand how other teams add value to their work?* Sometimes it's clear how one team contributes to the welfare of the other team, and to the organization at large, and not so clear how another team adds equitable value. How they can help you and how you can help them must be in balance. And that balance must be understood, especially if it isn't readily visible. (This understanding, by the way, isn't something that can be assumed. It often requires an overt educational process, like an internal trade fair.)

8. *Do you make it a point to publicize the value that one team adds to the work of the other teams, and to the organization at large?* Do you spread the word? This can (and should) be done both formally and informally. If it only appears in the company newsletter, it may come across as meaningless propaganda, or even disinformation.

9. *Do you actively help others work across teams, departments, and offices?* Have you put in place incentives to discourage the kind of behavior that would create silos in your organization?

We can't resist a short example here: A CEO of a large retail financial services company literally told his senior managers to "make synergy happen!" but did nothing to facilitate the process. There were clear opportunities, even given the regulatory issues involved, to take advantage of the consistency of the customer base across divisions, but no incentives to pursue any of those opportunities.

By contrast, consider the positive effect that an incentive to build synergy and trust had at a production and distribution company. This company produced only about half of what it distributed; the rest was product from outside sources. Over time, the people in the internal production company felt that they were getting short shrift from distribution, that there was no advantage to their being under the same corporate umbrella. As in the first case, the CEO publicly decreed his desire for synergy across divisional boundaries. The difference was that this manager backed up his words with a change in the executives' performance expectations, and incentives to position the company's own products to advantage in its catalogues and other distribution venues.

10. *Do you have people from each team to whom you can turn for an objective assessment of all of the above?* There is a tendency among senior leaders to have unreasonable expectations when it comes to trust between teams. And while there's nothing wrong with healthy optimism, and the goal of moving from good to better to even-better-than-that, you will cause problems if you forge ahead without consideration of the *volume,* the *time,* and the *complexity* involved in fulfilling the goals you set forth. If you say, for example, "You did a great job on that product profitability analysis. Now slice the numbers for a customer profitability analysis," do you know what you're asking for? If you say, "You did a great job on that analysis of region one. Now do it for all twelve," do you know how much additional work you've requested? In some cases, re-crunching numbers, or moving from phase one to phase two of a project requires only a little time at a computer keyboard. (Witness the ease with which architects now create mirror images of their designs; all it takes is a few keystrokes.) But in other cases, what looks to you to be a simple request may in fact mean a lot *more* work, or *new* work, or undue *time pressure.* Check these things out with a reliable source before you proceed.

If there was ever an area where a trusted leader has to work his or her hardest, it may well be in building trust across various parts of the organization. In most cases, the various groups feel as if they are doing the right things *now,* proceeding along the right paths, staying true to company values. In reality, though, each group operating with those assumptions is probably doing work in very different ways, none of which is in alignment. Though their intentions may be the best, it is your challenge, as their trusted leader, to make sure that they can align to the greatest extent possible.

Sea Changes

Although, as we've said, building and strengthening trust is an endeavor that requires constant, consistent care, there are some times when the process calls for more intense attention. We're talking about when something happens in your organization that could cause a sea change in the level or type of trust that exists among employees, between your employees and you, or between employees and the company at large. That something could be an organizational change, such as a new structure, or a reduction in force. Or it could be a crisis, either internal or brought on by the market or other external factors. The "something" could also be an event as "normal" as an employee leaving the organization for a more desirable position elsewhere, or for a life-style change. These are all defining times, with regard to trust. They are all times when trust is at its most vulnerable.

In Part Four, we'll also go into the remedies for rebuilding trust that has been destroyed. Most of you, at one time or another, will find yourselves walking into a situation in which trust has already been destroyed and you are expected to lead the charge to rebuild it. This too is a defining time; handled well, the trust that emerges can be stronger and more far-reaching than it ever was before.

DEFINING MOMENTS

10

In Times of Change

GAIL'S EMPLOYER, *a $2 billion women's apparel company, was being acquired by a much larger apparel company. The rumors had been circulating for months, and Gail, as the division vice president for one of the company's most successful apparel lines, had known that something was up based on the number of closed door meetings and the types of information she had been asked for recently. Now her immediate superior had confirmed the news.*

Of course, Gail was concerned about her own role. The acquiring company had its own very successful career wear line; in fact, until today, she had considered it her most formidable competition. She knew that there must be a "duplicate Gail" on their side already, but she had played leadership roles in other divisions in her own company, and she also knew that the senior executives considered her to be an extremely versatile performer. She was fairly certain that she would be kept on.

In fact, she was more concerned about her team. Gail had worked hard to build a sense of collaboration and fairness within her team; she was known as a very inclusive manager. Her people understood how decisions were being made, and were often active participants in even the highest level strategic decisions made within her division. They knew what they were being measured against and where they stood with her. They were also accustomed to being rewarded well and very publicly when they excelled. Now here they were, about to be acquired by an organization that had a reputation as being very "closed book" with its employees. Gail had heard that the leadership team at the larger company was very small and tight. What would that mean for her employees? How would it change the way they worked? The way they were evaluated?

And how could she explain what was happening now if the new company withheld information from her? If they asked her "Will we have jobs?" what could she say? How could she assure them that they would be treated fairly when she didn't even know—and didn't expect to find out—how decisions were going to be made?

It would only be days before the word leaked to everyone in the organization. Gail needed help. She knew that once her people found out about the acquisition, they would be watching her reactions, hanging on her every word. She needed assurances and answers herself from her boss before she could make her team feel better, but all of the SVP's seemed to be tied up in planning and negotiations. For the first time in a long time, she felt fearful of change. In fact, fearful wasn't a strong enough word. She felt backed into a corner, which was awful, because nothing had even happened yet.

Be it via merger, acquisition, reorganization, or layoff, every organization will go through times of tumultuous change. At these times, people's antennae are most finely tuned to any and all signals that might provide even a partial answer to the question "What does this mean for me?" Memos and e-mails from senior-level managers, snatches of remembered conversations—all of which might have been ignored under normal circumstances, are reread, rehashed, analyzed word for word.

Don't be surprised that the things that you say—even the most innocuous statements—can be given deep, sinister meaning. People are also going to hold you accountable for what they *perceive* you to have said (which may not necessarily be what you thought you said) for a longer period of time than you might think. Think about all of the organizations that stated they were "not currently planning any layoffs," that ultimately needed to implement reductions in force. While the statements might have been absolutely true at the time, and well-intended (trying to protect people from seemingly unnecessary distraction), two months down the road, when a layoff is announced, people are going to remind senior managers—in no uncertain terms—that they promised no layoffs. They'll suspect that the current actions were in the making when the first statement was made and their trust will rapidly erode.

"But that's a completely innocent statement!" you protest. "Why shouldn't we reassure people that we're not planning any layoffs if we're not?"

The answer is that you should. Of course you should. But there's a right and a wrong way to do it. The statement by itself—"we're not planning any layoffs at this time"—isn't the problem. It's what's missing in the way of fact-based supporting evidence and a description of the context that sets the company up to look bad later on.

If you haven't offered the full story, your employees will fill it in for you. And particularly in times of change, their filler is more likely to be negative than positive. (If senior leaders don't offer anything—as in Gail's situation—their silence is going to be analyzed just as intensely as would be any partial story. Trust erodes quickly in a vacuum.)

Our experience is that organizations that do well at managing change, and avoid the kind of scenarios we've just described, make significant deposits into the "trust bank." Managing your way through change need not be as perilous a journey as it seems, if you first put yourself through the paces we'll outline below.

When you're managing change:

Involve someone who really understands your people; what motivates them, how they react, what they need. Chances are, most if not all of the people in your inner circle are very involved in planning your organization's change initiative. Sometimes the people in the inner circle spend much of their working lives in the diameter of that circle. As a result, they don't understand the dynamics of the company's many "outer circles." You need to engage the help of someone who has a good sense of how the rest of the organization will feel about the change, as a reality check.

Who might that someone be? In one company we know, that person is a senior vice president who has been with the organization for 13 years. She has worked in a number of different offices and had a reputation throughout the company as a good mentor—she is good at developing people. And she has a similarly good reputation among clients. As the head of the human resources function at that company told us:

> She has a bead on the people dynamics throughout the company. So she's a great person to call in and run new ideas by. And if we have the feeling that something isn't going to go over well, she's a great person to explain things to in private, and in detail, before we address the entire company. People are in the habit of going to her to clarify what they think they've heard. She has a certain skill in framing whatever is coming down in realistic, optimistic terms.

The first few times the group used this senior VP in this capacity, they told her just what they were going to tell the company at large, and then analyzed their path based on her reactions. Now they tell her the whole story.

> After all this time, she knows that the expectation is that she'll behave like an owner of the business. She understands that there are certain things she can't share with others that we are going to share with her. And she welcomes that trust. You know, she's not gunning for a top management position here; she's made it clear that she's content at her level. But I think this added responsibility of sorts has enhanced her sense of herself in her job. It has given her something as well.

So one possibility is to look among the senior-level people who are not in the inner circle. But another avenue is to look even deeper in your organization. Rich is a mid-level finance person at a Boston-based company. The COO brought him into the inner circle initially because the company was going to go through a significant financial restructuring, and Rich was going to be doing much of the numbers work involved. Rich was by no means a policy maker; in fact, he was a pretty quiet guy, young (barely thirty), shy. But one day, as the group was discussing a significant reduction in force planned for one particular department, he piped up and said, "I think you all should reconsider that one. Those are the people who really hold the keys to the kingdom when it comes to knowledge of our customers." People were surprised; they didn't expect it from Rich. But they listened, and realized that he was absolutely right. In a subtle way, he became the voice of the "outside" thereafter, in the inner circle.

At one company we know of, when the inner circle was rethinking the organization's entire go-to-market strategy, the CEO sent four people from her inner circle out into the organization to select someone to become one of the team for that particular initiative. (The company's markets were changing, and although performance was still good, they were trying to stay ahead of the curve.) It was a brilliant move. Made more so by the CEO's attentiveness to ensuring that the four people selected—and their bosses—knew exactly why they were being diverted from their regular work and how that work was going to get done in their absence. And that those four weren't given access to information that might prove a distraction to them when they returned to their own jobs.

The voice of the rank and file, as it were, provided insights— and outlined potential challenges—that the inner circle, on its own, would never have seen, or anticipated. Those four people were able to bridge the gaps between the way in which top managers perceived that work got done and the reality of the day-to-day operations (which are often different, in some very important ways). And the reorganization effort was successful, in no small part because of their efforts.

Be wary of self-interest. Times of change are usually also times of uncertainty for some individuals. Consider one company we worked with that was about to acquire a small, fast-growing entity. The senior vice president of the acquiring company, who was charged with leading the integration effort, had some serious doubts about whether the acquisition was going to work. She told us:

> Everything appeared to be too good to be true. I was particularly wary because our one source of information from this firm was the president—an extremely capable guy, but one who had an awful lot at stake. He stood to gain tens of millions in cash if the

transaction went through. He also was being tapped to play a very senior, strategic role within the combined organization. I had no reason not to trust him, really. But I was suspicious of the fact that he was the gatekeeper, and that he seemed to be keeping us from too much contact with the rest of the people in his firm—under the guise of streamlining the process for us.

So I poked around. Turns out the deal *was* too good to be true. He had given us an impressive client list, for example, with some big names on it. But we found out that the firm hadn't really worked for that big name client. In fact, the firm had worked for a small company that happened to be acquired by the big name a year after the work was done!

And that wasn't all. He had told us that his key people were willing to travel. And when we finally insisted on interviewing a number of his senior managers, we found that they were, for the most part, *not* willing to travel. That was a critical discovery, because what we were really buying were the people, and if they were going to be at odds with our plans, what would that have left us?

I realized that even if the firm was a strategic fit for us—and it truly was—that I would have a hard time taking anything this man said at face value going forward. Ultimately, we pulled out of the deal; we just didn't trust him enough.

To give him the benefit of the doubt, we'll just say that the president in that last example had a difficult time being objective and straightforward because he had a lot at stake, but his story is played out every day in the marketplace. Our point is to be wary of self-interest in others, and also in yourself. Self-interest can lead a person to present the facts in a skewed way. And to make decisions based on impression and desire rather than on what is truly good for the organization.

Consider a layoff situation. It's relatively easy for senior managers to make decisions, based on superficial data, about people they don't know very well. But when they have to make those same sorts of decisions about their own direct reports, it gets a lot harder, and often, they'll find very creative ways to skirt the issue and circumvent the decision. They find the pressure points; they say things like "We can't cut that person; he is critical to our relationship with one of our most important clients. If he leaves, the relationship will be in jeopardy." Is that true? Maybe not. But is it difficult to assess? Definitely.

What can you do? Your most critical weapon against self-interest is reinforcing the expectation that senior leaders should behave like owners of the business. Sometimes that requires putting them through an exercise, like having them answer the question "If all of my personal assets were tied up in this business, what would I have to do?"

You have to remind everyone that the long haul is what matters. That the long-term health of the business is what people should have in mind when they're facing difficult, immediate changes. (If the president of that newly acquired entity had really thought about the longer-term implications of his actions, instead of allowing himself to be consumed by his potential short-term gain, he wouldn't have equivocated as he did.)

Often senior leaders find it very easy to make decisions on who will go at junior levels within the organization. But suddenly, when they are forced to make decisions on their direct reports or on team members whose absence would inconvenience them, they can't pull the trigger (and they often don't have to; they are in a position to make trade-offs that are less personally difficult). The result, though, can often be a smaller, but rather top-heavy organization. What's more, the junior managers, who may have had to have difficult conversations with their people, will inevitably resent those senior people who seem to have gotten off without the emotional difficulty that invariably faces the survivors in an organization. Where possible and appropriate, the rules of the game should be the same at all levels of the organization.

You have to remind them that other people in the company are making the same tough decisions, and that they need to play by the same rules. You have to be there for them when they come out of those difficult conversations. If there's an emotional barrier—they have to lay off a close friend—you have to help them work through it. If there is a perceived business barrier—"So-and-so is critical to this client relationship"—you have to help solve the problem—with a transition plan, or a part-time position—before you make them take action.

In the case of the president of the nearly acquired company, self-interest was smack-in-the-middle-of-the-forehead obvious. Many times it isn't. Many times it's difficult to spot, especially if it's your own.

Think through as many possible interpretations as you can of what you say. Natural resistance tends to intensify in times of change, particularly if the nature of the change means that you, the leader, cannot communicate as openly as you might like to. (Natural resisters, by the way, also tend to like center stage; when you're quiet, they'll be more than happy to offer their take on what's going on.)

That's why you should leave as little room as possible for misinterpretation. In times of change, people are even more hungry for information, more likely to hang on your every word or pause, and more willing to engage in "under the table" analysis.

Communicate often. People's information needs are so much greater than you might imagine. It's so easy to forget that, although you and the other senior managers have been wallowing in the same information for days or weeks, it may be news to most people in your company. Resist the temptation to say, "Enough already. Surely we've beaten this into the ground." Chances are you haven't. Be patient. Getting a message across an entire organization—any message—always takes more time than you think.

Resist, as well, the temptation to take the easy way out, and issue the same memo over and over again, in an e-mail, in an interoffice envelope, on a bulletin board. Change the medium in ways that require you to change the wording. Mix up the channels. Sometimes global channels are appropriate—the all-company voice mail, for instance. But sometimes doing that, and then convening smaller groups, or even having a series of one-to-one meetings, can go a long way to ensuring that the message is sticking.

Have a brown-bag lunch, a town meeting. Spend a deliberate hour or two walking the halls. Tuck the message into announcements about other topics. If you're trying to make people understand a drop in revenue, and you've already broadcast it directly in several ways, slip it into promotion notices as well. "Even in these tough times, we want to recognize the hard work of . . ."

Can you communicate too often? Yes! Give one too many pep talks and people are going to start to think "spin" rather than "sincerity." So don't plan to hit "re-send" every day at 2 p.m. Instead, after you've communicated the first message in a few different ways, ask yourself, "What is the next appropriate round?" Crafting another memo? Read it over. How broad is it? Is there any new information there? There should be at least something, and it shouldn't be buried.

Be wary of either extreme. Too little communication (the more common) and too much (the rarity). Both lead to a lot of long lunches and worried closed-door discussions. Both lead away from getting any actual work done.

Be careful of what you promise. Do any of these clinkers sound familiar?

- *I have no hidden agenda*
- *There won't be any more layoffs*
- *This time we've got it fixed*
- *This will not have an impact on bonuses*
- *I don't see any reason why this will slow us down*
- *This will actually improve (fill in your choice: our communication, our responsiveness, our processes)*
- *The customers will love this*
- *This will reinforce our commitment to our people*
- *We will be stronger as a result*
- *I have faith in our team*
- *We've got the right people on this*
- *This is the last time . . .*
- *This will be the first time . . .*
- *This is the hardest thing this company will ever have to do*
- *Read my lips. No new taxes*
- *We'll see results from this in three months*

- *This will dramatically increase our market share*
- *This will change the way our company operates*

Do we hear groans? You've been on the receiving end of more than a few of these, we're sure. Now you're on the other side. Review your facts. Paint the full picture. Really try to avoid blanket statements like the plague.

When you can't communicate, help people understand why. Often, change involves an initiative or set of initiatives that would be considered "disclosable events" for publicly traded companies. In other words, information that you cannot legally communicate to employees.

If you can't talk, say that you can't talk. People will sense that something is going on anyway, so be up-front (if possible) that you have to be quiet. Don't assume that everyone on staff understands SEC rules and regs, what's allowed and what isn't; they don't. If you explain the parameters you're working in, people might not like it, but at least they'll respect it. And you.

Watch the press. Unfortunately, even if you're up-front about withholding information, you still may find yourself in a defensive position—come the delivery of the morning paper. Unfortunately, it is not at all uncommon for the press to publish reports based on speculation of change. And those reports may make it seem as though you—or someone in your organization—is sharing more with the press than they are internally.

At large companies, huge, well-known multinationals, for example, where the organization—or some part of it—is in the news pretty much every day, employees are pretty inured to press reports. If you lead one of those, you're not going to have to deal with the repercussions of news articles unless they're particularly significant in nature—say, about a pending merger, or a lawsuit with a supplier. But in smaller companies, these less-frequent media reports—whatever their nature—must be taken seriously and addressed accordingly.

Annie remembers a news article that reported pending layoffs at Digitas. The gist of the report was correct—Digitas was in fact planning a small restructuring, and had already made a low-key communication to that effect internally and with investors—but the press got the numbers quite wrong. The article made it seem as though the figures had been supplied by Digitas, when in fact, as it turned out, they'd come from an analyst.

"We didn't respond immediately," remembers Annie. "And as a result, the article caused undue amounts of tension. The senior managers (with some dissenters) felt that responding would give the article credence it didn't deserve, but that wasn't the case. Instead, our silence was taken as an admission of guilt. We found ourselves digging out of a hole."

Even optimistic news reports can cause problems. In one case, the press picked up something that an electronics company CEO had said about a new product in the works, something about an accelerated launch schedule. The guy was at a conference, speaking informally with a group of people after his formal presentation, but the press picked it up and put it in print the next day. The result back home was pandemonium in the production department, in research and development, in marketing. No one was ready for an accelerated schedule. This was the first they'd heard of it. The time frame, as reported, was somewhere between wildly optimistic and wildly unrealistic.

Before the CEO had even returned from the conference, the company's various functions were suspicious of one another, spinning their wheels in futile attempts to speed up their output (unnecessarily), and worrying themselves to the point that they were *wasting* time. The CEO, in his open style, had waxed a little more enthusiastic than was probably appropriate. Turns out the press mixed up what he said about the introduction of the *prototype* with the introduction of the new product. The repercussions were huge.

Build intimacy and dialogue into communication forums. As you really start to analyze how and when you communicate with your employees, chances are pretty good that you'll discover your delivery method—while the venue may change—has been mostly of the "broadcast" variety. At many of the companies we've worked with, question-and-answer periods, however religiously offered, really rang flat.

Here's one of the ways you can truly start to encourage a two-way communication channel. Plant the tough questions. Yes, we're recommending something slightly devious right here in the middle of a book about trust-building. Call it a conversation starter. The fact is, you probably know what those questions would be. Planting the tough questions raises the topics that you would truthfully probably prefer not to have to talk about. You could have a member of your inner circle ask the question(s). Or, if you feel uneasy actually "planting," ask them yourself. Say, "I'm sure that even if no one has asked this, it's on people's minds." And then provide the brutally honest answer that isn't what people expect to hear.

At one company that had just completed a round of layoffs, the question was, "Did we make the right decisions about how many people we laid off, and who those people were?" The answer was, "I don't know. I hope so. We tried hard to make the right calls on this one, but I'll lose sleep over it for a long time."

Understand that your answers may not please everyone. Know that your answers may in fact cause additional distraction within the organization. But know, also, that by being honest, you've contributed in no small way to the organization's ability to move through the change and emerge in a healthy mental state.

And don't be afraid to personalize your comments. Tell about going home after the layoffs and facing a spouse who said, "Did you really have to let Jill go? I thought you really liked her." Tell how you said, "I did. I do. And this is going to stick with me for a long time."

Both of us (unfortunately) have had to make decisions to lay off people that we had truly come to care deeply about. It was horrible, but not hiding how we felt from the other "survivors" helped all of us move on.

Enlist middle managers' support to personalize the messages surrounding the change. It's not enough to send messages from the very top of an organization in times of change. Sometimes those messages, however heartfelt and honest, feel like "spin," or seem impersonal just because of their source. Middle managers, the people who have personal relationships with the majority of employees, can help personalize the purpose and outcome of the change so that people can truly understand what the change means for them.

Middle managers, in fact, are the ones who will put the spin—whatever it is—on your words because people will naturally gravitate toward their immediate bosses with questions. So make it a point to roll out any change initiatives in layers, so that your managers feel ready for the barrage they're going to face. Talk to your senior management group first, then deliver the message to a slightly larger group one level down, then go out to the organization at large. (If yours is a larger organization, you might add a few more layers as well. But keep the timing tight.) Your ability to get into the hearts and minds of your middle managers will have a significant impact on how well—or how poorly—change is received in your organization.

And remember that all of what we've just said is as true in times of positive change as it is in times of painful change. When you're rolling out a new brand initiative, expect the rank and file to turn to the next level up with their questions. Preparing that next level beforehand is a good idea. In fact, those prep meetings for the next level up, discussing the roll-out of something new, are usually "spirit builders." They can really provide an energizing experience, because of the opportunity they provide to give people the feeling that they are "in the know."

When you can, celebrate the success of the change. A wild celebration may not always be appropriate. But it is important to acknowledge the hard work being done, the fact that the change has taken place, and the commitment to looking ahead.

At one point, during a period where the inner circle—some 18 people—at Digitas were working long, long hours trying to organize a painful reduction in staff, Rob remembers that someone went out, late at night, and came back with a ton of Chinese food. "We littered the room with Chinese-food containers," he said. "It wasn't a party by any means. But it was a break in which we shared something, and it lifted us, for the moment, out of a very painful process. It was, in a way, an acknowledgment that there was a purpose to that pain we were all going through, and what we were going to put the company through."

If your company is going through a painful change—say, a round of layoffs—you do need to acknowledge, at some point, those who remain, what they've been through, their pain for the people lost, and what they're going to go through as a result of the change. Stick with subtle, small, low-budget food stuff. You don't need more (more, in fact, will cause resentment). Say, "Tomorrow morning at nine please come to the lobby (the large conference room, the cafeteria) and we'll talk about it." Then provide a giant bagel or donut buffet. Keep it small. Keep it local (don't take it off-site to some sterile hotel, for example.) Give people, yourself included, a chance to lick their wounds and regroup. It will do everyone good.

Allow people to develop their own impressions about the change. Don't tell people what to believe. The big question on everyone's mind during times of change—particularly when a company is going through a restructuring—is "How healthy is this company?" Sometimes the answer is that it's not very healthy, but it's the rare senior manager who will say that. They'll say, instead, something like "We're back on track, everyone should just focus on their work." The problem is, that message is the same if the company truly is back on track, so what's an employee to think?

Better not to tell people to feel confident. Better to let them reach that conclusion on their own. Go ahead. Risk some confusion, some tough question-and-answer sessions. Use data. Annie remembers:

> After several restructurings at Digitas, we realized that making the promise that there wouldn't be another one wasn't going to go over well. But we felt confident, and we wanted everyone to know that. David Kenny, our CEO, felt strongly that we needed to allow people to draw their own conclusions; he is very much in favor of open, honest information sharing. So he asked us to present far more financial data in front of the whole company

than we ever had before. And it made a big difference. People could see that there was much more visibility and less uncertainty in our forecasts than they might have imagined, absent other data.

We didn't say "We're in good shape now" and let it go at that. David showed people why we felt that way. And then they were able to decide for themselves if they shared those feelings.

Reestablish and rearticulate "people processes" immediately. Are the criteria for promotion going to change? Will people be promoted in June? How will assignments be made? Will raises go out in February, same as usual? Those things may change as the organization-at-large changes; they may not. It's never too early to let people know what the deal is. Knowledge of that nature helps people settle themselves. You'll realize a much faster return-to-normal time if you provide as much as you can in the way of parameters and policies as you go along. All too often, when such processes get changed, people feel as if things get announced, and then somehow disappear down a black hole. But the regular use of a simple "people process update" (such as an e-mail circular) that lets employees know that changes are being made, what to expect, and when—can go a long way to reducing skepticism and anxiety (and building trust) as people adjust to the new "norm."

11

When People Leave

Scenario No. 1: Jim had worked in sales for a consumer goods company for seven years. He was a terrific salesperson, a real star when it came to attracting customers and building strong relationships. He was also a great team player—very well regarded by his colleagues—but last month he had been passed over for the position of regional sales manager, which would have been a significant promotion. Two weeks after that, he had given his notice. He was going to work for a competitor, he told his fellow salespeople. The company had mistreated him; there were much better long-term opportunities for growth with the other company.

Pam, the head of human resources, didn't want Jim to leave thinking that the company to which he'd given his loyalty for so many years was mistreating him. She had talked with Jim extensively, immediately after he was passed over for the promotion. She thought he had understood the decision, and the kinds of things he would have to work on if he truly wanted to step into a managerial position. She also thought that he knew how much the organization valued him. She was concerned about him, but she was more worried about the remaining members of the sales force. The once-tight-knit group of people seemed to be unraveling before her eyes. She felt sure that Jim was poisoning the team—turning them against the organization, maybe even luring them to jump ship as well. The company Jim was moving to was small, but growing quickly. There were bound to be numerous opportunities for salespeople there.

She didn't know what to do.

Scenario No. 2: No one could say that Sam wasn't a hard worker. He was always among the first people in and among the last to leave. His nose was always to the grindstone. The problem was, he really wasn't suited to his job; he simply didn't have the skills he needed to excel or even perform at more than a marginally satisfactory level.

Now it was Fred's sad duty to have to let Sam go. And Fred was in a quandary. How honest should he be with Sam about the company's reasons for firing him? How honest should he be with those who remained? Would it be OK—even perhaps the right thing—for him to lie in this case? Sam was well liked, and widely considered a good employee. Maybe some folks knew, in their hearts, that Sam was a chronic underperformer, but would they allow themselves to admit it? Would honesty create paranoia in the rest of his department?

Maybe the thing to do was to work things out with Sam so that it looked as if Sam were resigning. That might mollify some people, but if it didn't, and the deception was discovered, wouldn't that be worse?

Why is "when people leave" a defining moment when it comes to building or destroying trust? Consider this: When someone leaves an organization—whether he decides to leave on his own or is asked to leave—employees pay more attention than they normally do to process, and to the actions and reactions of their leaders and colleagues. Whether they know it or not, they are paying more attention to the five A's (aspirations, abilities, action, alignment, articulation) than they normally do. They're asking questions like: Is the leader of this company living up to all that he or she has articulated? Are the leader's aspirations real, or are they situational? Has the leader said in the past, "We treat people with dignity and respect," but is he or she now acting differently toward the person who is leaving?

That increased level of visibility—and scrutiny—of the organization and its leaders is the essence of what connotes a defining moment.

Many organizations try to downplay departures, fearing negative repercussions, whether those departures are initiated by the company or by the employee. Many leaders believe that the relationship between company and employee essentially ends when that person leaves the organization. But when leaders fail to recognize "when people leave" as a defining moment, they inadvertently, and almost inevitably, allow the creation of a leadership or communication void. Resistance will step up to fill that void, sure as you're born.

When People Leave on Their Own

There are two significant opportunities to build trust when someone leaves an organization of his own accord: (1) the opportunity to build or strengthen trust with the person who is leaving, and (2) the opportunity to build or strengthen trust with the people who remain.

We'll start with the person who is leaving. It's easy, when someone announces his departure, to begin to think of him in terms of *what he represents to the company on paper*. What his skills are. What tasks will need to be completed in his absence. Whether or not his skill set was ideal for the job; whether you'll be searching for the same skill set in a replacement. Whether his departure offers you an opportunity to restructure the office or department or division to maximize efficient delivery of goods or services or whatever.

Thinking in those terms is a natural response; you are, of course, going to be concerned with filling the void, and with what lies ahead. But try to keep in mind the *person* in question, as well as the position. This person's unique contributions may have helped shape your company, and may continue to shape your company after her departure. She can and will refer other potential employees and customers to your organization—if she thinks well of you. By the same token, she will steer people and business away from you if she feels as if she was dumped on or duped when she decided to leave.

Now consider the people who remain. When a person announces his or her resignation, unless he's leaving for obvious reasons like a spouse relocating to another part of the country, or personal health issues, the rest of the crew are bound to ask questions.

"Is the grass greener somewhere else? Are other organizations offering more advancement opportunities? More money? A better opportunity to balance work with life?"

"What does the departing person know that I don't know? Is the company in trouble? When will the next shoe drop? Was he being paid enough? Am I being paid enough? Is our boss a bigger jerk than I thought? Was so-and-so having problems producing that I didn't know about? Is this a genuine resignation, or a disguised firing? How is my job going to change in his absence?"

"Should I be looking for another job?"

These are natural questions, and they deserve answers whether or not they are voiced out loud. You have an excellent opportunity to strengthen the bond of trust between you and your employees, and also between your employees and the organization. Think back to the characteristics and competencies of the trusted leader, in particular the personal trust equation. How you show your colors here will be evaluated along those lines (whether or not people are aware that they are, indeed, evaluating you). If you are normally forthcoming with information but silent on this particular topic, you'll set off an alarm. Ditto if you are defensive, if you change your response when talking with different factions from the organization at large, or if you're suddenly unavailable for comment.

By the same token, if you are forthcoming with information, able to quell any possible fears about the health of the company, or about hidden agendas, or about people's own abilities and your recognition of their abilities, you'll come out ahead.

Here are some general rules for dealing with an employee's voluntary departure:

Announce it. This sounds like such a simple thing to do, and yet many companies try to brush departures under the rug. As we said earlier, the urge to hide departures stems from a fear that people will perceive weakness in the organization, or follow suit. But those fears can be allayed quickly. That's a minimal worry compared with the fallout from a departure that was initially ignored or concealed. The more noise (genuine, accurate, heartfelt noise) that you make on the surface, the less chance there will be for questions, negativity, and fears to fester below the surface. Sometimes all it takes is the "first strike" to keep resistance at bay, and that's a small step for a big gain.

Allow people to tell their own stories, whenever possible. You do need to tread carefully here, especially if the person in question is leaving over a specific grievance. You don't want to encourage a debate that quickly degenerates into, "I did." "You didn't." "I did." "You didn't." But you can recognize their take on things, and disagree with them respectfully.

Say, for example, the issue that prompted the person's departure is compensation. The person who has resigned is leaving for a higher salaried job at another company, and she says so. If you make a blanket statement to the effect of "We have competitive salaries," not only do you run the risk of sounding defensive, you'll open the door to unproductive debate. But saying something truthful like "The value equation is going to be different for each person and we tailor it as best we can, while still trying to be fair across the board," is fine.

People's lives change, and as that happens, your organization may no longer be the right place for them, even if it once represented a perfect fit. As a leader, you have to accept the fact that your company will not provide the right job at the right time for all people, and you should let people know that you accept that fact, while at the same time trying to provide an optimal work experience and compensation package for the people who work for you. (A momentary digression: Think back to our story about the manager who began letting select people telecommute without thinking things through beforehand. It is important to try to provide an optimal package for your employees; but beware the dangers of customization without due consideration.)

One more thought on letting people tell their stories. When you encourage people who are leaving to be open and you treat them with respect, you're also reinforcing the signal to people still on board that their voices are important as well. Confident that they won't be punished for speaking out, they may let you know about issues that concern them—before those issues lead them to a "Should I stay or should I go?" decision point.

Actively solicit and listen carefully to feedback that the person leaving has to offer. In too many companies we know of, exit interviews are perfunctory, with an impatient person on one side of the desk, knowing that whatever she says either can and will be used against someone else, or will be dropped down a black hole. It doesn't have to be this way. Exit interviews can be a final, formal way of showing an employee that you value her input, right up to the last minute. They can also provide critical knowledge about what's working internally, and where the weaknesses are. (If ever there were a good barometer of whether or not a company's leaders are communicating enough and accurately, the open, honest exit interview with a departing, valued employee is it.)

In the midst of the economic and dot-com boom of early 2000, Annie found herself doing exit interviews with people leaving Digitas almost every week for one or another high-paying, hot new opportunity. Those interviews taught her a great deal, not the least of which was that when someone is leaving an organization, and having a conversation with a person whom he trusts, he will be brutally honest about things he thinks need improvement. She also learned the importance of trying to identify a common thread in what she was hearing before taking action. Sometimes when people leave an organization, they raise issues that are largely personal, but after Annie talked to several people, and each one mentioned a particular issue, she knew that the problem, whatever it was, was probably something that demanded attention. Annie recalls:

> I remember standing up in front of folks at a senior management meeting to talk about the exit interviews and what I was learning. I said, "Broadly speaking, this is what I've been hearing; this is how it has influenced my thinking about our aspirations, our actions, our abilities. And this is what I think we should do about it." It made me feel good to be able to show that we were learning something of value in those meetings; the changes we made as a result were important as well.

Exit interviews provide great fodder for honing the focus of a business and increasing the understanding of how the work of that business gets done.

The other insight that emerged from Annie's experience—and one that was also echoed in many of the conversations we had while researching this book—was that most of the time, people don't leave their places of employment because of the money. In fact, unless a new offer is so over-the-moon unbelievable, most of the time, the "heart of hearts" reasons people gave for leaving had much more to do with feelings about trust and the five A's or about trust and their boss or colleagues. "I felt as if we lost ground to competitors, and we shouldn't have" (aspirations). "We kept telling customers we could do things that I knew we couldn't do" (abilities). "Nothing ever changed, despite what people said. Promises were made and not kept" (actions). "The left hand didn't know what the right hand was doing, and I'd get caught in the middle" (alignment). "I just never understood the rules of the game here" (articulation).

One manager told us, "I don't know how many times I've heard things like 'Jane wants to leave; how much more money can we give her?' That's just misguided thinking. Most of the time, it really isn't about money. It's about a relationship that is lacking something."

Make it OK to leave. In reality, very few organizations are able to turn a valued employee's departure into a positive—or at least a "no fault"—experience. Professional service firms tend to do a good job in large part because they understand that the nature of their work has an enormous impact on the lifestyles of their employees. There are phases during which an exhaustive travel schedule works for some people, and phases during which it clearly doesn't. Some consumer goods companies similarly have a handle on it, because they understand that the general management track, which sometimes calls for a move every few years over the course of a decade or more, isn't for everyone over the long term. But for most organizations, in the final analysis, it's, "Either you're with us or you're against us."

Making it OK to leave is worth the effort. If you send the signal that it is OK for employees to talk about personal concerns when they leave, and by extension, before they even think about leaving, you'll be signaling that their opinions are valued all the time, on any topic. You'll also have to convey that there are appropriate times and places for airing such concerns. Their knowledge that their opinions are sought and valued—even within designated forums or through certain channels—is a fantastic trust-builder. Chances are very likely that you will learn things of value. Every day.

Nurture relationships after people leave (within reason). On her last day of work, a senior-level employee stopped in to see the president (her boss's boss, whom she had known for a long time) to wish the company well and to say good-bye and thank you. (The company was relatively small, about 200 people; this person had worked there for almost ten years; she was leaving for lifestyle reasons; she truly had enjoyed her tenure with the company; and she had been a valued employee.) The president was effusive with praise and goodwill. She said that she'd truly miss this employee, and that she hoped she would come back someday. She even said that she was in denial and would be calling the employee every once in a while to catch up, in the hopes that she would someday be able to entice her back into the fold.

The employee believed the line. She left feeling all warm and fuzzy about her former boss's boss, thinking that she would indeed hear from her again, thinking that the company really did care about the turn her life had taken.

She never heard from the president again. And these days, when she speaks of her former employer, it is with none of the goodwill she had on the day she left. She told us:

> It would have been better if she hadn't extended that quasi "we'll stay in touch" promise. I would have left with no expectations. But as it turned out, I'll probably always think that those parting comments were really insincere. And if she ever calls at this point, my assumption will be that she needs something; not that the company cares about me as a person. What's more, I'm happy to tell you all about my feelings. I have no compulsion to

protect or nurture that company, however important it was to me once. And that's got to say something too.

You can't always nurture a relationship with an employee who has left the company. Maybe the employee has gone to a competitor. Maybe the size of the company and the person's level mean that personal contact or follow-up is simply not plausible. Maybe the person leaving wanted to sever all ties; maybe it was a difficult departure. Maybe you asked him or her to leave. But if you can, it's worth your time. Consider the words of Jay Lorsch and Tom Tierney, in their book *Aligning the Stars: How to Succeed When Professionals Drive Results:*

> Pause for a moment on [the] word, alumni. Think about how alumni relate to their alma mater. Alumni are people whose help and participation are crucial to the success of their schools, even though they are no longer present on campus. Schools organize alumni conferences, publish alumni bulletins, and build alumni Web sites because alumni are such an important source of funds.
>
> Professional firm alumni, too, can be an important source of revenue for a firm. One consulting firm we know receives almost a third of its new business from its alumni. They are [also] a highly credible "inside" source of information about the firm's capabilities. Alumni from your firm may be talking about you this minute—to possible future clients and to possible future recruits. Are they saying "Yeah, you ought to call my old firm. They're the best in the world"? Or are they saying, "Yeah, I used to work there; they're terrible"? Or are they simply holding their tongues? You will never see the checks that are being written for you out in the marketplace, just as you'll never see the checks that aren't being written. But they exist, and their influence grows by the day.

Lorsch and Tierney were writing about professional service firms. We would hold that the same is true at least to some extent of any company. Once you've worked somewhere, left a little bit of yourself there, made a part of it your own, it's very difficult to leave it entirely behind.

Unless you had no personal relationships with any of those

colleagues, you may stay in touch with them for years. Rob still exchanges Christmas cards and updates with a former Citibank colleague, and they haven't seen each other since they both left that organization in 1977!

You may find yourself still following a company's progress years later. It's true if you left on your own terms, and it's even true if leaving there wasn't your choice. Which brings us to the next topic.

When You Ask Someone to Leave

There are, as you well know, a wide variety of circumstances under which people are asked to leave their jobs. There are times when you hate to let someone go, but you must because of financial concerns, or, as is the case in so many merger situations, overlapping skill pools. There are times when you hate to let someone go, but must because his performance just isn't up to par. There are "fit" issues, strategic issues, and, there are times when you may simply be firing someone because his or her behavior was grossly inappropriate, or even untrustworthy.

In the interests of maintaining whatever bond you can (or would like to) with the person who is leaving, and in the interests of preserving trust in the troops left behind, our guiding words for the times when you ask someone to leave your organization are "dignity" and "respect."

Yes, we know it sounds as if we're espousing Mom and apple pie. But if these are values that you hold dear in your organization (we're assuming that they are), and you suddenly take a different tack with the person who is leaving, then you've up and lost the alignment battle.

In short: Don't frog-march people out the door, unless prudent judgment would suggest that there is a real security risk—either physical or to your intellectual capital. Deal with those who behave badly on an exceptional basis. Grant most people the benefit of the doubt, and expect them to behave like grownups as they leave, just as you've behaved like an adult throughout the course of your interactions with them regarding their departure.

If you must escort someone out the door, or you find yourself dealing with a potentially volatile employee, handle that situation as quietly, discreetly, quickly, and humanely as possible. Don't pretend it didn't happen. Apologize to people around who may have witnessed bad behavior. And don't assume that just because you thought the person in question was behaving badly, that others agree with you. Anticipate that people will want to talk with you about what they witnessed, and be prepared to hear them out, and respond.

Beware the "survivor syndrome." When someone leaves an organization, the people who remain are bound to indulge in some worry, some re-assessing of their own skills and stability, and some reflection on whether the organization is still the right place for them. Answer what you can. Address the concerns in as straightforward and complete a way as possible. Where possible:

Show empathy and don't be afraid of your own emotions. When *Fortune* magazine published its annual list of the "Best Companies to Work For," the magazine highlighted Agilent Technologies (formerly a part of H-P), which was forced to lay off large numbers of people. The company retained its employees' trust (the group that left as well as the people who remained). Employees attributed their depth of positive feelings for the company in large part to the straightforward, emotional honesty of CEO Ned Barnholt. In the article, one employee commented, "And though all of us probably lost sleep worrying about our jobs and whether we'd have them or not, I know Ned probably lost more having to get up there in front of everybody and make this announcement and have to let go people in his family." The article continues, "Management couldn't have written a better response. Agilent had succeeded in turning the 'us vs. them' of corporate downsizing into just 'us.'" Barnholt let people see how painful the decision to lay people off was for him personally, and his employees responded to his pain. They knew he was treating them as human beings, rather than mere assets.

Ensure that everyone who is staying on understands the criteria for employment. A lot of times, particularly when someone has been fired, but also, certainly, in layoff situations, the survivors aren't at all sure why *they* were not cut. It's important, when a person or several people leave an organization, to reaffirm for those who remain what the employment contract is all about. What is expected of your employees? Is yours an "up or out" environment (in which someone did not progress quickly enough)? In some manufacturing environments, the contract is as simple as "show up for work on time and meet certain quality standards for production." Whatever it is, review it—in an e-mail, in personal conversations, through several channels and venues. We can't emphasize enough the value of reassurance at this time.

When possible, explain your decision. We say "when possible," because this is truly a delicate dance. If you are forced to lay people off, then by all means, explain the context. If the termination was the result of a situation in which someone has tried his best, but fallen short of performance standards, however, then we would generally recommend that you grant him his privacy. Legal liability questions may also leave you little choice in this arena. Sometimes, in situations where you've asked someone to leave because he's violated the company's policies and trust, you may feel the need to make an example of that person, or prove that you have the guts to take care of a problem by dealing with it in a very public way. That's your call as well, but bear in mind, if your actions are the result of a serious problem, most people will "get" the reason why the person left without your needing to broadcast it all over the company. People will respect your discretion.

Trust and Turnover

A final word on trust when people leave—and it has to do with how organizations handle turnover as a whole. We worry about organizations that measure turnover as an absolute number. "Here's our turnover rate. It's better than X-and-such a company's. It's worse than Y-and-such's rate." Turnover rates offer only a headline. They provide no context. And if you don't parse your number into something more meaningful, you're missing out.

If, for example, your company requires a great deal of travel, you can expect that employees who are starting families might find that their job is no longer a good fit for them. If you have a smaller, locally focused business, and your pay scales are modest, you can expect employees to start their careers with you and, in all likelihood, look to move to a larger-business venue in relatively short order. All these factors contribute to a turnover rate that might look unreasonably high taken by itself, but might in fact be just right for your organization.

Don't fixate on the number. Hold yourselves accountable, instead, for the people you know are leaving or have left for the "wrong" reasons—the ones you hated to lose, the ones who left because they had the feeling that they were mistreated or misled, the ones who left for a "better opportunity" at a competitor (where you know such an opportunity didn't or shouldn't exist). Watch out for a breach in one of the five A's, or for a rise in resistance.

The economy can dictate a shift in turnover beyond your level of comfort. Don't treat turnover as an accurate measure of whether your organization is a good place to work, or whether trust levels are high, or you might be tempted to make changes for the wrong reasons. Those kinds of moves could shake the company out of alignment. If you focus too much on retention, you're treating symptoms, but you may not be diagnosing the real cause of the problem.

12

In Times of Crisis

JILLIAN WORKS FOR A LARGE U.S.-based chemical company. She's the plant manager at a manufacturing and processing facility on the East Coast that employs 1800 people. Until last week, her plant had a spotless safety record, but then a small explosion left three employees with third-degree burns on their arms and faces and resulted in the release of trace amounts of toxic gases that forced the shutdown of a critical processing line pending investigation. Suddenly Jillian found herself thrust into the role of crisis manager.

Initially, Jillian felt that she was handling the situation well, on all fronts. For example, she responded personally to her employees, who were shaken. Several hundred had witnessed the accident—they'd seen the terrible injuries that their colleagues and friends had suffered. Jillian tried to acknowledge their pain, and to make them feel safe, while at the same time calling for a thorough analysis of what had happened so that they could ensure that nothing of the kind would happen again (that's why she shut down the line).

She also addressed the concerns of the sales force head-on. Worried about the people who worked in the plant, certainly, but also worried about their ability to meet commitments to their customer, they hounded Jillian for estimates on when the plant would be back up and running. She told them exactly what she knew, and asked for their patience. They were satisfied with her explanation; they trusted Jillian, and knew that she would keep things moving as quickly as possible.

She was also up-front with the public and press. Concerned citizens *demanded information, wanting to know if they were safe, and what, if any, precautions they should take. Jillian's candor resulted in coverage that both informed and reassured the public.*

But then the crisis management team from Corporate stepped in.

At first, Jillian was relieved to have some assistance—particularly with handling a very understandably needy community and sales force— and with customers, who were also lining up with questions and concerns. But she quickly became concerned about the people who worked in the plant. The crisis team had a reputation for focusing almost exclusively on process, blame, and the financial impact. They had harsh words for the line supervisor, and for the shift that had been on duty when the explosion had occurred. They stated immediately that heads would roll, and that the plant's processes were overdue for intense scrutiny. And Jillian quickly realized that their "take no prisoners; everyone is a suspect" approach was likely to destroy the sense of organizational trust she had worked so hard to create.

Whether it is an episode of workplace violence, an episode of corporate fraud, an accident in the workplace, or a serious product flaw or malfunction, a corporate crisis can have a profound effect on a company's health. All too often that effect is as much or more the result of how the crisis was handled internally than it is the direct result of the crisis itself. Too often, company leaders, or the designated crisis team members, become so distracted by external pressures that they simply don't take the time to address the crisis internally with care and attention. That's dangerous, because in times of crisis, employees feel unsafe. They look for reasons to trust their leaders, but they are also quick to find reasons why they *can't* trust them.

They ask these kinds of questions:

"Why did this happen?"
"Was it the result of someone's incompetence?"
"Am I safe here?"
"Does the company care that I am physically safe?"
"What does this mean for the future of the company and my job?"

"How do I be sure that it doesn't happen again?"
"Do my leaders care about how I am feeling?"

When answers prove elusive, trust erodes rapidly, and the after-crisis can have a greater long-term impact on the company's health than the actual crisis.

Mark Braverman is currently a senior vice president with Marsh Crisis Consulting in Washington, DC. He has been an advisor on crisis management to companies in virually every sector, from small manufacturing companies to national retail chains and government agencies. Braverman says, "Don't assume that companies who are managing their customers particularly well during times of crisis are also tending to the needs of their employees."

Recovering revenues is important; without revenue, you won't be able to take care of any of your stakeholders. But calls from the media about the financial effect of the event, and stakeholder and customer questions and reactions shouldn't be given so much attention that you ignore what's going on with the people who show up every day to work. You want to get through the crisis. You want a return to normalcy. So you feel the need to deal *first* with the people you don't normally have to deal with, on the assumption that you can take care of your own once the flurry subsides. This is not the best approach, because your people will not be able to wait. By the time you turn to "your own," they may be beyond repair.

We started writing this book before September 11, 2001, and had already begun to focus on the times of crisis that were defining moments for leaders in building or destroying organizational trust. But pre-9/11, we were thinking mostly in terms of events like the Johnson & Johnson's Tylenol scare or the Ford/Firestone fiasco. (The Enron collapse hadn't yet happened, of course, but that crisis is of similar ilk.) Leaders are more likely to encounter those types of rare, "contained" crises than the universal crisis that September 11 represented. September 11 created a new kind of crisis in the workplace for those of us who have only worked in post-Depression and post–World War II times. Such a horrific event is now part of the realm of possibility and it has challenged all companies—those affected directly, and those affected indirectly—and our assumptions about the role of a corporation in helping employees handle trauma and stress. The line between "work" and "life" is increasingly blurred; the role of the trusted leader now extends further into employees' personal circumstances than ever before. You'll see that truth reflected in the advice we offer in this chapter. Some of the lessons directly reflect the redefinition of crisis in the aftermath of 9/11; all have been influenced in some way by that day.

First Orders of Business

The advice that follows is in no particular order of importance, save for the first piece, on which all the others turn.

Authorize Yourself to Get Help—for Yourself

If you were not directly affected by the crisis, you may need only a quick check-in with an objective third party. But if so, you'll need to ensure that your view of the unfolding events is not skewed by your own state of mind.

The general idea in a crisis is to allow yourself to be as human as you can, while at the same time proceeding methodically to ensure (1) that your employees understand what's happening in the aftermath and why, (2) that their emotional needs are met, (3) that the workplace is safe and supplied so that work can continue, and (4) that the needs of other stakeholders are addressed as well. You can't and won't be able to do all of those things if you yourself are reeling from the effects of the crisis.

Don't assume that you have to live up to some Hollywood image of a leader. If there ever was a time *not* to fake something you don't feel, this is it. Don't assume—particularly if the crisis hit close to home—that your "clear thinking" about how to proceed is, in fact, clear. Your perspective may be off; your thinking may be cloudy. Acknowledging that fact could save you some painful mistakes, and could save your employees and other stakeholders a lot of pain as well.

The *Harvard Business Review* published an article in 1999 called

"The Toxic Handler." In it, authors Peter Frost and Sandra Robinson wrote about how certain people in organizations step up to shoulder the pain in times of crisis, and how those people are invaluable to the organization's well-being. It also discussed the toll that that role takes, and the special support that the people who carry the burden need in order to carry on themselves. We recommend that you read the article.

Understand the circle of impact. Mark Braverman told us this story about the aftermath of a bank robbery: Managers at the affected branch focused exclusively on the needs of the teller who was affected, and on the customers who were in the branch at the time. But they ignored the rest of the tellers in that branch, and also ignored the employees of the other branches in the system. The result was that one teller felt stable and able to go on with his work. One group of customers was reassured that their bank was taking every precaution to ensure their safety. But a whole host of employees, because they were not given the proper attention, still had concerns about their safety and were at increased risk of traumatic stress reactions. We would imagine that an increasingly large circle of shaky customers vowed silently to themselves that they would be using the drive-up window exclusively henceforth, or take their banking elsewhere.

Who has been affected by the crisis? Is the impact really contained to that group? Ask around. Put out an e-mail requesting any questions or concerns. Take what might prove to be unnecessary steps; reach out to a wider circle. Think about other employees, customers, vendors, partners—and also the community within which you do business. Parse your time among all those constituencies. It can't hurt.

Be visible. When we asked Mark Braverman about the most important thing a leader can do to build trust in times of crisis, he responded, "Visibility. Visibility. Visibility." That sentiment was echoed soundly by everyone else we talked to on the topic as well, and underscored by our own client work and experiences.

Visibility means far more than having an open-door policy, though access is important. It means being available emotionally as well as physically. People want to know that it is OK to have feelings at work about whatever is going on. They'll look to you to set the example. And that means that you have to allow yourself to do some of the things you may have thought that being a leader meant that you *couldn't* do. Crying, for example. If that's what you feel like doing, do it. Stop working for a day, or at least a few hours, to take the time to talk to people and process what is happening. (Let people know that you're doing this and why.) If you're shaken, say so, even as you strive to provide stable ground from which to move the organization forward. You can be a leader and still be human. Mayor Giuliani provided a great example of physically and emotionally visible leadership in the wake of September 11. Take his lead, as best you can.

Allow people time to process what has happened. We have observed, as has Mark Braverman, that many leaders believe that the best thing for an organization is a rapid return to normalcy. They don't want to stir things up by making a big deal of an event. People aspiring to be *trusted leaders* take the time to understand that things are already stirred up, and that in many cases, post-crisis, there is no such thing as a return to the way things were. There is, instead, the aspiration that what you build after the crisis will be stronger than what was destroyed by the crisis.

Experts who have studied treatment options for people suffering from post-traumatic stress disorder emphasize the importance of the need to process what happened to them. Processing time may be longer than we think, and the road to recovery is not always straight, and progress on that road may not be as consistent as we would hope. The treatment for employees who have suffered a corporate crisis is much the same. At the same time that they need to be shown how to move forward (and encouraged to do so), they also need to work through what they've been through, in a facilitated way, often with others who have suffered similar situations. "Closure" isn't just a fashionable term we all started using sometime in the 1990s. Its benefits are real.

Mark Braverman told us about an incident at the Royal Oak, MI, post office, in which an employee shot and killed other employees in the early 1990s (Mark was brought in to help the organization recover from the crisis). Typically, that office was stretched to process a day's worth of mail in a single day; the crisis, which occurred at the beginning of the week, shut down operations for four days while an investigation ensued. The workforce was terribly traumatized, understandably. At the urging of post office and union officials, Mark led them through several days of crisis counseling, focusing on their needs under the circumstances.

Come Saturday, the post office was set to reopen. Officials put out a call to all employees, saying, essentially, "If you would like to come back to work today, we have a lot of work to do and we would welcome the help, even if you are not normally scheduled to work on Saturday. We will reopen for business under regular schedules as of Monday. But it is completely up to you if you feel ready to come back; no one will be faulted for not coming." So great was the level of respect they showed for their staff, that 90 percent of the employees showed up, and together, they processed four days' worth of mail in one day.

In large part because the postal employees were given the time to process the event, and to make the choice for themselves whether or not they were ready to return to work, the level of trust at that facility soared. Out of tragedy, the leaders and employees in Royal Oak gained a respect for one another that they had never before experienced.

Ensure that a rapid-decision-making protocol is in place. When rescue personnel arrive at the scene of a motor vehicle accident, they have strict protocols, ingrained in their minds, which they are supposed to follow even as they tailor their responses to the situation at hand. Those protocols are in place to ensure that they remain as safe as possible, that the patients are treated as quickly and efficiently as possible, and that the whole rescue process keeps moving steadily toward completion. Crisis protocols for companies—though not necessarily spelled out or taught in the same way—are no less important. Even a little "prep work" can go a long way toward helping a company emerge relatively unscathed from many a crisis situation.

Some companies have crisis management teams set up for the kinds of crises that can be to some extent anticipated, like Jillian's corporate crisis team in the opening example; it is only natural that a manufacturing plant would anticipate and prepare for the (hopefully) unlikely event of an accident. In theory—and often in practice—crisis teams are a good idea. They snap into action to ensure that people move as quickly to recovery as possible.

Form at least some informal crisis teams, and spend some time talking through possible crisis scenarios. A series of "what if" sessions can provide just the footing needed in the event that the actual crisis, or one similar to what was discussed, occurs. The frequency of these session can vary; the key idea is to recognize that it takes a long time to get through a crisis and that even when things seem to be back to normal, they may not be.

TJX, parent company of retailers Marshalls and TJ Maxx among others, has been a long-standing client of Mark Braverman. It is one of the companies that lost employees (seven people, on American Airlines Flight 11) on September 11. Many people in the organization needed to step out of their usual roles and assume decision-making authority to deal with the crisis. What helped them, in part, was that they understood their guiding principles. They didn't need to stop and ask themselves what the company would want them to do; that much was already ingrained in them because TJX had invested the time regularly to educate employees on the company's priorities in terms of what was really important, for instance, respect and compassion for the individual and concern for and commitment to employees' extended families.

Employees who are weathering a crisis are going to be looking for competent leadership. They're going to want some initial direction, even if that direction is as simple as, "It's OK for us to feel bad about this and to spend some time, even a day or more, thinking/talking about it." But they're also going to want to be told when and how to move forward. The balance between letting people process an event at their own rate, and making the decisions that will mobilize them and get them back to work—get the organization back on track—is critically important.

Empower people to make their own decisions. When we interviewed people post–September 11, many of them told us that their leaders expected "business as usual" on September 12. Many said that their leaders truly seemed to believe that returning to work without pause would be the most effective way to "get through." Those leaders suggested to their employees that the brave, American thing to do was not to allow terrorism to defeat them. Invariably, these approaches led to a breakdown of trust.

TJX CEO Ted English reacted differently. The company depends on employee travel to carry out its business; for example, merchandise buyers routinely travel as part of their work, and TJX managers are constantly scouting store locations. Naturally, merchandising executives began to feel pressure to resume business operations as soon as possible once airports began to reopen. But Ted was unwilling to push people back into flying. His policy, and the official policy of the corporation was, "Nobody flies until they feel *ready*."

We heard that one high-ranking manager approached English several weeks after the attacks and said to him: "Ted, I'm scheduled to get on a plane next week. I'm nervous about it and my family is nervous about it. But I'll do it for you." Ted looked at him, put his hand on the man's shoulder, and said: "No you won't. You'll do it when you feel ready, and only then." English immediately convened his top management team and his EAP professionals to decide how to confront this critical issue. They organized seminars throughout the company to reinforce the "travel only when ready" policy, and gave people information about alternative travel options, up-to-date FAA information about travel safety and regulations, stress management skills, and counseling on dealing with family concerns.

One would think that TJX lost momentum and fell behind in its work in the weeks following the diaster. But that wasn't the case. Some employees got back in the air right away. But others, who did not, figured out alternate means of doing what needed to get done and kept up that way.

Ted English left the decision of how to get the work done up to his employees. And that approach, according Braverman, "drove a level of commitment and trust that is truly amazing." Braverman said the TJX workforce, in fact, "is one of the most committed groups of people" he's ever seen.

If you show that you care about your employees in times of

crisis, they will tend to make decisions that are for the good of the business.

Of course, merely making a decision is not enough; the obvious "Part Two" is to ensure that people feel safe acting on their decisions, as the TJX example shows. The empowered employee is an important part of any recipe for business success. Without empowerment, employees often find themselves stuck, unable to do things that would help or enhance the business, even if they know exactly what needs to be done and they know that the business will suffer if they *don't* act.

The same holds true in times of crisis. If employees feel that the leadership trusts their judgment to do the right thing for the business, they can move ahead, often solving small problems before they become large ones. Lacking that trust and empowerment, their frustration will increase, even as they see water leaking through a small hole in the dike turn into a raging rush of destruction.

Help people understand the "why" of the decisions you must make. As you're moving purposefully through a crisis, the decision path may be logical internally, but it may not be as clear to people in the larger circle. So as you take steps, it's important to provide some backup. You don't necessarily need to put out press releases on the "why," but an addendum—a short document, or something posted on the company intranet under the heading "If you'd like to know more"—can help.

Say, for example, your company is going through tough times and makes the decision to withhold annual salary increases as one of a series of cost-saving measures. The 400 people who are now not getting raises will be unhappy. But showing them the math—writing out that $4,000 \times 400 = \$1,600,000$ and explaining that that figure may save 40 jobs—can help smooth the waters. In addition, you could put the action in the context of other cost-saving measures and provide a full explanation for why these measures are being put into effect. Sometimes, for example, cost-saving measures are taken because of loan or debt covenants, but that knowledge may not be understood by people lower down in the organization, who may think, instead, that your actions are taken to satisfy greed at the top levels. A little explanation can do a lot of good.

Prepare Some Unspoken Guidelines for Yourself Before There Is a Crisis

We'll end this chapter on a relatively high note, given the nature of the subject. You may have heard this story about a group of people rehearsing a Broadway show. In the second act, there was a scene that called for a cannon shot. The lead actor was supposed to react to the sound with, "Hark, I hear the cannon" (or some such line). Each day at rehearsal, when the time came, the stage manager would clap his hands and drone, "Sound of the cannon shot." And the actor would say his line, "Hark, I hear the cannon." Right up until the performance itself, when the actual cannon sound effect was used for the first time, and the actor whipped around and shouted, "What the hell was *that*?"

Can you really prepare for a crisis? Not explicitly. But if your aspirations are clear—around how you treat your employees, how you talk to the press, how you address customers' concerns—your guidelines will be in place. Your track record will come to your aid, and the difficult decisions in highly emotional times will come to you more instinctively.

PART FIVE

BUILDING TRUST IN PERSPECTIVE

13

Trust Lost, Trust Rebuilt

Every man is a damned fool for at least five minutes every day. Wisdom consists in not exceeding the limit.—Elbert Hubbard, author, editor, printer (1856–1915)

WHAT WERE CHRIS AND HIS *management team thinking? How could they not have realized that people would catch on eventually, even if they did get away with it for over a year? Booking the same sale in two separate places might make it look like your region was superstar territory, but any auditor worth his or her salt would have spotted that kind of double-counting in a jiffy. But they were lucky. Quarter after quarter.*

It might even have started out as a genuine error, in the period when regional offices had responsibilities for national accounts. Chris or one of his sidekicks had undoubtedly spotted the double-counting, but just let it go, and then they kept it going, figuring that the boost in morale from moving up the sales rankings would at some point more than compensate for the irregularity. Who knows? What was known, however, was that in the time Chris and his two "right hands" ran the region, its track record got better and better. People asked for transfers in. Everybody wanted to be part of a winning team. The region won a series of awards at the company's national sales conventions, and the office was filled with high spirits, bonus awards, and company-sponsored cruises. Chris seemed like a shoo-in for VP–national sales manager.

After the sales reporting system was consolidated, however, it was less than a month before the irregularities emerged. Chris and the two "right hands" were called in to HQ one week, then came back to the office the following Monday, only to say they were leaving the company for "personal reasons." Each of them then just cleared out their belongings and left. The company sent out an e-mail saying that the regional sales management system was under review, and that the distribution of the quarterly incentive bonuses would be delayed indefinitely. Now, after a month of radio silence and nobody in charge, the new regional manager is due to start Monday. She has her work cut out for her.

Because of true-life episodes like the one described above, this may have been among the easiest chapters for us to write in the entire book. Whenever you talk with people about trusted leadership and its related topics, you hear about the destruction of trust first, and you hear about it with greater vigor than about its creation or endurance. Rebuilding trust is a significant part of trusted leadership. Very often, it's what new leaders are called upon to do.

After trust has been lost, employee morale erodes, customer loyalty declines, employees feel bereft, and, at the same time, embarrassed that they were bamboozled, angry that they had been kept in the dark, and unsure of what to do or whom to trust next. Customers affected by the breach are furious, those unaffected are suspicious, and those about to become customers backpedal very quickly. Competitors, whose natural tendency might be to gloat (and to profit from the situation), are usually quite circumspect, as they know it might just as easily have happened to them. Consider, just for a moment, how the goings-on at Enron, where Andersen was the auditor as that entity tumbled, might have been viewed by the other major accounting firms. They all knew, whether they expressed it openly or not, that it could have happened on their watch as well. Organizations and executives who quickly join the "It Couldn't Happen Here" Choral Society do so at their peril. Dealing with a loss of trust is likely to happen to most of us at some point, and the rebuilding of trust is often a defining moment in a leader's career.

At the same time (and this is *very* important to remember), not all trust is rapidly lost. It's not always a binary event, where one moment it's there and the next moment it's gone. Lots of times, trust has simply has eroded over time, and people take a while to be fully cognizant of its absence. In some cases, trust isn't destroyed, and hasn't even disappeared, but is operating at a chronically low level. Organizations and individuals that operate with low levels of trust lack the resources to fight potential or actual threats. They lack the ability to achieve desired results. They lack the ability to engage, or bring out the best in their people. So while we might often talk about the rebuilding of trust from rapid, immediate losses, please keep in mind that sometimes rebuilding must occur in a place where trust isn't gone, but lies dormant instead.

There's a flip side to all of this as well. This chapter is not just about others losing trust (be it in you, or your organization, or even with others where you are there as a rebuilder). This chapter is also about *you* losing trust (whether it is in others, or in a part of the organization that you oversee, or even in a third party), how to understand it, and how to handle it. Leaders have to deal with the loss of trust, whether it is a loss of trust *in* them or their organization, a loss of trust *by* them or their organization, or as an involved bystander in its loss.

The loss of trust is complex territory, but here is our attempt to give you a way to map it.

The Prism of Lost Trust

Looking at the loss of trust is like looking through a prism. The refraction of each of the surfaces affects how the object (in this case, the loss of trust) is perceived. Understanding those different perceptions can help us respond correctly in each case. While it may not adhere strictly to the principles of geometry or optics, our prism has 12 distinct facets.

They are:

1. *The relative speed at which the trust-destroying episode or situation occurred.* Was this a fast loss? When people talked with us about rapid losses of trust, the pneumatic analogies came fast and furious: "It took people's breath away." "They blew up." "It was like the air went out of the room." A rapid loss of trust is indeed like the puncture of a tire on a fast-moving vehicle.

The Prism of Lost Trust

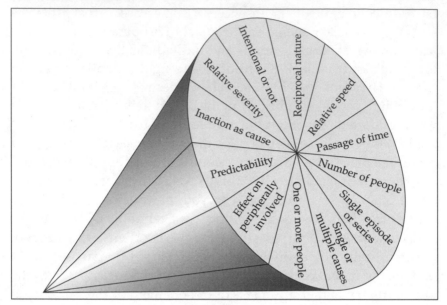

With a rapid loss of trust, there is usually a strong emotional component of either its cause, or its effect, or both. One logistics manager we know caused a loss of trust with an offhand comment, and it took substantial efforts on his part to attempt to repair the damage. One of the drivers under his supervision had been quite seriously injured in an episode outside his control, and was disabled for a number of months. On the first day of his return to work, even in the first moments, the manager assigned him his route and his truck (the same one he had when he was injured), and said, "Try not to hurt yourself this time." The driver bolted for the employees' break room, furious. The manager told us he knew immediately that he had been wrong, and followed the driver into the room, where he apologized publicly. The driver was far too angry to let it go, despite repeated attempts by the manager to apologize in front of the driver and his co-workers. The manager said it took months finally to make peace.

Implication: With a rapid loss of trust, even when there was no malice attached, don't expect commensurately rapid remediation. Most of us aren't as good at forgiving as we might like to be. Where trust wasn't rapidly lost, it's helpful to figure out what has gone on for this to occur, and what stop-loss mechanisms should now be installed.

2. *The passage of time between when the trust-destroying situation occurred and when it actually came to light.* A lag between the trust-destroying episode itself and its eventual discovery adds to the feelings of betrayal.

"How long has this been going on?" people ask. The revealing phrasing of the question that loomed large over the Watergate episode—What did the President know, and when did he know it?—was the one that eventually brought about Nixon's resignation. People sometimes feel more betrayed by the denial and ongoing cover-up than they do by the occurrence of the event itself.

Implication: Not acknowledging the loss of trust very quickly can have a long tail on it, and shorter tails are better. You don't have to go overboard with extreme acts of public self-criticism, but denying, hiding, or minimizing a betrayal will seriously jeopardize the rebuilding process.

3. *Whether the loss of trust was felt directly by just one individual or by a larger number of people, and whether the two are connected.* If you lose trust in a single person (or he's lost trust in you), it doesn't always mean that trust in the entire organization is destroyed at the same time. Very often, however, the two situations become closely intertwined. The organizational drums beat quickly, and reverberations are felt all over. That's why it's so critical to have a clear sense of how broadly the loss of trust extends. You have to ask yourself whether this loss is truly as contained as one might hope. After one looks at these situations closely, it's fair to say that the error lies more frequently in underestimating the reach of the breach. A single interaction with a single individual will make the problem disappear.

Implication: Trust can also be lost peripherally, by those affected only indirectly. The good news is that while there are obvious differences in undertaking the repair efforts with a single individual compared to a larger number of people, the overarching principles are the same.

4. *Whether the loss of trust was the effect of a single precipitating episode or situation, or was due to a series of events.* Dramatic losses tend to populate the landscape more visibly, but we would assert that the gradual erosion of trust probably occurs with greater frequency. A leader's loss of trust in a department's ability to get the job done may erode after a series of disappointments. It could be with a sales department that falls short of its projections quarter after quarter, a manufacturing facility that repeatedly misses production targets, a recruiting organization or a recruiter who fails to hire the necessary executives, promising that completion is just around the corner. When we lose trust in this way, we often feel quite embarrassed, along the lines of, Fool me once, shame on you. Fool me twice, shame on me.

As we all know, however, sometimes it takes a while before we lose trust. It may stem from the desire to be fair before casting judgment too quickly, or it may be a function of denial, where it takes a while before the scales fall from our eyes. In either case, some thing, some episode pushes us over the edge. If you talk to marriage counselors about the topic, you will likely hear that more relationships dissolve from inattention to a series of indicators than from a sudden big event. Those "big events" usually take place after the little indicators have been ignored for too long.

Implication: Small episodes that hardly hit the radar screen, if viewed or described in isolation, can be disproportionately large factors in the loss of trust. The seemingly inconsequential ain't so inconsequential. Leaders can have this greater awareness without becoming control freaks.

5. *Whether the loss of trust had a single cause, or multiple contributing causes.* Again, certain cases obviously hinge on a single terrible episode, featuring some major error that sends people running for cover. In the same way that a number of events can lead to the loss of trust, however, there can also be multiple causes. A situation in which multiple contributing factors caused the loss of trust would be the following:

Many securities analysts working for prominent brokerage firms had to walk a very fine line between the volatile nature and the uncertainties of some of the dot-com companies they were following, and the fact that their employers were, at the same time, underwriting or making markets in the shares of those companies. For a time, it seemed that the only recommendations were "buy," "strong buy," "hold," and "accumulate," and no discouraging word was ever heard. In fact, "sell" recommendations were rarely issued. The bounds of credibility were strained by all of these positive recommendations when it became clear that many of the analysts appeared to have expressed, privately, strong misgivings about the prospects of these companies. But they were caught on the treadmill and it was hard for them to get off. Sometimes it is hard to say "Stop. This is wrong." Or to call to public attention the nakedness of one emperor after another.

Implication: Lots of factors, not all of which are in your control, contribute to the loss of trust. It may look more like a pattern of morale-damaging events rather than trust-destroying behavior, but there are enough conspiracy theorists or fractal analysts around to turn it into one.

6. *Whether the loss of trust was the effect of one individual's actions or the effect of the actions of more than a single individual.* In many circumstances, it's not hard to establish whether the loss is attributable to the actions of one individual (such as in the logistics manager's confrontation with the returning driver), or to those of a group (such as in the vignette about Chris and his two "right hands" with which we started this chapter). The case isn't always clear, however. For example, in the situation discussed immediately above, it's hard to make the case that the CEO, or the new CFO, or any single person was the root cause of all that went on.

Implication: Sensitivity to the loss of trust, and responsibility for rebuilding isn't just your job (or theirs). Trusted leadership is a shared responsibility, and while you might have to be its most active partisan, your responsibility as a trusted leader is to infuse that mindset into the entire leadership group.

7. *How those peripheral to the specific trust-destroying episode or situation are affected by (or react to) its occurrence.* In the corporate arena, it's nigh on impossible for a loss of trust not to affect bystanders. Does it create a po-

larization, or a forced choice? Has its occurrence added fuel to the fire of others? The repair mechanisms for bystanders will differ from those directly affected, but repair mechanisms are needed in both cases. For bystanders, it may take the form of a town meeting at which they can ask questions, while those directly affected will usually need one-on-one attention.

Implication: Make sure you have an objective understanding of the impact this loss of trust is having on the larger community, as well as on those immediately affected. Whether or not it's as nominal as you hope, make sure you have good, objective data about that. Don't expect that you can always gather such data by yourself, which is particularly true if you're the one who has to repair the loss.

8. *The relative ease by which the loss of trust would have been discernible or predictable in hindsight.* Remember the moral of the Garrison Keillor story about the tomatoes we recounted earlier—that sometimes even the foreknowledge of negative consequences is not enough?

It often seems apparent in hindsight that the destruction of trust would necessarily have ensued from certain actions. In the heat of some organizational battles, there might not be sufficient time to reflect on potential negative consequences, or something may be need to be decided on the flip of a coin, or before all the relevant data can be gathered. Reflecting on the events leading up to the bankruptcy of Web portal Excite, its former CEO, George Bell, stated, "The lesson for me is go slower. When I look back on it, I wonder did we need to make important strategic decisions at 10 p.m. on Sunday night after another 80-hour week."

Implication: Calibrating the speed and quality of individual and organizational decision making is *really* worth it.

9. *Whether the loss occurred due to inaction on someone's part.* Lots of trust is lost through negligence (or inaction), rather than doing something and getting it wrong. In some ways, negligence is among the most insidious forms of trust loss, as the people on the receiving or implementing side of organizational decision making often spend countless hours waiting for something to happen. Since organizations and individuals, just like nature, abhor vacuums, they tend to fill it. And they tend to fill it with misinformation, or rumors, or strained, conspiratorial interpretations of the extraneous.

Implication: If the loss did occur through negligence or inaction, figure out how it happened fast, so it can't happen again.

10. *The* relative *severity of the loss.* Relatively innocuous losses, if part of a series or pattern, or if occurring at particularly sensitive times, get people into disproportionately greater amounts of trouble. A relatively low-impact loss that happens at a time when the workforce is feeling uncertain can have enormous repercussions.

Implication: For want of a nail, the shoe can be lost. For want of a shoe . . . (You remember the rest.)

11. *Whether or not the loss of trust was truly unintentional.* It's often hard to believe that a loss of trust occurs innocently or inadvertently. We talked to people about episodes when they or their organizations lost the trust of others, and everyone said it was unintentional. What we could hear, however, were the "if onlys." As in, *"If only someone had tipped me off that the slope was so slippery." "If only I hadn't opened my mouth too quickly,"* etc. It would be nice if the world were forgiving, if we got "do-overs" or "mulligans" for those times when we slipped up quite unintentionally.

Implication: Get yourself and your organization past the blame and into the resolution as quickly as you can.

12. *Whether it stemmed from a reciprocal loss of trust.* "I lost trust in them, so now they can lose trust in me. See if I care!" Yes, people can be like that. Often. Not you (of course!), but we all see it on a global scale, so why shouldn't we see it on a local scale, or even in and around an organization? It's not easy to stop the downward spiral of loss of trust, and radical action is necessary, often requiring a managed process of conflict resolution, perhaps even with high-quality outside assistance.

Implication: Acceptable to be pissed off? OK. Retaliatory? Not so fast. Matt Ridley, in *The Origins of Virtue,* says that humans differ from other beasts, and have societal norms that promote virtue by being clear, fair, nice, and retaliatory. But destroying trust probably ain't your best vehicle for retaliation. Better think that one all the way through.

And vindictiveness is off limits. That's how wars start. "Return to no person evil for evil." Even though a saint said that, it's worth remembering.

Rebuilding Trust

The nature of the trust that has been lost will dictate the specific requirements for its rebuilding. Although the guiding principles for rebuilding are valid across all circumstances, the precise remedy will depend greatly on what happened as trust was lost. To physicians, it's like knowing when to use rehabilitative medicine and when it's time for emergency reconstructive surgery. Many predicaments require both, some require only one, and the timing of each may vary dramatically, depending upon the circumstances. In yet other situations, different types of procedures, the passage of time, and perhaps even nontraditional therapies can contribute to healing. Trusted leadership means coordinating multiple treatments at the same time, all without killing the patient. Trusted leadership also means assuming responsibility for patients that you might have suddenly inherited, whose illness you did not cause, and who are looking for you to cure all that ails them.

You need luck, determination, skill, and appropriate approaches. Here's a guide to rebuilding trust with individuals and with the organization at large:

1. Recognize the intensity of the loss of trust: its depth; its breadth

2. Examine where the breach occurred, and where the damage was done: personal trust elements (credibility, reliability, intimacy, self-interest); organizational trust elements (aspirations, abilities, actions, articulation, alignment, resistance)

3. Place it out there: Fast!

4. Acknowledge its impact on the individual, the group, and/or the organization at large

5. Identify as precisely as possible what you'll be doing in an attempt to rebuild trust

6. Raise the bar of performance: Overdeliver on your attempt to rebuild

7. Reflect carefully on whether progress is being made, and what else needs to be done

8. Repeat the process for a good long time

For obvious mnemonic reasons, we have named the above approach the REPAIR model, and it will indeed foster the rebuilding of trust as robustly as possible. In the remainder of this chapter, we will offer a few words about each step and stories that illustrate why we believe in them.

1. Recognize the intensity of the loss of trust:

its depth

its breadth

Recognizing the intensity of the loss of trust means putting yourself in the place of those affected by the breach. How did they find out about it? What was their reaction? How did it make them feel? How does the reaction differ across individuals or groups?

You might find out, as we have, that one individual (or group) viewed a particular situation as a non-event, while another felt that the episode was a watershed in the organization's existence. Synthesizing the overall reaction into a consistent picture isn't always easy, but by undertaking the effort you can begin to gauge the overall impact, to develop a "sense of the meeting" that can guide you and your organization in response.

For example, a management committee meeting was convened after it was discovered that a stockbroker in a particular Midwestern branch office had defrauded clients out of many millions. The impact on other branch clients was severe. The impact on branches elsewhere in the Midwest was also substantial. The impact on firm clients on the West Coast, however, was highly varied. Many clients weren't even aware of the breach.

2. Examine where the breach occurred, and where the damage was done.

> personal trust elements (credibility, reliability, intimacy, self-interest)
>
> organizational trust elements (aspirations, abilities, actions, articulation, alignment, resistance)

It's not uncommon for trusted leaders to use their natural instincts in addressing the loss of trust. They usually do a good job of sensing where the most severe damage has occurred, and to devoting their efforts to relieving the most significant pain. This is right, but it's incomplete.

Unless the loss is so emergent, almost life-threatening, working by instinct alone leaves one open to missing the important elements and causes that a more thorough analysis would reveal. What systems have been affected? Where, personally or organizationally, did trust suffer? By undertaking at least a modest inventory of the trust elements, it becomes easier to identify the right things to fix.

Where do you think most losses or erosions of trust occur? Our experience tells us that the more sudden losses occur in the personal trust realm, and that the erosions tend to take place in the organizational trust elements, particularly around a lack of alignment and around bad articulation. Does that jibe with your experience? Let us know at http://www.thetrustedleader.com and we'll let you know what others think as well.

3. Place it out there:

Fast!

People already know when trust is at a low, or has been damaged. Ignoring it or pretending it isn't so bad just doesn't help. We've talked about getting rid of the elephants in the parlor, and talking about the issues that overshadow daily life. The earlier you talk about what has happened and what needs to happen, the better. In fact, not talking about it, delaying or downplaying it gets you into trouble not just for the situation itself, but also for not stepping up and discussing it! It only adds fuel to the naysayers' fire.

You'll need to choose your words carefully, as you will be under the microscope to an even greater extent at this point. People will be skeptical or suspicious, or both. Maybe even hostile. But getting it out there, acknowledging its occurrence, and getting the recovery process started as quickly as possible can only redound to your benefit. You don't have to have all the answers lined up yet. There can even be a lag between your placing it out there and the description of what you'll do. Don't even worry about the action plan yet. In fact, that's still two steps away. At this point, just acknowledge the loss and your awareness of it. You can ask for some time at this stage, or even tell people that it will be a few days (or however long) before you get to that point. But let people know you're aware of the issue, you're working on it, and you're committed to setting things to rights.

4. Acknowledge its impact on the individual, the group, and the organization at large.

Part of a successful repair process lies in being open about the loss of trust and the need to rebuild. A vital twin element is demonstrating that you have a clear understanding of the impact it is having.

For example, you have to make sure you've heard from someone on the front lines how hard it is to promise something to a customer that the organization may be erratic in fulfilling. It then means reflecting that understanding of the problem back to the organization, including it in your conversations with others in a meaningful way. It can mean, as we have seen in our own experience, conducting small group meetings with senior leaders to talk about the difficulties in carrying out a set of policies that will soon create greater organizational discomfort in an already uncertain organization.

There are lots of other ways to acknowledge impact; the following is a list of five suggestions for you to evaluate for use and modification in your own organization. If you take some number of these suggestions (not just one, and not all five, for heaven's sake!), the derivative (but highly desired) side effect will be that word will get out around your organization that you actually have a sincere interest in dealing with the issue at hand. The most effective means are probably best crafted and customized in your own shop, so you can adapt or discard these as appropriate:

- *Conduct one, or a series, of town meetings just to let people sound off.* You can even bill it as a two-stage process—the first, which is designed to elicit points of view and hear questions, the second, shortly thereafter (maybe about a week later), which is designed to offer your reactions and responses.

- *Offer an anonymous posting board* or Q & A phone line, and discuss what's showing up.

- *Monitor those community message boards,* especially if you're in a company of more than just a few hundred employees. These are often found on Web sites such as Yahoo! or Vault.com. You'd be surprised at what shows up. It may contain some trash, some inaccuracies, and a forum that you'd rather not popularize, but it's worth checking them out regularly to keep a finger on the pulse of what's being said in at least one forum.

- *Call individuals who you believe to be candid,* and talk with them. If you suspect that they won't be candid with you, ask other people to ask them (openly), and to filter the feedback to protect those who may be intimidated or fearful about talking with you directly. Then, follow it up with a "what I've heard" call.

- *Meet with key influencers in the organization who are not part of your regular circle,* and let them hear what you're hearing. Test it with them, ask them to validate it. You can't game or delegate this stuff. It has to be you doing it. You are, after all, the leader here.

5. Identify as precisely as possible what you'll be doing in an attempt to rebuild trust.

OK. Now we're at the implementation stage. You've thought about it, heard about it, reflected on it. Enough, already! Now you actually have to figure out what to do. The only thing more important will actually be carrying it out. But that can wait for the next two steps. First, let's plan a little.

a) *Create specific goals.* What specifically do you want to accomplish here? What are you trying to achieve? Write it out on a piece of paper, in front of you, in ink. First, write it out as a goal (or goals). For example, "To change the relationship between the people in the field sales offices and the people in Corporate from an adversarial one to a more cooperative one." Or "To have people stop doing end-runs around Caroline's department because it has a reputation for arrogance." Or "To stem the tide of departures from the technology group because they feel the company is no longer committed to staying on the cutting edge." Or "To eliminate the turf wars between the staff marketing group and my line marketing group." We could go on for pages listing these kinds of goals, but you get the idea. Plus, you probably have your own to write.

Next, write it out in "outcomes" form. What will it look like? Write it not just as an end-result, but as a set of examples of what it will look like on the way back. Not just in your eyes, *but in the eyes of those affected.* What might they do or say that will indicate you're on the right road? For example, "The quarterly review meetings will have 50 percent less time spent on mediating disputes, and 50 percent more time spent on planning new initiatives." Or "The volume of employee comments about unfair compensation or bonus decisions on the company's 1-800-line will be down by 90 percent." Or "The introduction of the new performance evaluation process will actually get employee praise." Or "The voluntary attrition rate of the finance group will decline to the level of two years ago."

b) *List the actual changes you will start to make.* Translate the theoretical into the practical. Get as detailed as you like (without driving yourself and those around you crazy). You can use whichever comprehensive progress-measurement framework (strategic, organizational, or personal) you prefer to identify these changes. If your company already has a helpful one in common use, this is a wonderful opportunity *not* to add yet another one to the mix. If there is no single framework to which everyone responds, then you might find it helpful to use a more organizationally focused framework here, as much of your repair work is likely to be around organizational trust, rather than the aspects of strategic or personal trust. If you like the balanced scorecard approach, and want to use that and look at customers, internal measures, financial stakeholders, and learning and growth, then fine. If you like the value chain, with its use of primary activities (e.g, inbound logistics, operations, outbound logistics, marketing, sales and service) and support activities (HR management, technology development, procurement, finance and corporate administration), use that.

In repairing organizational trust, we tend to lean heavily either on the Seven-S Model (looking at strategy, structure, systems, shared values, staffing, skills and style), or on a slightly shorthand version, examining structure, systems, people and culture. These latter two approaches tend to focus on what have been, for us, the most productive areas for the repair of trust. For example:

- *Systems and Process Changes:* What specific shifts (if any) will you make in how decisions are made, how information will flow, how it will be measured, reported on, compensated for, rewarded? How will you get that to happen? Is declaring "It shall be so henceforth and forever more!" enough? If so, then, boy, are you lucky!

- *Structural Changes:* What, if any, will the changes be in how you'll be organized, what will be the reporting relationships going forward, and which areas might be merged, consolidated, separated or put under common control? We have seen internal rivalries dissolve almost instantaneously when competing areas come under the control of a single person.

- *People Shifts:* Is now the time to make some of the people shifts you have been contemplating? You would think, after all these years, that we two authors would have stopped being surprised at how quickly trust (and productivity) improves when the move is finally made to replace a leader who hasn't done a notable job of building trust inside. We've never heard *anyone* say, "Gee, maybe I should have waited." Maybe it's one of those lessons that just gets reinforced time and time again.

c) *Create a mechanism for tracking tasks and responsibilities.* Now that you have identified all these valuable changes and initiatives, how are you going to make sure that they actually happen? How much of this work will you do by yourself, how much will be done in small groups or teams, what (if anything) will you delegate? What's the time frame for each of these? Some will probably be ongoing efforts without end-points, while others will be more finite in size and scope.

Some companies and some individuals are absolutely anal in tracking these efforts, assigning project managers to war rooms with the task of monitoring progress on a full-time basis. Others are a little less formal about assuring project integrity. You should decide by determining your own style, the organization's needs, and the nature of the trust you are trying to rebuild.

At a minimum, however, you do need some degree of tracking. The

RACI Matrix, which has been around for decades, provides a straight-forward way of making sure that progress is being made. RACI stands for responsible, accountable, consult and inform (as those are the roles that people must fulfill in the course of getting work done). The person(s) responsible are the ones charged with getting the task performed. While it is their responsibility, they may or may not be the ones fully accountable for its successful completion, so accountability may be a more serious burden. In some situations, you may reassign the same person(s) both the A and the R. In the course of the work, you'll need to consult others before certain steps are undertaken, and finally, you'll need to inform those whose advice or consent might not be necessary but who need to know the steps about to be taken, either in advance, or upon their occurrence. See next page for a sample RACI matrix.

d) *Check the tasks for consistency, completeness, and realism.* This may sound so basic, but not nearly enough people do it, and it nearly always reveals some pretty substantial gaps in the trust-rebuilding plan. Listing the tasks in some organized fashion (even if you go the "war room" route and post it all over a wall) provides you with a great opportunity to examine your trust-rebuilding plan from an overall perspective. Very often, trust-recovery plans suffer from an imbalance of short-term measures (at the expense of the longer term). They are frequently tilted too much in favor of those directly affected (at the expense of the broader organization). They can be unrealistic in their expectation of nearly immediate results. This overall look for consistency, completeness, and realism will serve you well. Be sure to ask one or two people who were not a part of its creation to give you their objective impressions.

e) *Link the obstacle-surmounting and progress-measurement processes in advance.* Even if you are an unbridled optimist, you know that most things take longer to accomplish than you hope, and that unforeseen events get in the way of progress. Given the fragility of organizations with low or lost trust, setbacks on the road to recovery can seem even more debilitating. That's why we suggest that you create a system that identifies logjams quickly and offers means of resolving them quickly, too. In large-scale efforts, an appointed individual can make the necessary decisions on the spot. In smaller-scale situations, in a daily or weekly "hit-list" meeting, the entire management team can participate. An out-of-the-ordinary decision process needs to be in place to anticipate such situations. Otherwise, you will be faced with the simultaneous tasks of fixing the problems that have piled up (quickly) and having to create a mechanism to deal with the future ones.

It's a good idea to link this mechanism for resolving logjams with measuring your progress in rebuilding trust. First, you *will* need to measure your progress. Your progress may be slow at first, and may not necessarily be as quantifiable as you may like. If or when progress isn't being made as rapidly as hoped, it's helpful not to be surprised. If the

Sample of RACI Matrix

Function	Engagement Manager	QA Manager	System Architect	Team Leader	Configuration Manager	Developer	QA Tester	Client
DEVELOPMENT TEST PHASE								
Configuration Management	I	A	C	C	R	C	I	I
Change Control	I	A	C	C	R	C	I	I
Metrics Capture	I	A	C	R	C	I	I	I
Traceability	I	A	C	R	C	I	I	I
TEST CREATION & EXECUTION								
Create Test Plan	I	I	C	A	C	R	C	I
Inspection of Test Plan	I	C	C	A	C	R	I	C
Create Test Cases	I	I	C	A	C	R	C	I
Execute the Development Test	I	I	C	A	C	R	I	I
Produce Metrics	I	A	C	R	C	R	I	I
Inspection of Test Results	I	C	C	A	C	R	I	C
Approval of Test Results	I	C	I	A	I	R	I	R
Conduct Quality Review	C	A	C	R	C	C	I	I

keeper of progress measurement is also a key player in problem resolution, the two will go hand-in-hand. Finally, if the two are not linked, you might have to go through a long root-cause analysis or a seemingly endless "he said, she said" discussion in sorting out the obstacles to progress. Linking the two will save you time in resolving them with deliberate speed and without blame when they inevitably occur.

f) *Build a forthright communications plan around your actions.* How are you going to tell people that you're working hard at rebuilding trust, and what's going on, and how it's going? We are reminded of the lovely story of the young prelate, working at the Vatican, who looks out his office window and is convinced he sees Jesus coming down the path. He runs to the pope, breathlessly tells him what he believes he has seen, and asks, "Your Holiness! What shall we do?" The pope pauses for a moment, and with a twinkle in his eye, says, "Look busy!" While we're not advocating window-dressing, some element of internal public relations has to take place to help convey the seriousness of your commitment to rebuilding trust inside.

There are lots of communications planning vehicles, and lots of communications experts who work in this field. Unfortunately, the number of experts working in the field may be considerably larger than the number of really good ones, so make sure you have real confidence in the person you might be using. On occasion, we have seen less than stellar internal communications impede the rebuilding effort. Regardless of whom you use, there are certain inbound (receiving) and outbound (transmitting) elements that will be a part of communicating about your rebuilding trust, as follows:

regular "temperature taking," helping you sense the internal market

describing your actions and your plans in a way that captures your personal intent and your organization's attention at the same time

responding to inquiries in a timely fashion, and making it easy for people to ask questions, get answers, and follow up

assuring that the timing of your actions and the communication surrounding them are synchronized

providing as good an outline as possible of what your organization can expect, and when

6. Raise the bar of performance. Overdeliver on your attempt to rebuild.

If you, like most leaders, are more possessed of a bias for action than a bias for analysis, it has probably driven you crazy that with the eight steps we counsel to rebuild trust, it has taken until No. 6 to start finally doing something. Up-front planning does a world of good, even if it is not deeply enjoyable. Yet now, your time has come to show how good you are at actually getting it done, and getting trust rebuilt.

You'll need to do more than just deliver on your promises, however. People in situations of low trust are sufficiently jaded or suspicious (or both) that merely doing what you said is, unfortunately, insufficient. You'll have to do more, and for longer, to help break down the animosity or disappointment that has accumulated.

All of your trust-building skills and tools, whatever personal charisma you have, all the brains, energy, persuasiveness you possess, are now called into use (to say nothing of good instincts, patience, impatience, and courage). There is no step-by-step guide or set of guidelines for actually doing the delivering of the messages, the walking of the floors, the tension-filled meetings, the hearing of the stories, the explaining of the road ahead. We'd like to be with you as much as possible, but for this particular step, you're on your own. But we'll be here whenever you get back.

7. Reflect carefully on whether progress is being made, and what else needs to be done.

How did it go? How is it going? What's working? What didn't work so well? Rarely does everything go perfectly on the road to rebuilding trust. But trusted leadership doesn't come about by flipping a switch. In those times during your career when you are called on to rebuild trust, this reflective element, figuring out what you have learned, will lay the groundwork for future situations when you will be called upon to do it again. And you *will* have to do it again.

8. Repeat the process. Again. Again.

Rebuilding trust is not a one-shot process. It is likely to take more time than you think and it will probably take more time than you think it should. You will feel that it has gone on too long. You, like others with whom we have spoken, might express a sentiment along the lines of, "How long will I have to feel like I need to keep apologizing for what happened, even though it is now long past, and even if I wasn't a part of it at the time?"

That reality, for better or worse, is actually part of the rebuilding of trust. People observing you as a leader will see that as among the strongest pieces of evidence of commitment on your part. They will see your ongoing involvement as evidence of trustworthiness, and as evidence of leadership. If you consider yourself a builder or a creator of new opportunities, spending seemingly inordinate amounts of time on the rebuilding of trust may not be the most interesting part of your work. But it will become the enabler for you to do more creating or more building of the kind you like. The people who will likely help you the most will be those who saw how you worked during the rebuilding process, who understood the importance of the rebuilding, and who became critical members of your team along the way.

14

When *You* Leave: The Legacy of Trust

Traveler, there is no path. Paths are made by walking.—Antonio Machado
(1875–1939, poet, essayist)

IT IS VERY POSSIBLE that you have been a participant on an executive education program or have completed a career assessment that included a segment asking you to write either a legacy statement or your own obituary. Most often, these tasks signal the struggle leaders face in trying to figure out just what their legacy will be. "Survive through next week!" or "How the hell do I know?" are common reactions. Yet these exercises highlight the fact that people have all too rarely focused on the topic of what their legacy will be, and so "How the hell do I know?" really means "Gosh, I've never thought about it . . . and I'd really rather not, thank you."

It's hard work, even if you *have* thought about it, but having a desired legacy (and acting on it) is an essential part of being a trusted leader. Although it might not be on your current to-do list or high on your top ten of fun activities, the earlier you address your legacy, the better. Trusted leaders may not have their desired epitaphs in place by their first day on the job. Bob Garland, of Deloitte & Touche, observed that people in earlier stages of their career, or at younger ages, have far higher priorities than thinking about their legacy:

It's like trying to convince your sixteen-year-old that there can be downsides to owning and driving that first car, such as insurance, maintenance, liability, or safety. He doesn't want to hear any of that. All he really wants are the keys. People need to be receptive and ripe to get concepts. Similarly, I'm not convinced that you can convince a thirty- or thirty-five-year-old of the importance of legacy. They're thinking about their career, getting promoted, their ability to influence, their finances. You may be wasting your time.

Nonetheless, the earlier you think about the endpoint, the better off you can be. When we interviewed good leaders (even trusted ones) in the preparation of this book, they often said that they wished they had given greater consideration to what their legacy would be, even before they took on their particular role. Might this be true for you as well? Would a little time thinking about your legacy earlier on have made (or, if you are still young enough, now make) a difference in your decisions about work? What form might this legacy take?

A Brief Typology of Legacies of Trust

There are countless ways in which corporate leaders leave their legacies. Bob Garland noted that too:

Legacy may also be a subtle definition of winning. It may be a version of competition. If the organization has endorsed and implemented your vision, that means you've won. It can mean moving from world class to best in class. That's like moving from running a four-minute mile to a three-minute-forty-second one. It's not just more conditioning the same way. It's a complete change, or breakthrough.

For some people, a winning legacy might be framed in terms of business accomplishment: organizational growth, geographic expansion, survival or salvation. For others, legacy has to do with more of a stewardship role, where their legacy is one of keeping the asset going, and handing it over to a new generation. Many of those who worked for Kathy Biro, co-founder and vice chair of

Digitas, and also adjunct professor of business administration at the Tuck School of Business at Dartmouth, would be in complete agreement about her legacy: It was to build an organization that was "totally groundbreaking and totally terrific." And she concurs:

> I was very conscious of creating a legacy. This idea started well before any particular job—even before I went into business. From the time I was a child I can remember thinking what it must be like to be in the history books. Knowing that I did something, or created something, or changed something. And by the time I started working on Strategic Interactive Group (which later became part of Digitas), I knew that I wanted to build a company from scratch in an industry that didn't even exist yet. And I wanted to make it last. I remember us saying, "Twenty years from now, we want to say we built something."

Building an organization, saving an organization, entering a new market, or a new geography—all of these are valid forms of legacy, all of them laudable in their own right. They are the foundations on which legacies of trust are built. So what makes the difference? Why are Bob Garland and Kathy Biro thought of as *trusted* leaders when so many other highly successful top managers are not? It's in what they leave, and it's in how they leave as well. Let's look first at what they leave.

When those more trusted leaders with (or about) whom we spoke reflected on (or responded to) the question of legacy, the answers that emerged with the greatest frequency included the legacy of *people*. When talking about legacy, these leaders talk about the people they have brought into, or retained in the organization. They talk about the people they have mentored or developed. They talk about the people to whom they gave an opportunity, a chance, a career path. You hear about skills taught, values imparted. You hear much less about the edifices built, the financial results achieved, or the processes improved. Kathy Biro wanted to build a groundbreaking enterprise; she is thought of by many as building an organization in which people were always motivated—in which people always felt the excitement of creating something new.

Based upon our work, and based upon the people with whom we've spoken on the topic, we have been able to discern three ways that these people's legacies are felt:

1. In their way of approaching a problem or doing certain things. How often have you heard someone say something to the effect that, "Well, if X were here, he would handle it this way"? People are remembered for their problem-solving technique, or their fairness. A typical recollected example was one where a trusted leader had to come between two warring staffers. He called them both in, together, and had them state their case openly, in front of each other, in order to stop all the back-channeling. They would barely look at each other as they said their respective pieces. He forced them to work together on the solution, and insisted on ending all the distracting warfare. That opening up of conflict, forcing people to stop dealing in innuendo, is a legacy of trust.

2. In their ways of dealing with people. This is a lot about listening and respect. Michael Bronner founded a direct-marketing firm in his college dorm room at the age of 20, which has grown into a $200+ million-a-year powerhouse. He is also the founder of Upromise, the company that links customer loyalty programs with college savings. People who have worked for Michael put him in the category of trusted leader, someone who engendered great loyalty from an extremely early age. When people reflect on Michael Bronner, one of the consistent themes that emerges is his ability to tune in so intently to people, and make them feel that they, and their conversation, are the most important things in the world. People who have not worked with Michael in five years or more continue to feel that way. That treatment of people, with equanimity, humility, and respect, is his ongoing legacy.

We know another Michael (Ward), not yet 40 years old, a president of a publicly traded company, who is building his legacy as a trusted leader in the same vein. What makes him stand out, however, is his extension of trust to others, as a trust. Those who work for him and with him express it in a desire to do whatever they can for him, even though he may not ask. Perhaps because he openly gives trust to them, they tend to give him their trust very quickly. Sometimes he has been hurt by being too trusting, too empowering. On balance, however, the trust he places in people has helped him build a great following very quickly.

Jim Lawrence, EVP and CFO of General Mills, emphasized the importance of patience and listening, when he spoke with us about being the "new kid on the block," being at the very start of the path toward building a legacy:

> I knew I had to make people feel that I was a trustworthy guy to make it work at General Mills. After I was here for about a year, I got some pretty straight feedback. It said that I talked about the "outside" a little too much, that I was probably not quite sufficiently appreciative of our in-house abilities. That I wasn't listening enough to the slower-speaking Midwestern folks who populate this organization. In short, I probably wasn't showing them enough respect. I learned to let the meetings take longer. To let the conversations go longer. There were certain things I wanted to do very quickly, but I learned that before I could go and do them, I had to build up the trust bank.

3. In their way with words. As Bob Garland says, "There's almost an assumption about how we all stand for quality and integrity. But you need to talk about it, you need to live it." In many cases, this is about the words they use. Is it a mantra? Is it a set of phrases they tend to live by? Warren Bennis, one of the great scholars of leadership, in his assessment of Jack Welch's legacy, made special note of the words and phrases that Welch brought into the daily business lexicon: speed, simplicity, stretch, boundarylessness, etc. The trick is doing it in a way that is unique to the individual, that isn't a hackneyed phrase, and that rings true. We all cringe whenever we see a not particularly sincere individual talk about sincerity, or a not terribly caring person wax on about how much they care. One of the distinguishing features of the legacies of people considered trusted leaders is in the words by which we remember them—their singularity of message, or faithfulness to a set of values.

Developing a Community of Future Leaders

One powerful way for you to think about whether yours will be a "people" legacy is to consider the community of leaders who will take the helm when you leave. These are the people you are mentoring, influencing, and shaping today, as you go about your daily work.

We went back and forth trying to select the right words to describe these future leaders. Should we call them a "cadre" of leaders? A "number"? A "network"? We decided on "community" because that implies an interdependence, complementary strengths and interests playing off one another, and an agreement between what might be very different people with different interests to come together and build something for a greater good. A community of leaders truly signals a legacy of trust on the part of the predecessor.

Think of a small town. Storekeepers, who may have disparate interests and beliefs at the personal level, respect one another nonetheless. They ask each other for favors such as, "Can you make change?" or, "Will you watch my store for a few minutes while I go to the bank?" They care about one another and share a mutual interest in the town's well being.

A community of trusted leaders is much the same. They take the idea of a company that has a strong leader and a number of skilled senior managers, each of whom might be able to take command one day, and ratchet it up a notch. This community is a skilled group of individuals who understand that although their own opinions might differ regarding how the company should be run, it is their *duty* to reach a meeting of the minds at some higher level and to work as a united front against the competition, and for their employees. They extend themselves accordingly to fulfill that duty.

Creating such a community is challenging. This type of leadership group implies an honesty and openness in communication that is rarely seen, even in great organizations. But fostering this community is a viable, realistic goal—even if it is difficult to achieve. We harbor no illusions that a community of trusted leaders is made up of a closely knit group of soul mates who never disagree about anything, and who share group hugs each day after lunch. Leaders can (and do) disagree with one another; in fact, it would be odd if they didn't. And they often compete with one another. *You* may have a particular successor in mind, but in this group, there should be several viable candidates for the top job, and they should be aware—but not wary of—each other's readiness to move up.

Put simply: the key difference between *a group of qualified senior managers* and a *community of future leaders* is the depth of understanding of what it takes to live in the other leaders' shoes, and the resulting respect and level of communication that stem from that understanding.

There are several ways in which you can foster the development of a community of leaders. Think first about the kinds of qualities that make up such a group. How would you finish the following sentence? "In an organization with trust inside, the future leaders would . . ."

Would one answer be, "The future leaders would respect one another"? Would another be, "The future leaders would have complementary skills?" Would another be, "The future leaders would have a solid understanding of how each department functions and contributes to the whole of the organization"?

Then think about the people who are in a position to step up. Is there more than one likely candidate for the top position? Are there several other people who will likely be promoted to senior management sooner rather than later? How are their current jobs designed? What would it take to help these folks become the future leaders you envision them to be?

Developing a community of future leaders is like succession planning, only *squared*. Once you've identified people of integrity with high potential (and in the process, possibly pinpointed some weaknesses in your organization that need to be addressed), the idea is to consider how, when, and why they're being groomed for their next positions in the organization, and how, when, and why they currently interact. Then think hard about whether your current setup is optimal for community-building. What forums exist for the kinds of interactions that build mutual support and under-standing? What formal and informal mechanisms are in place to get people into new situations and to get shared experiences?

We have seen and used a variety of approaches—some quite tactical in nature—that help turn groups into communities. You may find that using a similar variety lends great support to your efforts. A "trade fair" is one —a basic display of the various busi-nesses and assets in an organization that are put up in trade-fair style so that participants—your group of managers—can literally walk around booth to booth to see what their colleagues do. A trade fair can be a very successful approach to community-building simply because it provides a relaxed forum for knowledge-transfer.

Another tool we've seen used is a "language guide"—picture something along the lines of a British-American dictionary. Differ-ent people from different parts of the organization have what we call their own sets of TLAs (three-letter acronyms). Sharing the TLAs of a particular area is one of the ways to build a community simply because it breaks down linguistic barriers, which are often proxies for issues that are very important in the organization.

Another idea: Synergy committees, which *cannot and will not work unless* they are supported by an attractive set of incentives and a sense of sincere commitment on the part of senior manage-ment to give people some slack in their performance measures while they devote some time to their "synergy" work. When given the choice between "making your numbers" and "helping pro-mote synergy," is there really any choice when the chips are down? What would you expect people to do?

At one company we studied, so intent was the top manager on creating synergy among the troops, that he inadvertently created an excess of—we'll be blunt—*meaningless* meetings so that the higher-ups from various functions would be forced to interact with one another several times a month. An ancillary "new prod-uct discussion group." A "work/life-balance committee." Pre-dictably, the attendees quickly began to resent the additional demands on their time. They readily admitted that the new com-mittees were interesting, but also knew that they simply didn't have the time to participate fully in them and still perform their jobs up to the expected standard.

The problem was that these new groups were contrived simply to increase dialogue among the various managers, so they didn't have specific goals, or end-dates. No one really knew what to do with any good ideas generated during those discussions. These committees were simply left hanging there—to no end, for no tangible purpose, and with no reward. They didn't serve to increase productive dialogue. Nor did they set up their members as future leadership teammates. Instead, they fostered resentment: "How come he isn't here today? What's his excuse? I'm here, putting in my two cents, but for what? So that I'll have 150 new e-mails waiting for me when I get back, and I'll have to skip lunch trying to catch up?" And they fostered frustration: "That was genuinely a good idea we came up with during the prior meeting. But it's just going to be lost in the shuffle. It seems no one has the authority to put any of our ideas into action."

Lip service won't get you anywhere with synergy committees and their ilk.

You'll know that you're succeeding in developing a community of future leaders when you realize that the organization could indeed go on without you, and do quite nicely under the purview of its new leadership team. (Think the flip side of *It's a Wonderful Life*. What if, in George Bailey's absence, everything had been just fine? Now we know that's sort of comparing apples to oranges— we're not talking about what if you had never been around—but you get the gist.) Another litmus test? If you were to go to another company, would you want to bring along that same team that you've assembled? Perhaps more important, would they voluntarily reassemble as well?

Trust As the Default

When you think about leaving a legacy of trust, it is only natural to hope that your legacy will last as long as the company does. Building the kind of trust that lasts long after you're gone is about infusing trust as a modus operandi into the consciousness of everyone who has contact with an organization. It is about creating an absolute, unshakeable expectation of trust in those who work inside the organization, and in any and all stakeholders on the outside. Trust, in the long-term view, is the well-known, well-understood fallback. It is the default.

All of the things you do to build personal trust and organizational trust, to model the kinds of behaviors you'd like others to emulate, to keep your company's environment trusting even through times of change and crisis, help to create that default mode. But we'd like to add one more case to the file to emphasize how very deliberate the process can be.

For almost 100 years, the camps of the Aloha Foundation (based in Fairlee, VT) have been considered among the foremost summer camps in America, consistently ranked as one of the best in the United States. Second-, third-, and fourth-generation campers and staff abound—a tribute to the camps' consistent excellence. In an industry where extremely high year-to-year staff turnover is the norm, the Aloha camps provide one of the rare exceptions, with staff retention occasionally exceeding 80 to 85 percent. The combination of parent/camper satisfaction and unusually high staff retention led us to look closely at the Aloha camps as a place where long-term trusted leadership has not only taken firm root but also flourished over the long term.

Running a summer camp is not a cakewalk. Parents hand over their children to you, often for their first significant away-from-home experience. You've got several hundred kids to watch over, 24 hours a day, across cabins, tents, woods, fields, and lakes. Your staff is made up largely of 18- to 24-year-olds (who themselves present a unique set of dynamics for managing!). You have no more than seven weeks to create a meaningful experience for everyone who is there—one that will become a cherished memory over time.

It's easy to understand why there is such a vast range of quality among these camps—and how difficult it can be to maximize the value of the experience for parents, campers, and staff, and to maintain a good relationship with the community in which the camp is located, on whom you depend for resources and for quick response when there's a pressing need or a medical emergency.

We asked Barnes Boffey, the director of Lanakila, the Aloha boys' camp for 8- to 15-year-olds, for his thoughts on how, in such a fundamentally difficult business, the Aloha camps have excelled and created an environment in which trust is the norm. Boffey, who has a doctorate in education, has a long history with Lanakila. He started out as a camper there, held a counselor position for several years, and has been the director since the 1980s. His response was clear:

> There's no universally "right way" to build trust in the long term. But the key, I believe, lies in the understanding that building trust over the long term is multi-faceted. It's not simply being able to say, "I am a trusted leader." It's not simply being able to say, "This organization is trustworthy." It's being able to say, "I am a trusted leader in an organization that can be trusted." It's about ensuring that trust is absolutely a foundation of the environment.

Boffey told us that there are several things he does deliberately to instill trust as a way of living and working at Lanakila. Verbally reinforcing the idea that trust is important is one. Boffey and other camp leaders work the subject into staff exercises, projects, top-management retreats, and the like. As he told us:

> We talk about it constantly. And we look for opportunities to set up situations in which we'll talk about it. In pre-camp training, for example, we emphasize that anyone who attends this camp, or who works here, can trust the organization not to embarrass them on purpose. As you can imagine, that's a pretty unusual standard for a group of boys. But here's what we do. During pre-camp training, we'll have someone drop a tray full of food in the dining hall. Now, the typical reaction, in most places, when that happens, involves a lot of clapping, cheering, and jeering. Here we make it a point to help the person clean it up and move on.
>
> We have also set up a situation in which small groups of counselors tell each other jokes. Now as you can imagine, the jokes start to get pretty raunchy after a while. Then we form a larger group, and someone attempts to tell a story to the larger ensemble that was funny in the smaller group, but clearly inap-

propriate in the new context. There's generally a moment of uneasy silence. But then we step in and show how you can deal
with inappropriate behavior—swiftly, gently, without embar-
rassing people.

Making the subject of trust an integral part of your company's
day-to-day goings on—if you are indeed backing up your words
with actions—keeps the topic on everyone's radar. It's a powerful
way to remind people of what you and the organization expect
from them—and what they can expect, and demand, from you in
return.

Another way in which Boffey explicitly supports the idea that
trust is a way of life at the camp is to err on the side of trust, publicly, when given the chance. As a trusted leader, Boffey says, you
have the power to hurt people. Think about it. If you've built up a
reputation as being credible and reliable—if people are willing to
appear vulnerable in your presence, and you violate their trust by
turning on them, or behaving in a way that goes against the nature
of the expectations you've led them to believe in—the impact will
be enormous. Everyone knows this, so the impact is equally great
when you choose *not* to hurt people.

Boffey told us about one very public instance in which he had
to deal with a counselor who, for the moment, had lost control:

> He was furiously angry, and publicly screamed at his antagonist,
> "Get the f— away from me or I'm gonna kill you!" It would
> have been very easy for me to have destroyed this young man
> for having shouted. There was ample reason, if we wanted to go
> that way, to fire him. He had a moment on the edge, and he was
> vulnerable. Instead, we talked through it. And as a result, he'll
> be loyal to me and to this institution, forever. Also, those who
> witnessed the incident now knew that we were serious about
> choosing trust over punishment and that compassion was not
> just lip service; it was real. If there are values in place against
> which you can examine your decisions and resolve conflicts,
> you're OK. You may argue about what to do in a particular situ-
> ation; you may instinctively want to do something that goes
> against your values; but you won't. Ultimately, you'll adhere to

those values that the community has committed to and you'll strengthen your own reputation as a trusted leader, and by extension, the organization's reputation.

Giving people the benefit of the doubt doesn't mean that eventually you'll reach a point where no one ever disappoints you or lies to you. What it does mean is that, person by person, situation by situation, you'll be helping people reflect on whether they want to be trusted, and trusting, individuals. You'll be setting people up to extend the same thoughtfulness to other people in turn. You'll be initiating and reinforcing behavior that has a very powerful and positive ripple effect.

The Power of Myth

Several times, in the course of researching this book, we heard tell of the power of myth. A number of our interviewees used the word "myth" as they talked about the legacies of trusted leaders and the legends that grew up around them in the course of or after their tenure.

This is a touchy subject, because "myth" gets us into the larger-than-life categorization of leaders, and what we have come to believe about trusted leaders is that they are more often than not, *not* larger than life. At the same time, sometimes what sets them apart from other leaders are the stories that develop about them over time.

Henk Broeders, head of Cap Gemini, Ernst & Young for the Netherlands, gave us an example of one such myth, about the leader of a large European company who wanted to make his organization more effective:

> One day early, as the story goes, the CEO went out to the airport close to the headquarters of his company and asked every manager who showed up at the company's help desk there the same questions. Where they were going, why they were going there, and if there was not another way of accomplishing their goal (phone, video conference, e-mail, mail). He sent back anyone

who didn't have the "right" answer. And he sent back a lot. Now, whether he actually was there or not—and whether he actually did carry out that exercise—is not the point. The point is that he became known as someone who was not afraid to face anyone in the organization personally on the issue of effectiveness. A reputation that stuck to him long after he retired as the CEO of that particular company.

There's a definite downside to the power of myth, of course. Consider a man who comes from a long line of real estate developers in New York City and who is now the head of the family business. His office takes up an entire floor of a tall building in midtown Manhattan. One day, when he returned to his office from lunch, he reportedly found a workman sitting in his chair, at his desk, repairing something. He was furious, and immediately had the chair destroyed to emphasize to all of his employees that No One Could Ever Sit in His Chair. Supposedly a true story—hopefully not—but that was the myth. His company pays well—offers a good benefits package, and the like. But employees almost universally cut as wide a swath as possible around this guy; they're terrified of him.

Broeders noted that as an organization gets larger and as the span of control gets more difficult to manage, it becomes increasingly difficult for leaders to have the same direct level of influence on their people (and on the organization) as they once might have enjoyed. That's why myths can be valuable—and why we've mentioned them here. As Broeders told us, "A trusted leader can only exist over the long term in a large organization if there are good myths about him, and particularly about his consistency."

How Trusted Leaders Leave

It's no surprise that people, and leaders in particular, wish to be remembered positively. While not all of us have a need for immortality, most of us have sufficient ego to want to believe that our existence has mattered. When our own individual thoughts about legacy rise in importance or frequency, it's often a sign that we are coming to terms with our own mortality, or at least with the conclusion of a stage in our lives. How we leave becomes important to us.

There are several components of how you leave your legacy as a leader (and hopefully, a trusted one). First, there is the intentional part—that part of your legacy where you can presumably exert some influence or control. Much of the chapter thus far has focused on the intentional legacy. On the other hand, we are not always in a position to control our entire legacy. Macroeconomic conditions, extraneous events, and random or unintentional occurrences can have a significant impact on what we are required to do in our lives, and thus what we might be remembered for.

How (and even whether) you think about your legacy is likely to change over the course of your adult life. You are bound to have early stage views, make course corrections (planned and unplanned), changes in the roles you play and the responsibilities you face that will all have a profound impact on your thinking. We are rarely blessed with control over the timing or circumstances of these events. Sometimes we are made by them, however. It all depends on how we handle things thereafter. Again, the stature and legacy of former New York mayor Rudolph Giuliani was dramatically enhanced by his conduct in the period following September 11, although his remaining tenure was barely another hundred days.

Legacy is strongly affected by the circumstances of one's departure; retirement, layoff, firing, a new opportunity, health reasons, a lifestyle shift. All affect how our legacy is framed. As a result, how we leave casts a shade on our legacy that we have to factor in. Even when these departure circumstances might not always be welcomed or voluntary, the more that can be done to leave in a manner befitting one's personal aspirations, becoming that person we'd *like* to be, the better off we are. And precisely how does one do that, one might ask.

Here are two guiding thoughts to keep in mind for departing with a legacy of trust, whether or not you have the luxury of a long lead-time to anticipate or plan:

One small thing will get you started

Just start.

First, you can ask yourself the question that Barnes Boffey often poses: "If I were the person I'd like to be . . ." What's the nicest gift you could leave to the people with whom you've worked? Not in terms of a beautiful or expensive item, but in something that would have the most meaning for them on a regular basis? It may be a binder of how certain valuable things get done, or the things that have helped you succeed. It may be the establishment or the resurrection of a particular tradition that brings out the best in people, or that reinforces the value of the community of which they are a part.

Second, you might ask yourself specifically by whom you'd like to be remembered. This could be a successor, or someone to whom you are a mentor. Focus on that particular individual. Is there something that, either in a single episode, or if time permits, periodically, you could do with this person that would be valuable? Is it a single dinner, or a monthly lunch? A trip to another facility? Inclusion in a particular meeting or event? These episodes are very much where legacies can be built. If you think of the legacy that others have left to you (intentionally or otherwise), chances are it has a component of going somewhere or doing something with them that has stayed with you as a treasured memory. It probably wasn't consciously planned as a legacy-building event in mind, as that sort of thing rarely has the desired impact. This doesn't have to be grandly planned, either. Just do it because you care about the person.

Don't feel that you must leave a legacy with a capital L

Sometimes our tenure, or the nature of our work hasn't had sufficient impact to generate much of a legacy at the time we leave an organization. Sometimes we haven't built enough trust to make a legacy meaningful or credible. (Some people fall into this category, yet don't know it, and have an overblown sense of their importance. Some may confuse their longevity (or survival) in a particular organization with thinking they have had some treasured impact for others to emulate.) Don't berate yourself if you haven't done enough to make a mark in a particular area. There's nothing wrong with going quietly into that good night. It may actually be a better legacy than trying to leave an imprint where one doesn't belong.

Saying Goodbye

The final dimension of legacy that is worth considering is *what* we do as we leave. You may now be reading this, thinking to yourself, Here we are, thinking big thoughts, talking about mortality and meaning, and now we're going to drop down to the micro level, and discuss how we say *goodbye*? If it hadn't been so striking how often, in the discussion of legacies, this topic came up, we would not have included it, but it happened too many times for us to ignore. Even if you've built a great history and track record, the one additional element to your legacy where you really can have an impact is all about *how* you leave. Here are excerpts from just a few of the true stories that we know or have heard personally in looking into this topic. Each of them reminds us that how you leave, and how you behave around the time of your departure will have a disproportionately large effect on how you are remembered, and what you are remembered for.

The first involves someone who has become a prominent CEO in American business. This person (let's call her Jane) was the COO of a well-known company (let's call it TFC), and she came in with the mandate of assembling an entirely new management team. She built a cadre of more than a dozen rising stars, with the kinds of credentials and experience that most entities would envy. After the new team was in place and beginning to make a difference, Jane had a major philosophical disagreement with the CEO, and the handwriting was on the wall. Jane effectively stopped coming to work. She disappeared, quite abruptly. So abruptly, in fact, that she never said goodbye to any of the cadre of Jane loyalists she had assembled. This entire group of promising managers, ostensibly her dream team, were all bewildered by her lack of contact. Not by the circumstances of her departure—they were politically far more clued in and savvy than that—but by her lack of personal connection with them at the time of her departure, and any time thereafter, up to and including today. That original episode at TFC took place close to a decade ago. All the members of that team have now gone on to senior roles across a variety of large corporations. Yet when those individuals look at Jane, or look back on their tenure with Jane at TFC, her legacy will be forever clouded by how she interacted (or failed to interact) with the team she built at a crucial moment for all of them.

One might argue that at the time of the episode Jane might have been ashamed, angry, humiliated, legally constrained, or anything else, and she simply couldn't bring herself to talk, but the entire team knew her (and the entire situation) well enough to know that simply wasn't the case. In the words of one of those affected, "She literally turned her back on us." No matter how good she might have been, Jane's legacy as a leader will be tainted as a result.

The second story was recounted by Bob Garland of Deloitte & Touche:

> Transitioning, taking one's hands off the wheel, may be the hardest part of a career. To counsel behind the scenes and let [others] make mistakes is hard. It's hard because it does get you to your own career mortality. Yet it's about finishing up. Letting go. Not trying to control things from the grave. I remember an important senior leader who, as he left this organization at the end of his career, had been trying to kill off the successor, whom he viewed as competition. It was because [the departing leader] wanted to be viewed as indispensable. I promised myself I'd never do that. So the right thing for me to do is *not* to leave that way.

We have heard numerous similar stories that serve to remind us of the importance of how we leave, and what it says about us. Some of them border on the tragic. The head of HR of a major Boston-based financial institution recalled one in particular, when the organization's COO departed: "His legacy was interrupted by his own doing, as he fought a political battle and lost. He left so quickly, with almost no goodbyes. He went home and sat by himself in his kitchen, feeling like he lost it all."

In an effort to prevent you from becoming the subject of any similar stories, and to help preserve your own legacy of trust, here are a handful of things you should consider doing prior to or con-current with a departure, be it voluntary or involuntary:

1. Get yourself some closure, No. 1: Acknowledge unfin-ished business. Even if you've had ample time to plan your last few days, weeks, or months, there is still a good chance that you haven't completed everything you might have hoped, in the style you might have hoped.

Rather than leaving with your jaws clenched, be prepared to let certain matters go, or to pass them on to someone. You can (and should) prioritize the open items, and figure out those you can complete, those you'd like to complete, and those that will tor-ment you eternally should you leave them uncompleted. This last category may be larger than you'd prefer, so it will be time to bite the bullet on them. Pick the precious few. Pass the others on. And please, don't bury them uncompleted, for others to discover sev-eral months later. When Rob was leaving one job earlier in his ca-reer, he knew that, even with the best-laid succession plans and planning, his successor would be left to deal with certain situa-tions that were not of her doing. What he failed to realize, how-ever, was just how much he had left unresolved (or unorganized), and how sticky these situations would eventually become. He still harbors some remorse for having left too many things unresolved. He was blessed with having a successor possessed of competence and grace, but not everyone is so lucky.

2. Get yourself some closure, No. 2: Acknowledge unre-solved relationships. OK, so there are some people in your world of work who are not among your favorites. You might have had a run-in or three, maybe even lost a political battle to them. Maybe just never liked them. Now is your chance, your only and last chance to get even. As we used to say when we were kids, "No backs!"

Don't do it. Tempting, nay irresistible as it may be, don't. This is also your only and last chance to rise above it, and to go out with real dignity. It means actually considering (if not acting on!) walking into their office at some point (before your last day, if pos-sible), and talking to them about the fact that there were differences between you that never got resolved. Words to that effect. You don't have to resolve those differences (besides, there's probably too much baggage and possibly not enough time or reason to do that), but it sure doesn't hurt to acknowledge the fact they have been around and didn't go away. You also don't have to go in proffering or seeking apologies (nice as getting or giving an apology might be). Conversations of this nature can lead to all sorts of confessions, revelations, or confirmations of earlier suspicions that may give you greater understanding (if not compassion) for this nemesis. People leave these conversations feeling really good. You will also leave a better person for having done so.

3. Even if you must leave in haste, leave not in haste! Be as purposeful as possible, even in hurried circumstances. A departure from a job that has been a big part of your life is, in its own way, like leaving your parents' home when you are a young adult. It represents a significant change, perhaps to something long anticipated, but you are leaving something that has been important to you and to other people. Rob still regrets the hasty way he left the chairmanship of a not-for-profit board when other demands arose. While others have carried on and succeeded him with even greater accomplishment, he still has misgivings about the disruption his exit might have caused, and how he might have spent time working on a more gradual withdrawal.

4. Give words of encouragement to those you believe in, have fostered or mentored. While this chapter has been directed at you as the leaver of the legacy of trust, remember that there is also a set of counterparts in this departure, in those you are leaving behind. Those people are what legacies are all about.

As this chapter emphasizes, for many trusted leaders, the legacy they consider most important is the people they have influenced. As your interactions with those individuals will become ever less frequent, this is a good time to focus what you want your final imprint to be. A hearty handshake and a "Good luck!" is pretty pallid. Those who care about you want (and deserve) something more to remember you by. You don't have to get all mawkish or mushy. It's more than a purely sentimental goodbye that we're counseling here. We're suggesting (strongly) to offer them a goodbye gift of some thoughts from you that will have enduring value. You won't have many chances like this in your life. Take advantage of it. Over dinner. Over drinks. Wherever. It will have real impact.

5. Reflect on what you did and didn't accomplish in your tenure. Regardless of the duration of your time with the company or in this particular job, it makes sense to take stock, and to do so while the memory is fresh and it still has meaning. Do this for yourself.

When someone is at the end of their run, it can be difficult for them to apply much in the way of rational retrospective to their work. They may be pushing to complete open items, they may be wrapping up transitions or projects, they may be selecting or grooming successors, they may be doing all of those things. Whatever is on your plate in the last weeks, be sure to do some inventory of your personal accomplishments and disappointments. What are the half-dozen things of which you are most proud? What about the converse? This is not intended to be a scorecard or a report card. It's a chance for you to sum up, for yourself. No one is likely to do this for you.

6. Keep the channel open. This is more than "don't burn your bridges" advice. Keeping the channel open means staying connected to the individuals who have meant something to you, with whom you have worked closely in recent times.

Whether you are transitioning to a new role elsewhere, retiring, or simply escaping, you have probably been part of a tight set of working relationships. Don't let those relationships wither away too quickly. Time and circumstances have a naturally erosive effect on business relationships as is. Even if you continue to hang around your old workplace, they will take their toll. You'll have to nourish those relationships over time. Over time, they will also sort themselves out, and some will falter. The more meaningful relationships will survive and even grow. They can endure for decades, and these people will form part of your inner circle. They will bring out the best in you. It is a legacy of trust, for them and for you.

This legacy stuff is hard. It may be the last thing you want to do. Yet it *shouldn't* be the last thing you do. And we can almost guarantee that you won't regret your efforts in this regard. It might even grant you the best legacy of all—that of the trusted leader.

AFTERWORD:
THE TRUSTED LEADER CONTINUES

You've now read the book. Chances are good that there won't be a movie. And we're not likely to go into the business of marketing inspirational corporate giftware. So, if you have found the thoughts contained in *The Trusted Leader* to be useful, how do you keep it going? How can we make this something more enduring for you than simply residing on a bulging bookshelf? We have pondered that question frequently in the course of our writing, and we have come up with a few suggestions that might help. The first is to revisit the self-assessment tool we introduced in Chapter 2, not just once, but with greater frequency (in fact, we suggest you look at it at least twice yearly—if you'd like, we'll even send you a reminder!).

The second offering is to become part of our circle of interest through our Web site, at www.thetrustedleader.com. There you'll find more about our work on trusted leaders and trusted leadership, as well as a spot to submit your own observations on the topic as part of a discussion forum. In addition, there will be a Q & A section, and information on our ongoing work on the topic. We hope you'll visit us there.

NOTES AND REFERENCES

Chapter One: What Is Trusted Leadership?

There are references throughout the book to *The Trusted Advisor,* by David H. Maister, Charles H. Green, and Robert M. Galford, Free Press, 2000.

There is a valuable discussion of the scarcity of focus on trust in Thomas A. Stewart's thoughtful book, *The Wealth of Knowledge,* Currency/Doubleday, 2001, pp. 238 et seq.

Tom Valerio, interviews with Rob Galford, 2001–2002.

Unnamed technology company, Galford meetings, Cambridge, MA, 2001.

Forrester Research conversations, 2001–2002.

Jim Lawrence, CFO of General Mills, interview with Rob Galford, December 2001.

Media conglomerate with shared services, California offsite, July 2001.

J. Peterman quote, interview with Regina Maruca, 2001.

Unnamed CEO, "Walk up the hill" with Rob Galford, Waltham, MA, 1999.

Chapter Three: The Characteristics and Competencies of the Trusted Leader

Story regarding corporate layoffs, recounted by Kathy Lubar of the Ariel Group, to Rob Galford, 1998.

Description of "Leo" from Christopher Fleming, St. James Properties, 1986.

Trusted Leader surveys, conducted 2001–2002 by Galford and Drapeau, respondents promised confidentiality. Survey respondents in a variety of staff and line roles with companies in Massachusetts, Ohio, Michigan, California, operating in financial services, research, consumer marketing.

Regina Pisa, managing partner, Goodwin, Procter and Hoar, interview with Rob Galford, 2002.

Chapter Four: The Enemies of Trusted Leadership

George Hornig interview with Rob Galford, New York, December 2001.

Regina Pisa interview with Rob Galford, 2002.

"Big Daddy" syndrome, Rob Galford case, 2001.

Firm with small accounts, Rob Galford, 1990s.

"Cheryl" story, Annie Drapeau, 2001.

Head of sales moves to sales training, Rob Galford, 1999.

Michael Rice interview with Rob Galford, New York, 2001.

Paris and London office story, confidential interview with company executive, Rob Galford, 2002.

Company layoffs, Annie Drapeau, 2001.

Stock options, Annie Drapeau, 2001.

Interviews with investment firm CFO, Rob Galford, 2001–2002.

New president in research company, confidential source, Rob Galford, 2001.

"Milk" story, Annie Drapeau, 2000.

Patrick McGeehan, "At a Wall Street Firm, Juniors' Voices Roar," *New York Times*, April 8, 2000, p.1.

Chapter Five: The Tools of Building Personal Trust

Five stages of personal trust, *The Trusted Advisor,* Chapter 9 et seq.

College PR officer, Regina Maruca, 2002.

"Peg" story (disguised), Rob Galford source, 2001.

Man with five televisions, Regina Maruca, 2002.

Radio story, Regina Maruca, 2002.

Discussion with Rev. Gary Smith, senior minister, First Parish in Concord, MA, Rob Galford, 2001.

Pay raises after layoffs, Rob Galford client, 2002.

Major-account manager, adapted from Annie Drapeau, 2001.

Chapter Six: The Tools of Building Organizational Trust

Alan Colsey, police chief, interview with Rob Galford, 2002.

George Hornig of Credit Suisse, interview with Rob Galford, 2001 and 2002.

"Doug Baker" in a media company, Annie Drapeau, 2002.

Diane Hessan of Communispace, interview with Rob Galford, 2002.

Paul Clark of National City Corporation, interview with Rob Galford, 2002.

Story of president of her own business, Regina Maruca, 2002.

"We-they," union family, Annie Drapeau, 1999.

James and the new CEO story, Annie Drapeau, 2001.

Interview with Bob Garland of Deloitte and Touche, Rob Galford, 2001.

Medical story, Regina Maruca, 1998.

Chapter Seven: From the Top

Emily and Frank story, Regina Maruca, 2002.

Interview with a "twenty-something," Annie Drapeau, 2002.

Paul Clark of National City Corporation, interview with Rob Galford, 2002.

Chapter Eight: Inside Teams, Departments, Offices

Jon Skinner, interview with Annie Drapeau, January 2002.

Fons Trompenaars and Charles Hampden-Turner, *Riding the Waves of Culture: Understanding Diversity in Global Business*, McGraw-Hill, 1997.

Telecommuting story, Regina Maruca, 2002.

"Victim Mentality" example, Annie Drapeau, 2002.

Entrepreneurial manufacturing company example, Regina Maruca, 2002.

Chapter Nine: Across Teams, Departments, Offices

Malcolm Gladwell, *The Tipping Point: How Little Things Can Make a Big Difference*, Little, Brown and Co., 2000, p. 11.

Michael Welles, interview with Rob Galford, 2001.

Volcker comment, as reported in *The New York Times*, February 26, 2001.

Ephraim Brecher, meeting with Rob Galfold, 2002.

Marketing agency story, Rob Galford, 2001.

Layoff story, Rob Galford, 2001.

Law firm partner ("Strickland") story, Rob Galford, 2001.

Diane Hessan of Communispace, interview with Rob Galford, 2002.

Retail financial services firm story, Rob Galford, 2001.

Chapter Ten: In Times of Change

Story about seasoned senior vice president, Rob Galford, 2001.

"Rich" story, Annie Drapeau, 2001.

Story about rethinking go-to-market strategy, Rob Galford, 2001.

Strategy consulting firm acquisition story, Annie Drapeau, 2001.

Electronics company CEO story, Rob Galford, 2001.

Chapter Eleven: When People Leave

Unnamed manager interview, Annie Drapeau, 2001.

Unnamed senior-level employee interview, Annie Drapeau, 2001.

Jay Lorsch and Tom Tierney, *Aligning the Stars: How to Succeed When Professionals Drive Results*, Harvard Business School Press, April 2002.

Daniel Roth, "How to Cut Pay, Lay Off 8000 People and Still Have Workers Who Love You," *Fortune*, February 4, 2002.

Chapter Twelve: In Times of Crisis

Interview with Mark Braverman, Annie Drapeau, January 2002.

Peter Frost and Sandra Robinson, "The Toxic Handler," *Harvard Business Review*, July–August 1999.

Chapter Thirteen: Trust Lost, Trust Rebuilt

Logistics manager, confidential interview with Rob Galford, 2001.

Saul Hansell article, *New York Times*, December 27, 2001.

Matt Ridley, *The Origins of Virtue*, Viking, 1997.

Robert S. Kaplan and David P. Norton, *The Balanced Scorecard: Translating Strategy Into Action*, Harvard Business School Press, 1996.

Michael E. Porter, *Competitive Advantage: Creating and Sustaining Superior Performance*, Free Press, 1985.

Tom Peters, *Structure Is Not Organization*, Business Horizons, 1979.

Authors' note: We have been unable to locate the origins of the RACI model, but see it employed with some frequency in software development and project management.

Chapter Fourteen: When *You* Leave: The Legacy of Trust

Interview with Bob Garland of Deloitte and Touche, Rob Galford, January 2002.

Interview with Kathy Biro, Rob Galford, 2002.

Michael Bronner story, Annie Drapeau and Rob Galford, 2002.

Michael Ward story, Annie Drapeau and Rob Galford, 2002.

Interview with Jim Lawrence, Rob Galford, 2002.

Warren Bennis, Sidebar in Harris Collingwood and Diane Coutu, "Jack on Jack: The *HBR* Interview," *Harvard Business Review,* February 2002.

Interview with Barnes Boffey of the Aloha Foundation, Rob Galford, 2002.

Interview with Henk Broeders of Cap, Gemini, Ernst & Young, Rob Galford, 2001.

"Jane" story, Annie Drapeau, 2001.

Confidential interview with the head of HR of a major Boston-based financial institution, Rob Galford, 2001.

INDEX

ABOUT THE AUTHORS

Robert Galford is managing partner of the Center for Executive Development, which was founded by several former Harvard Business School professors in 1987. He divides his time across teaching on executive education programs and working with senior executives on the issues that lie at the intersection of business strategy, corporate organization, and leadership. He has taught on the executive programs at the Columbia Graduate School of Business, the Kellogg Graduate School of Management at Northwestern University, and, most recently, Harvard.

Earlier in his career, Rob was executive vice president and chief people officer of Digitas (NASDAQ: DTAS), a 1500+ employee marketing services firm based in Boston with offices worldwide. He was also a vice president of the MAC Group and its successor firm, Gemini Consulting, focusing largely on the strategic and organizational challenges facing *Fortune* 100 companies, international financial institutions, and professional services entities. While there, he worked for a number of years in Western Europe prior to returning to the U.S., where he took on a variety of firm administrative and managerial responsibilities. He has practiced law with the international firm of Curtis, Mallet-Prevost, Colt & Mosle in New York, and has also worked in investment management, first for Citicorp in New York, and later in Boston. In addition, he has taught management policy in the MBA program at Boston University Graduate School of Management.

Rob is a three-time contributor to the *Harvard Business Review*, including "When an Executive Defects" (case comment—1997), "Why Can't This HR Department Get Any Respect?" (1998) and "What's He Waiting For?" (1999). His work has also appeared frequently in the

Boston Globe, where he has served as one of the "Job Doc" advice colum-
nists. Rob is the co-author of *The Trusted Advisor* (with David Maister and
Charles Green), initially published by The Free Press in 2000, and subsequently reissued in paperback by Simon & Schuster in 2001. He currently
sits on the boards of directors of Forrester Research, Inc., and Access
Data Corporation. He also hosts the business video *Talk About Change!*
with the popular cartoon character Dilbert.

His educational background includes Liceo Segre, Turin, Italy, a BA
in Economics and Italian Literature from Haverford College, an MBA
from Harvard, and a JD from Georgetown University Law Center, where
he was an associate editor of *The Tax Lawyer.* Rob lives with his family in
Concord, MA. He may be contacted through the Center for Executive
Development (www.cedinc.com) at rgalford@cedinc.com.

Anne Seibold Drapeau is the successor to Rob Galford as chief
people officer at Digitas, where she has responsibility for learning and
development, compensation and benefits, knowledge management and
leadership coaching. She has been with Digitas for about five years in a
variety of roles, most recently as the head of Digitas's e-Dialogue practice, consulting to clients on building customer relationships through
live channels.

She took a brief dot-com sabbatical from Digitas to serve as vice
president for customer experience at start-up Send.com. Prior to joining
Digitas, she led new business development for FTD, where she was in-
strumental in building international business partnerships and new di-
rect-to-consumer businesses. Before FTD, she spent many years at
PepsiCo and Pepsi-Cola in a variety of strategy and general management
roles, including an assignment in a Pepsi-Cola distribution facility,
where she first developed an interest in organizational dynamics and
leadership and motivation. She began her career as an investment
banker at J.P. Morgan in New York.

Annie's educational background includes a BS in chemical engineering from Bucknell University and an MBA from the Amos Tuck School of Business Administration at Dartmouth.

Annie lives in Boston with her family, and her interests include downhill skiing, classical music, and traveling. She can be reached at adrapeau@digitas.com.